PHANTOM BILLING, FAKE PRESCRIPTIONS, AND THE HIGH COST OF MEDICINE

A volume in the series
The Culture and Politics of Health Care Work
edited by Suzanne Gordon and Sioban Nelson

A list of titles in this series is available at
www.cornellpress.cornell.edu

PHANTOM BILLING, FAKE PRESCRIPTIONS, AND THE HIGH COST OF MEDICINE

Health Care Fraud and
What to Do about It

Terry L. Leap

ILR PRESS

AN IMPRINT OF

CORNELL UNIVERSITY PRESS

ITHACA AND LONDON

First published 2011 by Cornell University Press
Printed in the United States of America

Library of Congress Cataloging-in-Publication Data

Leap, Terry L., 1948–
    Phantom billing, fake prescriptions, and the high cost of medicine: health care fraud and what to do about it / Terry L. Leap.
        p. cm. — (The culture and politics of health care work)
    Includes bibliographical references and index.
    ISBN 978-0-8014-4979-6 (cloth : alk. paper)
    1. Medical care—Corrupt practices—United States.   2. Fraud—United States.   I. Title.   II. Series: Culture and politics of health care work.
    RA395.A3L4125   2011
    364.16'3—dc22   2010041491

Cornell University Press strives to use environmentally responsible suppliers and materials to the fullest extent possible in the publishing of its books. Such materials include vegetable-based, low-VOC inks and acid-free papers that are recycled, totally chlorine-free, or partly composed of nonwood fibers. For further information, visit our website at www.cornellpress.cornell.edu.

Cloth printing   10 9 8 7 6 5 4 3 2 1

In memory of my father, Henry W. Leap, and my brother-in-law, William Howard Wisner, MD

Contents

Preface

The health care systems in developed countries today employ diagnostic methods and treatment regimes that are light years ahead of the health care available when even the youngest readers of this book were born. Medical conditions once considered incurable or life threatening are now treated routinely, causing only minor disruptions to the patient's life. Bioengineering and health care in the early part of the twenty- first century seemingly border on the miraculous.

But a dark side also exists. Fraud and abuse are pervasive elements of the vast health care systems of advanced industrial nations such as the United States and the European Union. A small but troublesome minority of health care providers submit bills for services they have never performed. Others provide treatments that their patients do not need, and they steal hundreds of millions of dollars from the Medicare and Medicaid programs through false billings. Still others take kickbacks from pharmaceutical manufacturers, hospitals, and ambulance companies. To make a quick buck, a few of the most nefarious health care "professionals" are willing to place the welfare or even the lives of their patients in jeopardy.

Health care is what criminologists call a "criminogenic industry." This book illustrates how the U.S. health care system provides a fertile environment for fraud and abuse on a scale that makes it among the most serious of all white-collar crimes.

Acknowledgments

I owe a deep debt of gratitude to Suzanne Gordon, coeditor of the Culture and Politics of Health Care Work series of Cornell's ILR Press. Her insights and meticulous reading and rereading of the manuscript forced me to think critically about the complex social problem of health care fraud and abuse. Also, Fran Benson, editorial director of ILR Press, provided her usual strong support and encouragement. This book is the fourth project that Fran and I have worked on together during the past three decades. I also thank Myron Fottler, who served as a reviewer for the book, as well as a second anonymous reviewer. In addition, I would like to express my appreciation to staff at Cornell University Press, including Kitty Liu, Ange Romeo-Hall and Katy Meigs for their extensive editorial work, and to the production and marketing departments. Finally, I want to thank Bo, my cat and wonderful friend for nearly eighteen years. He sat at my feet throughout the preparation of most of this manuscript—as well as two previous books that I published with Cornell University Press. Unfortunately, he died before this book was published.

PHANTOM BILLING, FAKE PRESCRIPTIONS, AND THE HIGH COST OF MEDICINE

THE BIG PICTURE

A Social Problem That Comes in Many Shapes and Sizes

After spending two weeks recovering from heart and lung problems, a Florida man in his early nineties was released from an Orlando-area hospital. His condition was too unstable for him to return home, so his doctor arranged for a short stay at a nursing facility. On his discharge from the hospital, the patient told staff members that someone was available to drive him to his new quarters. But the hospital staff insisted he make the short trip by ambulance, assuring him that "Medicare will pay for it."

The ambulance ride went smoothly, and the patient, fully conscious and aware of what was happening during the trip, arrived safely at the nursing center. Several weeks later, he received a $627 invoice from the ambulance company. The bill for the eight-mile journey included charges for services such as the availability and actual use of oxygen (two separate charges) as well as something called an "OSHA sanitary procedure." The oxygen, for which he was charged, was never provided, and, contrary to what he was told by hospital personnel, Medicare balked at paying for the ambulance service.

This case is a personal one because the elderly man I am describing is my father. At ninety—two, his mind was sharp. He kept up with current events through his three reading staples—the *Orlando Sentinel,* the *Wall Street Journal,* and *Time* magazine. And with a lucidity that was rare for his age, my father knew exactly what services he received during his short ambulance ride, a ride that forced him to deal

1

with Medicare red tape (he was told his appeal was "on file") as well as threats by the ambulance company to refer his bill to a collection agency "within ten days." To protect his credit rating, I advised him to pay the charges and then seek reimbursement from Medicare. After making a dozen or so telephone calls and enduring needless hassles, he finally settled his account by paying a $42 fee. My father always tried to play by the rules. He should not have been forced to waste time dealing with a shady ambulance company and Medicare bureaucrats during the last months of his life.

Many of the cases discussed here involve frauds totaling hundreds of millions of dollars. By comparison, my father's unwanted ambulance ride seems positively banal. But I use it to introduce this book, however, precisely because of its banality. The cumulative effect of the many "nickel-and-dime" frauds is perhaps even more devastating to the U.S. health care system than the high-profile cases that make front-page news. Clearly, reform is needed.

But will reform occur? Federal prosecutors have long been aware of Medicare and Medicaid fraud.[1] The Health Insurance Portability and Accountability Act of 1996 (HIPAA) established the Health Care Fraud and Abuse Control Program (HCFAC) under the auspices of the U.S. Attorney General and the Department of Health and Human Services (HHS). And funding to the HHS, Office of Inspector General (OIG) and the FBI—both key players in the fight against health care fraud—has increased significantly since the late 1990s.[2]

The Obama administration proposed an initial budget of $634 billion for health care reform. These measures were designed to provide Americans with greater access to health care. As was the case with the Clinton and Bush administrations, President Obama claimed that fighting Medicare and Medicaid fraud was a priority. Obama's Medicare Fraud Strike Force, operated jointly by the Department of Justice and the Department of Health and Human Services, with the cooperation of state and local law enforcement, set its sights on persons who were filing false Medicare claims, billing the government for unnecessary or bogus treatments, and soliciting illegal kickbacks. In the wake of indictments against fifty—three doctors, health care executives, and beneficiaries during June 2009, HHS secretary Kathleen Sebelius said, "The Obama administration is committed to turning up the heat on Medicare fraud and employing all the weapons in the federal government's arsenal to target those who are defrauding the American taxpayer."[3]

A month later, thirty health care providers, including doctors, in New York, Louisiana, Massachusetts, and Texas, found their bank accounts frozen and assets seized—including Rolls Royce automobiles and million-dollar houses—as part of a Medicare fraud bust. In this series of frauds, providers were billing Medicare between $3,000 and $4,500 for "arthritis kits" that contained nothing more than knee and shoulder braces and heating pads. The perpetrators also billed Medicare for thousands of dollars in liquid foods such as Ensure that were never delivered to patients.[4]

In late January 2010, the Obama administration held a health care fraud summit.[5] This initiative was followed in March 2010 with the announcement of new measures to employ private auditors or "bounty hunters" to look for erroneous Medicare and Medicaid payments. In 2009 alone, bogus payments amounted to an estimated $98 billion, of which $54 billion came from Medicare and Medicaid. The plan calls for paying bounty hunters a portion of the recovered funds.[6]

But are these efforts enough to stop white-collar criminals who are stealing from consumers, insurers, and tax payers? Is this reform real and lasting, or is it political grandstanding? The billions of dollars spent by the Clinton, Bush, and Obama administrations to fight health care fraud and abuse sounds impressive until we realize the enormity of health care fraud and abuse. The numerator—that is, the federal government's spending almost $2 billion a year on antifraud measures—sounds great until we see the size of the denominator—that is, the $75 billion to $250 billion a year that is being stolen by health care fraudsters.

Except for a handful of lawmakers—most notably Senator Charles "Chuck" Grassley, R-Iowa—Congress has given little attention to this major social problem. And they have not shown the same indignation over fraudulent health care billings as they did over financial crimes at Enron, WorldCom, and Bernard L. Madoff Investment Securities.

A lack of attention to this pressing social problem goes beyond the halls of Congress. Health care reform was a hotly debated topic during 2009 and 2010. Except for oblique references to waste and mismanagement, however, the pundits were silent on the topics of fraud and abuse. Price Waterhouse Coopers did release a report in 2009 that placed a "focus on fraud and mistakes" at number four on its top-ten list of health care concerns.[7] But the Price Waterhouse Coopers report appears to be the exception, not the rule. Although think tanks, interest groups, and the media have paid close attention to many of the problems plaguing U.S. health care, they have said little about fraud and abuse.

The fact remains, however, that the U.S. health care system, with its network of providers, consumers, and insurers, is a major target for criminal activity.[8] A report issued by the Department of Justice and the FBI indicates that health care fraud is the most prevalent of the major frauds in the United States, far outdistancing corporate fraud, securities fraud, identity theft, mortgage fraud, insurance fraud, and mass-marketing fraud.[9] According to the FBI:

> All health care programs are subject to fraud, however, Medicare and Medicaid programs are the most visible. Estimates of fraudulent billings to health care programs, both public and private, are estimated between 3 and 10 percent of total health care expenditures. The fraud schemes are not specific to any area, but are found throughout the entire country. The schemes target large health care programs, public and private, as

well as beneficiaries. Certain schemes tend to be worked more often in certain geographical areas, and certain ethnic or national groups tend to also employ the same fraud schemes. The fraud schemes have, over time, become more sophisticated and complex, and are now being perpetrated by more organized crime groups.[10]

At the outset, it is important to note that most health care providers place their professional obligations above their personal and financial needs. These individuals and their organizations provide quality services and products to patients and clients at a fair price. They abide by the laws, regulations, and ethical guidelines of their regulatory bodies and professional associations, and they play by the rules when seeking reimbursements from Medicare, Medicaid, or private insurers. But unscrupulous health care providers—and these include a surprising number of supposedly upstanding professionals—often have a different agenda.

Many of the perpetrators of health care fraud and abuse come from the upper crust of society—board-certified doctors, surgeons, hospital CEOs, attorneys, and even renowned physician-academics working at some of the world's top medical schools. In some cases, they steal or misappropriate resources. In other cases, they engage in scandalous over- and undertreatments that cost people their health or even their lives. Yet few of these "perps," as they are often called on TV cop shows, ever go to jail. Indeed, some of them are among the most disturbing of repeat offenders. What does this predicament tell us about our health care system and about our society and values?

In a scenario that has become all too commonplace, a physician practicing in South Florida was sentenced to forty—six months in prison and three years of supervised release. She was also ordered to pay over $2.3 million in restitution for her participation in a massive kickback scheme involving pharmacies, medical equipment companies, and Medicare patients. In addition, she was sentenced on charges of conspiracy to violate the antikickback and false claims statutes, along with tax evasion. The doctor landed in hot water after she agreed to provide bogus prescriptions in return for cash.

Beginning in spring 1999, this doctor established referral relationships with the owners of medical equipment companies. The owners brought "patients" to her office and specified the medications and equipment they wanted her to prescribe. She conducted cursory physical examinations and then signed the requests, regardless of their medical necessity. For these services, she collected kickbacks ranging from $50 to $200 per patient. The medical equipment companies delivered the unneeded items to the patients and submitted Medicare reimbursement claims. In addition, prescriptions signed by the physician were filled by Miami pharmacies in return for a referral fee. As a result of this scam, Medicare paid more than $2.3 million for unnecessary equipment and medications.[11] One aspect of this case, however, is different—this fraudster was sentenced to time behind bars. Many other white-collar criminals who steal from the health care system never see the inside of a prison cell.

Pharmaceutical and medical equipment companies are often in the health care fraud limelight. In 2009 two major pharmaceutical fraud cases were noteworthy—Pfizer agreed to pay $2.3 billion and Eli Lilly $1.4 billion for their illegal off-label promotions of major drugs.[12] Furthermore, medical equipment firms, ranging from small-time operators of phony shell companies to providers of kidney dialysis machines, have been subjected to fraud charges and huge monetary settlements.

Some newsworthy cases center on the largest institutions in the United States. Hospital chains such as Tenet Healthcare Corporation, the Hospital Corporation of America (HCA), and HealthSouth have forfeited hundreds of millions of dollars to settle a variety of fraud and abuse charges. Extended care facilities, home health care firms, and even hospices have also been charged with a laundry list of fraud and abusive practices.

Persons from all walks of life—some highly paid professionals and others common street criminals—are attracted to the tremendous moneymaking potential of health care fraud. Law enforcement agencies have discovered that organized crime groups are leaving the dangerous work of trafficking drugs and migrating to the safer and more lucrative work of health care fraud.[13] Crooked business people and lawyers with no formal training in the health care professions have also gotten in on the action, licking their chops and viewing the U.S. health care system as a proverbial gold mine. Health care fraud seems to offer high payoffs with few risks to people whom we do not usually regard as "criminals." These developments do not bode well for government efforts to protect patients, honest providers, insurers, and taxpayers against more fraud and abuse.

But the United States hardly has a corner on the market for health care shysters. Fraud is a global issue that plagues both developed and developing countries. A key point to remember is that fraud and abuse arise in all health care systems, regardless of their size, structure, or methods of finance and delivery. The magnitude and scope of health care fraud and abuse in the European Union is proportional to that in the United States. Laurie Davies of the NHS Counter Fraud and Security Management Service estimated that of the one trillion euros spent on health care in the EU, 3 to 10 percent (30–100 billion euros) is lost every year to fraud.[14] Despite the enormity of the problem, the antifraud and abuse measures in the EU lag well behind those of the United States. Beginning in 2004, the European Healthcare Fraud and Corruption Conference held annual meetings throughout the EU to discuss strategies for fighting health care fraud. According to the European Healthcare Fraud and Corruption Network:

> The problem of fraud and corruption is likely to grow with EU enlargement and increased free movement of people, money, rights of establishment and rights to provide service. With expansion comes a greater freedom for EU citizens to live and work in other EU Member States. Although this is a positive step for a better, more productive Europe, it also means an increased risk from healthcare fraud. Whether they are individuals or organised crime cartels, fraudsters will be able to duplicate their crimes throughout the EU due to the unrestricted passage from state to state of people, capital and the provision of services. It is important that the EU realises that healthcare fraud is a cross border problem.[15]

Concern for this serious social problem is also growing in post-Communist Europe as well as in Asia, Africa, and Central America. According to Transparency International, a civil anticorruption network founded in 1993:

> Corruption in the health sector is not exclusive to any particular kind of health system. It occurs in systems whether they are predominately public or private, well funded or poorly funded, and technically simple or sophisticated. The extent of corruption is, in part, a reflection of the society in which it operates. Health system corruption is less likely in societies where there is broad adherence to the rule of law, transparency and trust, and where the public sector is ruled by effective civil service codes and strong accountability mechanisms.[16]

It is beyond the scope of this book to discuss in depth the global problem of fraud and abuse. Instead, I analyze the profusion of fraud cases arising within the U.S. health care system. I examine a variety of corrupt acts and crimes, ranging from the padding of trip miles by ambulance operators to inflated Medicare claims by large hospital chains to shady marketing practices by major pharmaceutical companies. The dollars lost to health care fraudsters are dollars that could be used to fund more care for underserved populations. Dollars recaptured could also provide better wages and benefits to nurses, aides, and caregivers who have traditionally been underpaid.

To fully explore the problem of health care fraud in our system, this book centers on the following questions:

1. Are the current definitions of "fraud" and "abuse" too broad? How does one reconcile the dilemma between a physician's zealous advocacy for her patients and the physician's ordering tests and treatments that might be regarded as excessive or unnecessary? Are legal counsel, government officials, prosecutors, judges, and juries with little or no formal training in the health disciplines able to distinguish between quality health care and abusive overutilization?

2. How effective are the current laws and regulations for fighting health care fraud? Do these laws micromanage and hinder the efficient delivery of health care, or do they ignore certain health care frauds? Are more anti-fraud laws necessary or should greater emphasis be placed on enforcing existing laws? How much money is needed to ensure an optimal level of support for fighting health care fraud and abuse? And how will regulators know when enforcement measures have reached an optimal level?

3. Are certain institutional arrangements such as fee-for-service or capitation plans more (or less) conducive to fraud and abuse? What is the role of for-profit health care in reducing this major problem? What health care arrangements, financial incentives, and technologies can be used to curb fraud and abuse?

4. To what extent do health care providers, patients, shareholders in private hospitals, fraud control experts, health insurers, fiscal intermediaries, and government officials share a common ground insofar as reducing health care fraud is concerned? If the interests of these diverse groups are not in sync, what measures can be taken to align them?

5. What demographic changes will affect the future of the health care system? Will these changes exacerbate or diminish health care fraud and abuse?

The U.S. Health Care System: The Genesis of Fraud and Abuse

The U.S. health care system is a Garden of Eden for thieves. As the late Walter Cronkite once put it, U.S health care is "neither healthy, caring, or a system."[17] It is, however, a fragmented and diverse collection of 580,000 public and private health care providers employing approximately 14 million workers (out of a total labor force of over 150 million).[18] In the United States, health care generated $2.5 trillion in transactions, or about 17.3 percent of the nation's GDP, in 2008.[19] Because of the rising cost of health care and the aging U.S. population, the system is expected to grow to $4.3 trillion or 20 percent of GDP by 2017.[20]

People often refer to health care as an "industry." But health care in the U.S. is not really an industry (i.e., a group of firms producing the same or similar products and selling them in the same markets).[21] It is actually a loose system or network of overlapping industries—a diverse collection of businesses with different strategies, markets, and competitors.[22] The U.S. Department of Labor, Bureau of Labor Statistics divides health care into nine segments: hospitals, nursing and residential-care facilities, physician offices, dentist offices, home health care, other health care practitioners, outpatient care centers, other ambulatory health care services, and medical and diagnostic laboratories.[23]

Although immense, the U.S. health care system consists mostly of small businesses. Over three-fourths of the system is made up of offices run by physicians, dentists, and other health care providers. Hospitals constitute only 1 percent of all health care establishments, but they employ about 35 percent of all health care workers.[24] A great deal of variation exists within each of the nine segments. Hospitals, for example, range from small community facilities offering basic inpatient care and surgical services to major university hospitals serving as centers for teaching, research, and state-of-the-art medical care. The Bureau of Labor Statistics segmentation of health care providers excludes public insurance programs such as Medicare, Medicaid, and TRICARE (the military health care plan) as well as private health insurance companies.

In most developed countries, the government plays a central role in administering and financing health care. The United States, however, is the only industrialized country without a national, tax-supported health care system. The majority of people in the United States under the age of sixty—five—and not participating in Medicare—finance their health care through private insurers rather than through public programs such as Medicaid, Veterans Affairs, or the State Children's Health Insurance Program (SCHIP).[25] As the population ages, the Medicare program will expand. By 2017 the government's share of health care spending will increase to about 49 percent (up from 46 percent in 2006).[26] (The appendix to this book describes the Medicare, Medicaid, SCHIP, and TRICARE programs.)

Advocates of the capitalistic private-sector market in health care contend that, at least in theory, a for-profit health care system should encourage innovations and efficiencies that reduce health care costs and improve quality. In reality, the U.S. health care system is a model of inefficiency. Woolhandler, Campbell, and Himmelstein studied the differences between the private U.S. health care system and the socialized Canadian system. They discovered a widening gap between the two countries in per capita health care expenditures.[27]

> Market theorists argue that although competition increases administration, it should drive down total costs. Why hasn't practice borne out this theory? Investor owned healthcare firms are not cost minimisers but profit maximisers. Strategies that bolster profitability often worsen efficiency. US firms have found that raising revenues by exploiting loopholes or lobbying politicians is more profitable than improving efficiency or quality.... Evidence from the US is remarkably consistent; public funding of private care yields poor results. In practice, public-private competition means that private firms carve out the profitable niches, leaving a financially depleted public sector responsible for unprofitable patients and services. Based on this experience, only a dunce could believe that

market based reform will improve efficiency or effectiveness. Privatisation trades the relatively flat pay scales in government for the much steeper ones in private industry; the 15-fold pay gradient between the highest and lowest paid workers in the US government gives way to the 2000:1 gradient at Aetna.[28]

According to surveys conducted by the World Health Organization (WHO) and the Organization for Economic Co-operation and Development (OECD), the United States spends more on health care per capita than any other high-income country. In 2007 per capita health care expenditures were $7,900.[29] By 2017 these annual expenditures are expected to exceed $13,000.[30] According to *America's Health Rankings: A Call to Action for Individuals and Their Communities* released in December 2008 by the United Health Foundation, the health of Americans had failed to improve for four consecutive years: "Key factors contributing to these results included unprecedented levels of obesity, an increasing number of uninsured people, and the persistence of risky health behaviors, particularly tobacco use."[31] Yet countries having smaller per capita expenditures on health care are superior to the United States on measures of infant mortality, obesity, and average life expectancy.[32]

Another criticism of the system is the rapid rise in health care costs. In most years, these increases have outpaced inflation by a significant margin. Skyrocketing health care costs have been attributed to greedy health care providers, consumer ignorance, bureaucratic inefficiencies, the failure of market forces, and, of course, fraud and abuse. Although Medicare, Medicaid, and other public programs have a fixed price structure, prices in the private sector of the U.S. health care system are largely unregulated—something that can lead to fraud and abuse. Consumer advocate Cindy Holtzman has pointed to outlandish charges, such as a Florida patient being charged $140 for one Tylenol pill and a South Carolina patient paying $1,000 for a toothbrush: "Usually any kind of bill under $100,000, they [the insurance companies] don't look at the details. And that's where something like this can be paid in error."[33]

As the Obama administration worked feverishly on health care reform during the summer of 2009, hospitals, health care plans, physicians, and unions offered to make changes that could reduce aggregate health care costs by as much as $2 trillion over the following decade—largely by bundling services and charging one fee for an entire course of care. Does this offer suggest that the major players in our health care system were already well aware of its "slack," inefficiencies or, simply, its "room for improvement?"

But the most overlooked cause of rising health care costs are the dramatic advances in medical technology. Because health care has improved, it has also become more expensive.

Probably the harshest criticism of U.S. health care—and a major concern of the Obama and earlier administrations—is the number of persons who lack insurance coverage. The federal government estimated that 47 million individuals (15.8% of the population) were uninsured in 2006.[34] Although the number of uninsured persons declined by 1.5 million in 2007, millions of Americans still go without health care coverage.[35] According to Sara R. Collins of the Commonwealth Fund, a private foundation supporting research on health care, "What is notable is how these problems are spreading up the income scale."[36]

What about those fortunate enough to have health insurance? During tough economic times, even persons with health insurance may be hard-pressed to pay the deductibles, copayments, and for the treatments that are not covered by their health insurance plans. Researchers from Harvard Law School, Harvard Medical School, and Ohio University found that about 60 percent of personal bankruptcies have been fueled by onerous medical debt.[37] And, according to a report issued by consumer advocacy group Families USA, uninsured persons in 2008 received $42.7 billion in unpaid health care. The Families USA report went on to say that this amount forced providers and insurers to pass these costs on to consumers in the form of a "hidden health tax." This tax amounted to $1,017 per insured family (or $368 per individual).[38]

Some evidence suggests that the U.S. health care system is also becoming more impersonal. A study by University of Chicago researchers published in the *Archives of Internal Medicine* revealed that patients were often unable to name any of the physicians who cared for them during their hospital stay.[39] A lack of personalization, in which no bond exists between patients and providers, may make it easier for the providers to commit fraud and then to believe it was a victimless crime.

In the *World Health Report 2000*, WHO cited three goals of a health care system: (1) good health across the entire range of ages, (2) health care providers who respond to people's expectations and treat them with respect and dignity, and (3) an equitable system of health care financing based on one's ability to pay.[40] The U.S. health care system has been blamed, to varying degrees, for falling short on reaching all these goals. Since the mid-1960s, politicians, policymakers, and health care experts have debated how to overhaul a group of industries described as "a non-system, an incoherent pastiche that has long repulsed reforms by private and public stakeholders."[41] A piecemeal overhaul of the health care system will simply shift problems and costs from one consumer group or industry segment to another. Conversely, little political and industry support seems to exist for a socialized health care system that is controlled by the federal government.

The future of the U.S. health care system is still unclear. The Obama administration's mislabeled "health care reform"—probably better described as "insurance reform"—is supposed to be phased in over a period of several years. If the plan withstands legal challenges and opposition by politicians, most Americans will be required to buy insurance, perhaps using a government-run exchange with tax credits to defray the cost. But an increase in the number of people covered by health insurance will likely lead to more health care transactions (e.g., more doctors' visits and more prescriptions filled). And as the number of transactions increases, so too will the amount of fraud and abuse.

The Flow of Services, Information, and Money: A Criminal's Delight

In its simplest form, the U.S. health care system has been depicted as one of money flowing in and money flowing out (represented in bird's-eye view in figure 1).[42] More accurately, the system is a constant movement of health care services, products, information, and money. Each arrow in the figure represents millions of possible transactions among U.S. health care's vast network of providers, consumers, and financing mechanisms. From the white-collar criminal's perspective, this fragmented system has numerous points of entry and a level of security that is incapable of preventing fraud.

Money is the commodity most valued by white-collar criminals. Money may be stolen directly when a physician files Medicare claims for dialysis treatments that were not provided to patients. But, rather than stealing money directly, white-collar criminals may convert information, products, or services to cash. A crooked employee working in a hospital or clinic may transcribe Social Security numbers from patient records as a first step toward committing credit card or insurance fraud. Another might convert stolen or misappropriated goods to cash. Pill-mill schemes employ criminals working for clinics. These individuals divert prescription drugs from their intended use and sell them back to crooked pharmacists or to drug dealers. And outsiders not working in a health care setting may also get in on the act; medical identity theft occurs when an uninsured person uses an insured person's identity to obtain treatment for an illness or injury.

Causes of Health Care Fraud

Individual Influences

Forensic psychologists and criminologists study the individual causes and patterns of crime. Theories attempting to explain or predict criminal behaviors and patterns of crime are diverse. Some theories focus on individuals, others on crime-facilitative or "criminogenic" environments, and still others on some combination of individual and environmental influences. Each theory of crime

The flow of services, information, and money

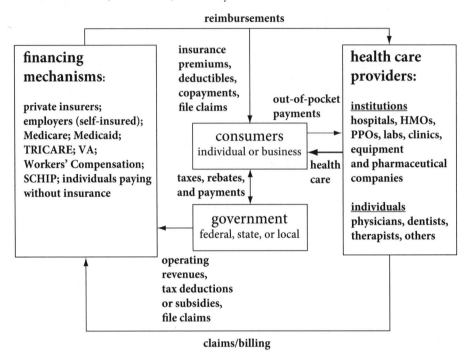

FIGURE 1. The U.S. health care system

probably contains an element of truth, but none fully explains why certain people engage in criminal or corrupt acts.[43]

An individual's decision to commit health care fraud is a rational choice. Few criminals have lost touch with reality. To the contrary, most white-collar criminals are rational; they carefully weigh the risks and benefits of a crime. But some health care fraudsters, although legally sane, may have a personality disorder. Aaron Beam, the cofounder and former chief financial officer of HealthSouth, described the company's infamous former CEO, Richard Scrushy, in the following fashion: "As brilliant as Richard was in his business dealings, he was equally diabolical, callous and cruel in his justification for attaining success. Unbeknownst to me from the outset was the fact that Richard was an egoist of the highest order, a consummate narcissist, likely a sociopath, and one of the biggest liars and fraudsters to ever lead a Fortune 500 company."[44]

Persons committing health care fraud—and white-collar criminals in general—can be divided into four categories: crisis responders, opportunity takers, opportunity seekers, and inadvertent offenders.[45] Crisis responders commit crimes out of financial desperation. They may be overwhelmed by medical bills, a past-due mortgage, gambling debts, a drug habit, or other "unsharable" problem. Crime, they believe, is the only way out of their financial embarrassment. Most crisis responders are first-time offenders with no prior arrests. They claim their crime is both their first and their last.[46]

Opportunity takers, though not experiencing a financial crisis, encounter an illicit offer they cannot refuse. Persons who are enticed into accepting lucrative kickbacks often fall into this category. As with crisis responders, opportunity takers may have no criminal record. In some cases, opportunity takers are first seduced by others into participating in a minor act of corruption. Once ensnared in the trap, they are forced into more serious crimes and, ultimately, into an inextricable situation.

Opportunity seekers are habitual criminals. They may engage exclusively in a life of crime or they may commit crimes on the side, often using their legitimate job or profession as a front for their illegal work. Some opportunity seekers prefer specific crimes such as health care fraud, whereas others are willing to participate in any criminal activity that offers high benefits and low risk. Opportunity seekers have usually had one or more encounters with the criminal justice system.

Inadvertent offenders mistakenly violate a law. The Stark Law, a federal civil statute, prohibits physicians from referring Medicare and Medicaid patients to a business such as a laboratory or radiology service if the physician—or an immediate family member of the physician—has a financial interest in that business.[47] The term "financial interest" under the Stark Law is confusing, especially to a physician with no business or legal training. What makes this statute especially treacherous is that it imposes a strict liability on offenders; a physician who unknowingly violates the Stark Law faces civil sanctions no matter how well intentioned he may have been.[48]

Because fraud and abuse are hard-to-define terms, it is useful to ponder two questions: Are current definitions of "fraud" and "abuse" too broad? And are those who judge these actions—legal counsel, prosecutors, judges, and juries—able to tell the difference between a real crime and an honest attempt by a doctor or a therapist to provide needed care to a patient? The following are some dilemmas encountered by health care workers.

Medicare allows home care services only to patients who are "homebound." These patients can leave their residences only infrequently and for a short duration; such absences must pose significant difficulty, inconvenience, or danger for the patient. In recent years, the definition of "homebound" has been relaxed to permit home health care patients to go to adult daycare facilities or to attend religious services. But this definition, some home health care nurses might say, is too stringent. Medicare investigators may observe an elderly patient sitting in a park across the street from his apartment and use this as proof that he is not homebound. Yet the man, desperate to leave the confines of his small apartment to enjoy a breath of fresh air on a nice day, may be unable to clean his house, make his bed, or do his shopping and laundry. Is the visiting nurse service, which receives Medicare payments for providing home health care to this man, committing Medicare fraud?

Or what about hospice care? According to Medicare, patients are only eligible for hospice services if they are expected to survive six months or fewer. Patient prognoses, however, are often inaccurate. The Medicare program permits a patient's physician to recertify her for an extended period of hospice care if she survives beyond the six-month limit as long as her condition is still regarded as terminal. Are physicians subject to prosecution for Medicare fraud if their patients live longer than expected or if the patient beats the odds and recovers from a terminal illness? Is this definition so stringent that it places an otherwise honest physician in an untenable position?

Or what of the obstetrician who knows her patient's insurance plan does not cover annual checkups? In a well-intentioned effort to get her patient's visit covered, she makes a notation in the patient's medical records that she was complaining of a headache when, in fact, she was not. Does the doctor's fudging the facts constitute fraud?

I also consider the flipside of this issue—whether the definitions of fraud and their associated penalties are sometimes too lax. Government prosecutors have extracted huge fraud settlements from large pharmaceutical firms and hospital chains. And, amazingly, it is usually the organization that bears the brunt of the punishment—along with its customers, shareholders, and other stakeholders. While these corporations take the heat, the actual perpetrators who engineered the fraud—the crooked administrators, doctors, or pharmaceutical-marketing representatives—may get away scot free. The real crooks not only avoid prison, but they often continue on with their professional lives without missing a beat. What does this historically lenient attitude toward white-collar criminals—especially those in the health care professions—tell us about our judicial system?

The stature of some health care fraudsters makes them unlikely criminal suspects; they may be board-certified physicians or professionals with advanced degrees who are leaders in their medical specialties and who are looked up to as role models and teachers. This fact raises questions about our health care system as well as about the educational institutions that produce the nation's physicians. Given the undue influence of commercial interests on physician practices, are doctors being educated and mentored in ways that sometimes promotes unethical behavior?

But not all health care fraud perpetrators are highly educated professionals. Some are little more than street thugs who have acquired a superficial level of medical knowledge. Others have acquired an in-depth knowledge of health care information systems and insurance claims procedures. Professional differences aside, however, they often share traits such as insatiable greed, a sense of entitlement ("I will take what is rightfully mine"), super optimism ("I am too smart to get caught"), and a superb ability to rationalize their illegal acts and assuage their guilt. Criminals may justify Medicare or Medicaid fraud, for example, by claiming these programs are operated by corrupt government officials bent on shortchanging health care providers and consumers. As Stanton E. Samenow, a forensic psychologist with more than forty years of experience evaluating criminals, has observed: "Despite a multitude of differences in their backgrounds and crime patterns, criminals are alike in one way: *how they think*. A gun-toting uneducated criminal off the streets of Southeast Washington, D.C., and a crooked Georgetown business executive are extremely similar in their view of themselves and the world."[49]

Organizational Influences

Organizations both encourage or discourage criminal activities through their culture and compensation practices. As noted, organized crime groups traditionally involved in gambling, prostitution, drugs, loan sharking, and pornography have begun to turn their attention to health care fraud. Some health care institutions not associated with organized crime, however, have also grown increasingly corrupt. Health care executives in these institutions may engage in unethical behaviors, sending a strong message to their associates that mendacious practices are acceptable. The for-profit sector of the health care system—hospital chains such as Tenet, HCA, and HealthSouth as well as the major pharmaceutical companies such as the former TAP (now the Takeda Pharmaceutical Company) and Serono Laboratories—has witnessed some spectacular health care frauds. It seems that unprincipled executives in these corporations have developed a groupthink mentality that fosters feelings of invincibility. For repeat offenders, it appears that this sense of invincibility is chronic.

Some health care organizations have fixated so intensely on bottom-line finances that fraud seems to be an integral part of their business strategy. Others inadvertently encourage crime through poor financial controls, lack of secure information systems, and lax peer review. Furthermore, large organizations with complex structures and flexible work environments allow criminals to hide their illegal activities. And, if they are caught, these fraudsters may use the byzantine structure of their organization to sidestep responsibility or to diffuse blame. Thus, when a medical error, false prescription, unnecessary treatment, or inflated insurance claim is detected, it may be written off as an honest mistake rather than viewed as an illegal act.

Widespread health care fraud may be facilitated by hospital boards failing to exercise adequate oversight over institutional executives and managers. Major scandals at Enron and WorldCom were enabled, in part, by compliant boards functioning as rubber-stamp entities rather than as vigilant watchdogs. Similarly, corrupt health care executives may hide their misdeeds from trusting board members. Hospital boards have been kept in the dark about clandestine illicit activities by hospital executives, or they have turned a blind eye toward fraudulent practices that, in some cases, have become part of the institutional fabric.

The Obama White House health reform director Nancy-Ann DeParle earned more than $6 million during the time she served on the boards of several major healthcare corporations. At least two of these corporations—DaVita and Guidant—were accused of fraud, mismanagement, and regulatory violations during DeParle's tenure on their boards. DaVita, a chain of dialysis centers, was being investigated for its billing and drug prescribing practices. Guidant, a medical equipment supplier, was being investigated for not disclosing the failures of some of its devices. No evidence has been found that DeParle contributed to or was even aware of the alleged illegal activities, but she did serve on board committees that were charged with overseeing legal and regulatory compliance.[50] Is DeParle yet another Obama appointee—along with the "income-tax challenged" Ron Kirk, Timothy Geithner, Nancy Killefer, and Hilda Solis—with skeletons in the closet? And will DeParle's possible lack of vigilance detract from her ability to help bring reform to U.S. health care?

Furthermore, the Joint Commission on Accreditation of Healthcare Organizations, the accreditation body for health care institutions, has been the target of controversy because of ties between Joint Commission members and hospital board members—especially Tenet Healthcare Corporation, a company with a beleaguered history.[51] In the case of Tenet, shareholders also got in on the act and formed the Tenet Shareholder Committee under the leadership of South Florida physician and attorney M. Lee Pearce. The shareholder committee spent eight years publicizing fraud and abuse at Tenet before dissolving itself at the end of 2008. The committee's parting shot at company executives came in the form of a lengthy web page that, among other things, leveled scathing criticism at Tenet's "overpaid, conflicted, and passive" board of directors.[52]

Compensation practices can also encourage health care fraud and abuse. Many health care providers are paid by the number of patients they see or by the number of treatments or services they render, tempting them to overstate the amount of work they actually perform. And high-salaried health care executives may receive a significant portion of their compensation through stock options. Anyone familiar with recent financial scandals knows about the corrupting influence of equity-based pay—linking executive pay to a company's stock price. The UnitedHealth Group agreed to a settlement of $895 million with two pension plans, the California Employees' Retirement System and the Alaska Plumbing and Pipefitting Industry Pension Trust. The lawsuit was precipitated by a stock option backdating scandal centering on UnitedHealth's former CEO, Dr. William McGuire. For his end of the settlement, McGuire agreed to forfeit

$420 million in stock option gains and retirement pay.[53] Antitrust violations represent yet another avenue of health care fraud and abuse, when health insurance companies or providers fix prices at unreasonably high levels. At this writing, the Massachusetts Attorney General's Office was investigating whether the state's largest insurance company, Blue Cross Blue Shield of Massachusetts, and its largest healthcare provider, Partners Healthcare, engaged in illegal price collusion. This case is discussed more fully in chapter 4.

Societal Influences

Society influences crime in a general way. The most important societal influence on health care fraud and abuse is the health care system itself. The emphasis on generating high earnings in the for-profit segment of U.S. health care often breeds cutthroat competition. Many cities have several hospitals, creating battles over personnel, patients, contracts, and resources. This commercial warfare may encourage hospitals and suppliers to offer kickbacks, physicians to self-refer, admissions personnel to treat unprofitable Medicaid patients with scorn as well as engaging in other fraudulent, wasteful, and unethical practices.

Western societies, in general, and the United States in particular, equate economic well-being with individual advancement and personal worth. Geert Hofstede's analysis of cultural differences among countries worldwide ranks the United States as the single most individualistic nation: "The high individualism (IDV) ranking for the United States indicates a society with a more individualistic attitude and relatively loose bonds with others. The populace is more self-reliant and looks out for themselves and their close family members."[54] A focus on the individual, rather than on the social good, can encourage people to ignore how their actions might impact others. Furthermore, individuals in the health care fields are among the brightest and most ambitious of all professionals.

Before the economic bubble burst in 2008, the accumulation of wealth—seemingly without much consideration as to how that wealth was obtained—became an obsession for some highly driven, narcissistic, and even antisocial doctors, politicians, lawyers, and executives (both on Wall Street and off). Add to this the fact that health care occupations rank high in status and autonomy. Many physicians—although not always perpetrators—may act as enablers to many forms of fraud and abuse. Why? Is there something about the high status of doctors that, at least in their minds, exempts them from legal and ethical guidelines?

As analysts of professionalism have pointed out, society historically has given physicians the power to regulate themselves because they were supposed to act altruistically to protect their patients. Modern critics have debunked the myth of self-regulation. But has society's traditional hands-off approach encouraged or enabled some health care professionals to misuse their status?

A strict hierarchy of authority exists among health care providers, placing the medical doctor at the top. Being in an unassailable position allows the acts of a crooked doctor to go undetected or unchallenged. Some people joke that M.D. stands for "major deity." In the case of fraud and abuse in health care, it seems that some M.D.s—albeit a minority—believe they have sole discretion in deciding whether an act is justifiable and ethical and whether to obey the law. Fleecing patients and their insurers by providing overpriced or unnecessary services and then justifying these excesses in the name of free-market forces or better health care is a temptation that some providers cannot resist.

Another aggravating issue is that, when it comes to the health care professions, information asymmetries are everywhere. Doctors, nurses, and other health care professionals have more knowledge of medicine than do their patients, reducing the likelihood that their professional decisions will be questioned. Furthermore, information technology has become an integral part of health care, and it has improved tremendously the management of patient medical information. This technology, however, has also enabled persons—both authorized and unauthorized—to make illicit transfers of money, to steal information, to submit fraudulent insurance claims, to gain unauthorized access to patient medical records, and to cover up acts of fraud.

The Salient Features of Health Care Fraud and Abuse

Health care frauds come in all shapes and sizes, but they are similar to other white-collar crimes.[55] One obvious similarity is the illicit transfer or misappropriation of money and resources. But there are more.

The success of many crimes, whether perpetrated by an urban street hustler or by a sophisticated white-collar criminal, often depends on gaining the victim's trust. And health care fraud and abuse often entail an abuse of trust between patient and provider. A Wisconsin psychiatrist was arrested after a criminal complaint charged him with three acts of sexual misconduct with a female patient. The patient told detectives that she and her doctor had sexual contact "during a number of their therapy sessions."[56] A fifty-six-year-old Delaware pediatrician was charged in February 2010 with the molestation of 103 children. Labeled as "pure evil" and as one of the "worst pedophiles in U.S. history," the doctor faces a 471-count indictment. If convicted, he faces a life sentence without parole. But putting these doctors behind bars will probably do little to lessen the horrible psychological damage to their innocent victims and their families.[57] These two cases exemplify some of the worst that our health care system has to offer.

As with the Blue Code of Silence for police officers, health care workers and other professionals may feel pressures to protect their own. But perhaps a less-obvious concern of whistle-blowers is the fear of "no good deed going unpunished." Doctors at a Tennessee eye clinic turned in one of their colleagues after they discovered he had cheated Medicare out of $1.6 million. For their honesty and because they were saddled with a dishonest business partner, the eye-doctors-turned-whistle-blowers had to pay back hundreds of thousands of dollars to the federal government. They also had to write off about $300,000 in expired drugs (the medicine was seized by federal authorities as evidence), cover the costs of an internal investigation, and endure a civil lawsuit.[58]

Health care fraud often inflicts bodily injury or even death on its victims. Medical injuries and deaths may be precipitated by incompetency, negligence, fraud, and abuse. These injuries have led to a degree of unnecessary human suffering—a suffering that has been described as "the equivalent of a 747 airplane crashing every day of the year."[59] White-collar crimes are often regarded as nonviolent. But, according to the FBI, a significant trend observed in recent health care fraud cases is the willingness of medical professionals to devise schemes that risk harming patients.[60] Recommending unnecessary surgeries, prescribing dangerous drugs, and engaging in other abusive or substandard practices imperil the lives of unsuspecting patients. In many jurisdictions, the fee-grubbing surgeon who wields a scalpel to remove a healthy gall bladder is subject to the same criminal charges as the street hoodlum who wields a knife to stab his victim during a back-alley mugging.

The Dynamics of Health Care Fraud

Health care fraud is always a moving target. White-collar criminals commit fraud because health care systems or organizations and society provide them with the opportunity to do so. When fraud becomes widespread, society and organizations take measures to stop it. The U.S. Congress and state legislatures have enacted laws to deal with white-collar crimes in general and health care frauds in particular. Furthermore, public officials may beef up the enforcement of existing laws. Media exposure and heightened public awareness of health care fraud may also make such crimes more difficult to commit. Organizations may attack health care fraud by bolstering security, reconstituting auditing practices, training employees in fraud detection, or aggressively prosecuting those caught engaging in illegal activities.

As society and organizations try to curtail fraud, criminals also make adjustments. Some fraud artists may decide that certain crimes have become too risky, so they shift their efforts to other crimes or forego illegal acts altogether. Other criminals adapt to the new societal and organizational measures and continue committing health care fraud by employing new strategies.

Thus, health care fraud is ever changing. Types of frauds committed twenty years ago may have fallen by the wayside only to be replaced by newer and more innovative ones. Although criminals as a group score lower on intelligence tests than do law-abiding citizens, those committing health care fraud are often quite ingenious, especially when it comes to developing new fraud schemes.

Victims of street crimes such as robbery or assault are immediately aware of their predicament. Victims of financial crimes such as identity theft or credit card fraud are usually aware within a few days of the transgressions against them. Many health care frauds, on the other hand, are invisible.[61] Criminals use the vastness of the health care system or the trust and ignorance of their victims to hide their misdeeds. They depend on the fact that a bogus insurance claim appears normal or that a health insurer is more concerned about processing claims efficiently than about detecting fraud. In other instances, criminals bank on their victims either not realizing a fraud has occurred or not reporting a suspected case of health care fraud to authorities—possibly because of personal embarrassment, fear of legal action by the health care provider, or concerns that they will lose their health insurance coverage.

If a category of crime cannot be detected or reported consistently, then it cannot be measured accurately and analyzed intelligently. Although health care fraud remains an enigma, clear evidence exists that it is a major social problem costing U.S. consumers and taxpayers billions of dollars a year. As health care expenditures also increase, fueled by an expansion of health care insurance coverage and an aging population, fraud and abuse will continue to affect millions of potential victims. It is clear that perpetrators of health care fraud and abuse are usually intelligent individuals who are skilled at avoiding detection, rationalizing their misdeeds, and adapting to changing conditions. They have learned how to leverage their professional status or to capitalize on security weaknesses and legal loopholes in the health care system. Public and private organizations will have to step up their efforts to combat fraud and abuse, and our society will have to examine cherished values and entrenched hierarchies if we want to stop the fraud and abuse that is draining our system of billions of health care dollars and putting patient lives at risk.

The criminals described in this book steal billions of dollars from consumers, providers, insurers, and taxpayers. Thefts committed by these crooks not only inflict pain and suffering on their victims, but they undermine the workings of the U.S. health care system. An understanding of health care fraud and abuse should begin with a discussion of health care law—a topic addressed in the following two chapters. But antifraud and abuse laws are of little value unless resources are provided to enforce them. So, as another presidential administration takes a stab at health care reform, such efforts—no matter how well intentioned—are doomed to failure unless we have both a plan and the resources to fight this monumental problem.

HEALTH CARE FRAUD AND ITS FACILITATING CRIMES

The False Invoice Scheme

Two business partners, one living in Texas and the other in Tennessee, had a good thing going. Despite being separated by hundreds of miles, these middle-aged women worked together, making money hand over fist through a simple invoicing scheme that lined their pockets with hundreds of thousands of dollars.

The woman in Texas was employed by a medical center as the director of physician recruiting. The woman in Tennessee ran her own physician-recruiting service. After meeting online in 2002, the pair agreed to a physician-recruitment scam. The Texas partner told her Tennessee counterpart what items to bill the medical center along with the billing amounts. Then the crooked Tennessee partner created and sent the invoices for the bogus services to her friend in Texas. Both women knew that the work represented on the invoices had not been performed at all or had not been performed as represented. Once the Tennessee physician—recruiter received a check for "services rendered" on the invoices, she kicked back between 25 and 50 percent to her accomplice in Texas.

From 2002 to 2007, the Texas medical center paid the Tennessee businesswoman $851,416.83 based on the fraudulent invoices. Of that amount, her friend in Texas received $283,126 in kickbacks. The scheme was eventually detected, and the two women pleaded guilty to theft in January 2009. U.S. District Judge Sam R. Cummings sentenced them each to thirty months in federal prison and ordered them to pay a total of $905,166.05 in restitution.[1]

This health care fraud case is extremely simple. Since the medical center was deceived into making payments for services that it never received, the women committed fraud. Yet, in addition to the primary crimes of fraud and theft, white-collar offenders such as these two women usually face charges for a variety of facilitating crimes. By acting together, they engaged in a conspiracy to commit an illegal act. Because their scheme involved using the mail system as well as the telephone and the Internet, the pair opened themselves up to mail and wire fraud charges. Furthermore, if they had tried to hide their money or disguise its source, the women could have been charged with money laundering and tax evasion. Finally, many criminals who attempt to deceive investigators may face charges of lying to federal authorities, obstruction of justice, and perjury.

The point to remember is that even a simple health care fraud case such as the one involving these two far-flung business partners can have severe consequences. By pleading guilty instead of putting themselves at the mercy of a federal jury trial, the two women avoided twenty-two additional charges that could have lengthened their sentences considerably.[2]

Fraud Defined

The backbone of all white-collar crimes is fraud, and the primary ingredients of fraud are misrepresentation and acts of deception. When we use the term "fraud" in common language, it always has a pejorative meaning. "That's fraudulent behavior," we exclaim when we hear about someone behaving less than honestly. Certain conditions must be met, however, before an individual can be judged guilty of fraud in a legal proceeding.[3]

Fraud differs from abuses such as price gouging or mistakes such as billing errors. Price gouging usually occurs when someone takes advantage of a vulnerable person and charges them an exorbitant sum for goods or services. In the wake of a natural disaster such as a hurricane, unscrupulous price gougers charge devastated residents inflated prices for basic necessities. The second example—a billing error—is a mistake that will not result in criminal charges or a civil suit, unless such "mistakes" are blatant or follow a repeated pattern. Fraud also differs from a bad result (e.g., a frail patient dies after a successful surgery), an incorrect prediction or forecast (e.g., a doctor's prognosis for a patient was wrong), and even malpractice (e.g., a doctor failed to provide adequate postoperative care and his patient developed a life-threatening infection).

Three conditions are required to prove fraud. Prosecutors must demonstrate that the perpetrator lied to or mislead the victim to conceal the fraud. Then they must show that the victim believed and acted on the perpetrator's fraudulent statements. Finally, to constitute fraud, it must be documented that the victim suffered economic or other damages at the hands of the perpetrator.

The person committing a fraudulent act must knowingly or recklessly make a misrepresentation of a material fact. The misrepresentations they make include lies of commission and lies of omission. A lie of commission occurs by saying something that is not true about "a fact that is significant or essential to the issue or matter at hand" (in legalese, this is known as a material fact).[4] When a physician intentionally overcharges a health insurer, he or she has committed a lie of commission. Some health care providers contend that overbilling compensates them for accepting low payments, wasting time on claims disputes, or dealing with insurance company red tape. But no matter how justifiable their complaints, they do not have the right to decide on what payment they believe befits them. Such misrepresentations constitute fraud.

A lie of omission occurs when a health care provider hides an important fact such as a medical mistake endangering a patient's life. According to a study by HealthGrades, over three hundred thousand deaths of Medicare patients between 2002 and 2004 resulted from medical care errors.[5] Most of these deaths were due to mistakes, not fraud. But fraud may be used to mislead investigators, to cover up serious medical errors, to avoid malpractice suits, or to protect one's professional reputation.

The case of Esmin Green became a Pandora's box for New York's Health and Hospitals Corporation. Green's case received widespread media coverage after she fell and died while waiting for psychiatric care at HHC's Kings County Hospital Center in Brooklyn. A subsequent investigation of HHC by the *New York Daily News* revealed missing records at HHC facilities as well as discrepancies and false entries in hospital records. Some entries were faked to cover serious mistakes by HHC personnel.[6]

Demonstrating the first condition of fraud can be vexing to prosecutors because they must show that the defendant meant to defraud and then took actions to cover his or her tracks. For this reason, prosecutors may prefer pursuing civil rather than criminal charges against an offender. The "preponderance of evidence" burden of proof standard in civil cases is less demanding than the "beyond a reasonable doubt" standard in criminal cases. Providers accused of fraud often claim they had no intention of deceiving their victim (i.e., they had no *mens rea* or "guilty mind"). For example, a physician may describe the liberal use of diagnostic tests on a patient not as abusive overutilization but as crucial to the thorough evaluation of that patient.[7]

As mentioned earlier, definitions of fraud may be too broad and thus entangle clinicians who have only the best intentions toward their patients and society. Remember the obstetrician who tried to get her patient's annual checkup covered by claiming falsely that the patient had a headache? She knew quite well that her patient suffered nothing of the sort, but she also believed that the patient's health insurance should cover annual physical exams. Is this otherwise honest physician a perpetrator of fraud because she wanted to serve the best interests of her patient? One could argue that the physician was innocent of wrongdoing because she was protecting her patient. On the other hand, a cynic might argue that if the physician was so concerned about her patient's welfare—perhaps then being accused of favoring one patient over another—she could have provided the annual checkup free of charge. Another counterargument is that by giving the patient a thorough physical exam and charging it fraudulently to the patient's insurer, the physician was acting in the best interests of both the patient and the health care system. Had she spotted a serious medical problem early, she could have nipped it in the bud before it later developed into something more debilitating. As can be seen, the line may be blurred between a physician's making a medical decision that is in the best interests of the patient versus a decision that might be regarded as health care fraud.

A promise or opinion made in good faith and founded on reliable knowledge does not constitute fraud. Suppose a physician prescribes an expensive antibiotic and tells his patient he will feel better within a week. Even though the antibiotic did not later perform as promised, no fraud occurred as long as the physician had made an informed judgment based on current medical knowledge.

The second condition required for establishing fraudulent intent is for the victim not only to believe but also to take action based on a misrepresentation. A Boston-area psychiatrist fabricated medical diagnoses and made insurance claims for patients, some of whom he had never met. His false diagnoses included "depressive psychosis," "suicidal ideation," "sexual identity problems," and "behavioral problems in school." Many of his diagnoses were documented using fictitious counseling session notes. In this case, the health care insurers accepted these bogus evaluations as legitimate, and the insurers paid the psychiatrist over $1 million in reimbursements. He was later caught and convicted of fraud and money laundering.[8]

Health care fraud cases often hinge on the trust patients place in health care providers. "Fraud in the inducement" is a misrepresentation that entices a person to enter into a transaction with a false impression of the risks.[9] Bernard Madoff did exactly this sort of thing in the field of financial management when he lied to his clients and pocketed their investment monies. A patient who is paralyzed by a controversial and dangerous experimental treatment after his physician tells him the procedure is "routine" and "normal" is a victim of fraud in the inducement.

A San Francisco executive was sentenced to forty-one months in prison and ordered to pay $1.3 million in restitution after he defrauded thousands of people across the United States by selling them worthless health insurance. The phony insurance company collected over $2.8 million in premiums, but most of these funds were not placed into insurance trust accounts. Instead, the perpetrator spent the premiums on expensive cars, football tickets, and commissions to promoters who helped market the fraudulent plan.[10]

Finally, the act of fraud must cause harm. Nearly all health care frauds result in economic damage. Economic damages include the loss of money, products, or services as well as inflated health care costs, higher health insurance premiums, extraordinary legal expenses, additional regulatory and compliance costs, beefed up fraud detection measures that slow the processing of insurance claims, and time wasted in dealing with the fraud (an opportunity cost). Health care frauds, however, add a pernicious element to white-collar crime and fraud in general. They often cause physical harm to sick and vulnerable individuals. For example, fraud, in the form of fake or substandard laboratory tests, may allow a patient's serious health problem to go undiagnosed and untreated.

Counterfeit diagnoses, on the other hand, may lead to unnecessary, painful, or dangerous treatments. A hospital in Maryland has been at the center of a federal investigation over the accusation that doctors there inserted coronary implants (stents) in as many as 369 patients who did not need them. Medicare and private insurers will pay for these implants only if the patient has at least a 70 percent blockage. One sixty-nine-year-old patient was told that he had a 95 percent arterial blockage when, in fact, the blockage was closer to 10 percent. Another patient, who was told she had a 90 percent blockage, later learned that she had no problem. But for the rest of her life she will be saddled with an irremovable stent. At over ten thousand dollars a pop, cardiac catheterizations are a tempting and lucrative business for an unscrupulous physician.[11]

A network of doctors and clinics based in California devised a rent-a-patient scheme to defraud health insurance companies. As many as 4,500 patients from forty—four states and Puerto Rico were recruited and paid small sums of money to undergo unnecessary colonoscopies and other surgeries. The doctors then billed private insurance carriers at inflated rates, resulting in a $30 million civil suit against them by twelve Blue Cross plans.[12] This fraud resulted in lost income and legal expenses for Blue Cross.

Phony diagnoses may also stigmatize a patient, later limiting employment opportunities or making it difficult to obtain health or life insurance. Charges for unnecessary tests or treatments have also caused patients to exceed their lifetime health care insurance benefit limits—something the Obama administration is eliminating in its health care reform proposals. But persons without major medical coverage are walking a tightrope with no financial safety net, which is especially dangerous if they are faced with a catastrophic illness or injury.

The psychological damage to victims of health care fraud can be devastating. Fertility scams are among the most despicable of health care frauds. One notorious case involved a Virginia physician, Dr. Cecil Jacobson. Jacobson misled some patients into believing they had conceived, and, in other cases, he secretly impregnated female patients with his own sperm. Although Jacobson duped couples into paying him tens of thousands of dollars, the psychological damage he caused undoubtedly exceeded the economic damages.[13] Why did these patients sign on with the likes of a Cecil Jacobson? The answer might lie in their desperation to conceive a healthy child. That same desperation might explain why some terminally ill patients agree to almost any form of treatment, no matter how radical, far-fetched, or expensive.

Many fraud artists view public and private insurance programs as veritable treasure chests. On March 4, 2008, an Ohio man was sentenced to thirty-seven months in prison to be followed by three years of supervised release. A few days earlier, his brother had been sentenced to thirty-three months in prison and three years of postrelease supervision. Both defendants were charged with conspiracy to commit health care fraud and money laundering. They were each ordered to pay over $1.7 million in restitution, a $75,000 fine, a $200 special assessment fee, and $550,000 for prosecution costs.

What did the two brothers do to deserve this punishment? As it turns out, they put their brains to work trying to fleece millions of dollars from Medicare, Medicaid, TRICARE, and several private health insurance programs. And, before they were finally caught, they succeeded in submitting over $4.8 million in false claims on behalf of their company, a group of chiropractic and medical clinics doing business in seven northern Ohio cities.

The brothers hired medical doctors to work in the clinics where chiropractors performed noncovered chiropractic services disguised as covered medical services. Using the hired medical doctors as a ruse, the company's noncovered services were billed to the insurers using false billing codes. If one of the insurers questioned or denied an improper claim, the impudent brothers lied, saying the billings were for medical services, not chiropractic services. This scheme enabled their medical clinics to circumvent the insurance coverage limits on chiropractic treatments, and unsuspecting insurers were duped into reimbursing the company for more than $1.7 million. In cracking the case, agents from the Federal Bureau of Investigation, the Internal Revenue Service, the U.S. Postal Inspection Service, the Defense Criminal Investigative Service, the Ohio State Medical Board, the Ohio State Chiropractic Board, and the Ohio Bureau of Workers' Compensation interviewed eighty people associated with the clinics, including doctors, chiropractors, staff, and patients. Agents also seized some 973 boxes of records along with twenty computers. In addition to the false claims, the defendants conspired to commit money laundering by using funds from the billing scheme to make almost $1.6 million in salary payments to the medical doctors.[14]

Facilitative Crimes

Health care frauds such as filing phony insurance claims, making false diagnoses, organizing a rent-a-patient scheme, or promoting the illegal off-label use of a drug are all "object crimes." These crimes have a purpose and that purpose is usually to steal or misappropriate money. In August 2010, a Chicago-area cardiologist was sentenced to five years in federal prison for receiving more than $13 million in improper reimbursements from Medicare and other insurers. The cardiologist allegedly obtained confidential health care information on unsuspecting patients from three local hospitals between January 2002 and July 2007. He faxed phony handwritten treatment notes to hired "billers" to complete claims to Medicare and other insurance companies for high-end cardiac treatments that he never performed.

In another Chicago-area case, a forty-seven-year-old general practitioner bilked Blue Cross Blue Shield of Illinois out of $900,000 for bogus treatments. A number of bloggers familiar with these two cases weighed in. One wrote: "As a guy who knows a lot about doctors, I would say 80% of them do this type of thing and is quite common. There is a reason why some primary care physicians are able to afford $400,000 cars for telling some people to take aspirin." Another had this to say: "I saw [the doctor] Dec 05, I was very diligent about reviewing my bills. I received bills from him for dates I did not see him, 4 or 5 separate occasions. My husband also saw him once and received numerous bills. They even tried sending me to collections. I called the office and kept getting the runaround. I finally called BCBS and filed a complaint with the fraud department. I'm glad they finally put a stop to this."[15]

The crimes that support or enable the object crimes are known as facilitative or auxiliary crimes. Facilitative crimes include conspiracy, money laundering, tax evasion, mail and wire fraud, and obstruction of justice. No one commits a facilitative crime (with the possible exception of tax evasion) without an object crime in mind. You might say that the facilitating crimes provide the traction for the object crimes. For example, the facilitative crimes of mail or wire fraud are necessary for the commission of the object crime of filing false insurance claims. It is difficult to imagine how those Chicago-area physicians whose frauds I have described could have committed this primary crime without using the mail system or some form of wire communications such as a telephone, fax machine, e-mail, or other component of the Internet.

Federal prosecutors have found a silver lining in facilitating crimes. It is often easier for them to convict a white-collar defendant of conspiracy, mail fraud, tax evasion, or money laundering than it is to convict someone of an object crime such as embezzlement or fraud. Evidence to support a Medicare fraud charge against a physician may be weak, but evidence to convict the doctor of tax evasion, money laundering, or obstruction of justice may be strong. Furthermore, tax evasion and money laundering convictions alone carry prison sentences that may be lengthy enough to satisfy federal prosecutors.

Charges of facilitative crimes also enable prosecutors to present a comprehensive view of the case before a judge and jury including timelines and background information on the defendants, their motives, their victims and the harm they suffered, and the statutes violated.[16] Information pertaining to the facilitative crimes may then be useful in demonstrating the defendant's guilt for the object crime.

Individuals charged with a white-collar crime are almost always charged with at least one (and usually more than one) facilitative crime. The two brothers from Ohio, for example, were charged with the object crime of health care fraud as well as the facilitative crimes of conspiracy and money laundering. And the Miami physician discussed in the introductory chapter, was charged not only with making false claims and receiving kickbacks (both object crimes), but she was also charged with conspiracy and tax evasion (both facilitative crimes).

In February 2008, a woman was sentenced to twenty-four months in prison followed by two years of supervised release and ordered to pay $596,429 in restitution for funds she had stolen from her employer, Blue Cross Blue Shield of Massachusetts. Over a period of five years, this $90,000-a-year systems manager created a false self-insured health plan and defrauded Blue Cross Blue Shield into issuing refund checks to the plan.[17] She then cashed the checks, using the money for personal expenses and failing to report the income on her federal tax returns.[18] Thus, we have the object crime, defrauding Blue Cross Blue Shield of Massachusetts, and at least one facilitating crime, income tax evasion. This woman could have been charged with two additional facilitating crimes, mail and wire fraud, if she had used the mails or online banking services to deposit the stolen funds into her Boston-area bank account.

Conspiracy

Charges of conspiracy arise when two or more individuals participate in the planning or execution of a crime.[19] The Blue Cross Blue Shield employee described above appears to have acted alone, so she cannot be charged with conspiracy. But many white-collar crimes—including health care fraud—involve more than one participant. Conspiracy is also an amorphous crime. Because participants in a health care fraud case are involved to different degrees, it is sometimes hard to know when knowledge of a crime or participation in a crime crosses the line into an illegal conspiracy. For this reason, prosecutors favor conspiracy charges because it enables them to cast a wide net, ensnaring anyone who might be even slightly involved in a crime.

Conspiracy is an agreement or meeting of the minds to achieve an illegal end. One such illegal end, health care fraud, often entails complex arrangements and a concerted effort by several individuals who have specific expertise or specialized access. They may use their expertise or access to navigate unobtrusively through information systems, insurance-claims procedures, and money-laundering channels.

That is why criminal statutes treat conspiracy as a charge that is separate from the object crime.

When health care frauds are conspiratorial, they work either as a chain or as a wheel conspiracy. The chain conspiracy is one in which, in "a single conspiracy," "each person is responsible for a distinct act within the overall plan."[20] A fraud in which one person steals patient information, a second person files fraudulent Medicare claims, and a third person launders money derived from the scam is an example of a chain conspiracy.

A Texas couple, along with a third conspirator, admitted to defrauding Medicare and Medicaid in a two-year durable medical equipment (DME) fraud conspiracy. Federal District Court Judge Leonard Davis sentenced the couple to twenty-seven months in prison for conspiracy, money laundering, and fraud. They were ordered to pay $284,689 in restitution and to submit to three years of supervision after completing their prison terms.

Through medical supply companies in East Texas, the defendants obtained information about legitimate beneficiaries, submitted fraudulent claims to Medicare and Medicaid for the cost of motorized wheelchairs and accessories, and hid the money from law enforcement and tax authorities. The seven-count indictment listed frauds totaling $427,150. The third conspirator in this chain cooperated in the prosecution of the other two defendants and was sentenced to two years in prison for defrauding Medicare of more than $800,000. He contributed to the chain conspiracy by filing Medicare claims for motorized wheelchairs and scooters on behalf of recipients who were not eligible for these benefits.[21]

When we do not have links in a chain, we have spokes in a wheel. Here we are dealing with a conspiracy in which a single member or group (the hub of the wheel) colludes with two or more conspirators—the spokes. The person or group at the hub is the only party liable for all the conspiracies.[22] In the case of a New York podiatrist, we see that almost any health care service or piece of equipment might be used to commit fraud. The podiatrist was indicted by a Westchester County grand jury on the charge of stealing $1.8 million by submitting fraudulent Medicaid billings for special footwear. He billed Medicaid for expensive custom-made foot appliances even though he provided patients with cheap stock goods or no goods at all. The indictment accused him of masterminding what a special prosecutor for Medicaid fraud called "the largest and most sophisticated podiatry fraud yet perpetrated on the nation's Medicaid system." Between 1983 and 1986 he paid kickbacks to New York area podiatrists for steering business to his five custom footwear businesses. Inventive to a fault, he even tried to mislead state investigators by creating a mock laboratory, complete with leather dust, in the basement of his office.[23] In this case, the crooked podiatrist was the hub of the wheel with the other New York podiatrists, who may not have even known each other, serving as the spokes.

Even those playing a minor role in a criminal activity are subject to conspiracy charges. A custodian who is paid by other conspirators to "accidently" leave a door unlocked so that unauthorized personnel can enter a room and steal laptop computers containing confidential patient information may be charged with conspiracy even though the custodian was at home when the thefts occurred. But someone who merely suspects that others are involved in criminal activity, however, will not be charged with conspiracy. Getting cold feet and withdrawing from a conspiracy does not necessarily protect a party from criminal charges. Furthermore, prosecutors may grant leniency to those playing a less significant role in the conspiracy in exchange for information or testimony against the more culpable participants.

Whether chains or wheels, conspiracy is an "inchoate" crime. That is, perpetrators of a health care fraud may be arrested for planning a crime even before they have the opportunity to execute it. Suppose that three former information technology employees at a medical center plan to steal patient medical information and use the information to commit identity theft. If the former employees hack into the center's computer system but their plot is foiled before they have a chance to steal any information, they will be charged with conspiracy even though the object crime never reached fruition. Discussing a crime over drinks in a bar without doing anything to set it in motion, however, does not qualify as a conspiracy.

Federal rules govern the introduction of evidence in both criminal and civil cases. In conspiracy cases involving hearsay testimony, the rules have a twist. Hearsay might include rumor, gossip, unverified statements, or evidence based on the reports of others rather than on the personal knowledge of the witness—what we call secondhand information. Because hearsay evidence is often unreliable, it is not admissible in most legal proceedings—except conspiracy cases. By relaxing the hearsay rule, prosecutors are able to use information about coconspirators that was obtained through out-of-court or secondhand sources. The hearsay rule is relaxed because conspiracy cases offer little or no direct evidence, and inferior evidence is preferable to no evidence at all.[24]

Using the Racketeering Influenced and Corrupt Organizations (RICO) Act

When we think of health care fraud, we do not usually think of mobsters such as John Gotti and Charles "Lucky" Luciano (or fictional ones such as Tony Soprano or Vito Corleone). As mentioned earlier, a $2.5 trillion industry is not only a magnet for run-of-the-mill crooks, but it is also becoming a magnet for people who have made crime an organized business. Not surprisingly, the Racketeer Influenced and Corrupt Organizations Act of 1970, which was enacted primarily to combat organized crime, can be used to pursue the mob's entrance into the health care arena.[25] But the law has also been used—at least to a limited extent—against health care institutions, pharmaceutical manufacturers, and health insurers. Indeed, in 1985, the U.S. Supreme Court in *Sedima v. Inrex* made it easier for civil plaintiffs to use the RICO Act by expanding its coverage beyond organized crime. The Court's decision in *Sedima* has transformed the act into an integral weapon against white-collar criminals.[26]

According to the RICO Act, it is a crime for someone to gain control of a legitimate business through intimidation, violence, or other illegal means.[27] The RICO Act defines a pattern of criminal activity as the commission of two or more related instances of racketeering within a ten-year period. "Racketeering" is defined by a wide range of "predicate acts," which are spelled out in the RICO Act. Predicate acts include murder, extortion, theft from an interstate shipment, embezzlement from pension and welfare funds, and many more. In addition to targeting organized crime, the Act's broad definition of racketeering has been applied to corporations, partnerships, associate-in-fact enterprises (a loose-knit group of associates who engage in both legal and illegal activities), and even individuals.

Federal court decisions have dealt extensively with definitions of what constitutes an "enterprise," or what is meant by the terms "management" and "racketeering." The courts have also had to wrestle with whether a proximate cause, or close relationship, exists between the actions of an illegal enterprise and the damages inflicted by that enterprise.

And what constitutes a pattern of criminal activity? To constitute such a pattern, a set of crimes must have a common element. Crimes all linked to defrauding Medicare, for example, constitute a pattern, whereas a variety of unrelated crimes (e.g., drug trafficking, securities fraud, and automobile theft) might not constitute a pattern. To qualify as a "pattern" such crimes must share a degree of continuity—that is, the frauds must be committed by a core group of perpetrators over a period of time.

Under section 1962(d) of the RICO Act, it is unlawful for a person to conspire to violate subsections 1962(a), (b), or (c) of the RICO Act, which make it illegal for persons to have a financial or business interest in an organization engaged in racketeering.[28] So when it comes to health care fraud, the RICO Act prohibits the associated crimes or predicate acts of bribery, money laundering, counterfeiting, extortion, dealing in narcotics or other dangerous drugs, mail and wire fraud, and obstruction of justice. It not only establishes stiff criminal penalties, but it also permits civil suits and the forfeiture of assets derived from criminal activities. Victims of health care fraud may pursue civil action under the RICO Act section 1962(c) against persons who have caused them harm. The following cases illustrate the ever-widening scope of RICO Act litigation.

A national class action was certified in March 2008 against First DataBank and the McKesson Corporation. The suit alleged that First DataBank and McKesson engaged in a racketeering enterprise by falsifying the average wholesale price for numerous prescription pharmaceuticals in violation of the RICO Act and California state law. In late 2001, First DataBank, a drug-pricing publisher, and McKesson, a drug wholesaler, reached a secret agreement to increase the spread between the wholesale acquisition cost of certain drugs and their average wholesale price. According to a health care policy report released by the Bureau of National Affairs, the average wholesale price (AWP) for most brand-name drugs is 20 to 25 percent above the wholesale acquisition cost (WAC).[29] The agreement between McKesson and First DataBank increased profit margins on over four hundred drugs. McKesson communicated these new markups to First DataBank, and the company then published them.

Prior to the secret agreement between McKesson and First DataBank, little uniformity existed between the WAC and the AWP for hundreds of brand-name drugs; differentials were based on information supplied independently by the drug manufacturers or by First DataBank's surveys of wholesale costs and prices. Once the secret AWP-WAC agreement went into effect, the prices of most drugs were raised to artificially high levels and fixed.[30] By 2004, 99 percent of all prescription-drug manufacturers were using the inflated markups. The scheme resulted in higher profits for retail pharmacies because these firms purchased drugs on the basis of the wholesale acquisition cost, but they were reimbursed on the basis of the marked-up average wholesale price.

McKesson was accused of implementing the scheme to increase profit margins for major retail pharmacy clients such as Rite Aid and Wal-Mart as well as for its own pharmacy businesses.[31] Court documents revealed differences in customer profits between the "old spreads" and "new spreads" for drugs such as Lipitor (20 mg. 90s from $6.86 to $17.18), Prilosec (20 mg. 30s from $4.92 to $8.92); and Befaseron (from $20.00 to $58.25).[32] Douglas Hoey, chief operating officer for the National Community Pharmacists Association, has said that First DataBank's pricing scheme was of little help to community pharmacists who continue to be burdened by slim profit margins.[33]

Although a federal judge had earlier dismissed the price-fixing suit against McKesson, the company agreed in November 2008 to pay $350 million to settle a suit brought by the New England Carpenters Health Benefits Fund and others.[34] McKesson settled the suit without admitting any guilt, and CEO John H. Hammergren commented, "We believe the plaintiffs' allegations are without merit, and that McKesson adhered to all applicable laws. We did not enter into any alleged conspiracy, did not manipulate drug prices and did not violate any laws." Hammergren remarked further that McKesson's settlement agreement was motivated by the company's desire to avoid the "inherent uncertainty" of litigation, a tactic that has been used repeatedly in other fraud settlements against pharmaceutical firms.[35]

To establish a civil claim under section 1962(c) of RICO, the plaintiff must demonstrate that the defendant engaged in a pattern of racketeering activity in association with an enterprise affecting interstate commerce. The plaintiff must then demonstrate that the pattern of racketeering activity caused harm to his or her property or business.[36]

A physician in New York filed civil charges under the RICO Act against two large health insurers. The doctor claimed the insurers conspired with medical evaluation companies and associated physicians to perform rigged boilerplate medical examinations meant to deny his patients future treatments.[37] According to the complaint, the insurers pressured the independent medical examination (IME) companies to conclude that the doctor's patients did not require future treatments. This pressure, of course, deprived the doctor of revenues that he would have received for the treatments. In essence, IMEs were expected to issue reports that were favorable to the insurance carriers and detrimental to the insured patients. In one complaint, the doctor said that "[the insurer] made it known to the other defendants that if they did not provide sufficient denials within the evaluation reports then [the insurer] would not use their IME services."[38]

Mail and Wire Fraud

The lifeblood of health care—information—moves primarily through the mails or wires. Medical billings, insurance claims, laboratory test results, and patient medical histories are sent to patients, providers, and insurers by the U.S. Postal Service, package delivery services, telephones, fax machines, electronic mail, and Internet websites. So, not surprisingly, transmitting phony diagnoses, filing insurance claims for services not rendered, or upcoding medical treatments all carry potential charges of mail and wire fraud.

The same applies to false advertising. Health care consumers—especially senior citizens—are often the targets of mail or telephone sales pitches by con artists with no medical training who are selling elixirs for aging, weight loss, baldness, or impotency. Other quacks use the telephone or Internet to peddle remedies for heart disease, cancer, arthritis, rheumatism, and Parkinson's disease. These miracle cures are supposedly derived from "secret ancient sources" or from "recent scientific breakthroughs," and they are bolstered by phony money-back guarantees and staged testimonials from "satisfied customers."[39]

The federal mail fraud statute is the oldest federal criminal statute, and it continues to be used extensively by prosecutors.[40] The mail and wire fraud statutes make it a criminal act for anyone to use the mail service or the wires to advance a fraudulent scheme across state lines. Mail fraud applies not only to items shipped by the U.S. Postal Service, but also to items shipped by package delivery services such as UPS and FedEx.

Although the transmission of sales hyperbole does not constitute mail or wire fraud, true but misleading statements may violate federal law. An advertisement claiming that a certain vitamin will make a person "feel like a million dollars" is sales hyperbole. Telling prospective customers that a brand of vitamins, if taken for the rest of their lives, will cure cancer is a true but misleading statement. If customers take the vitamins for the rest of their lives, their cancer will be "cured" when they die. But the proclamation is fraudulent because a reasonable person might misconstrue the actual meaning and act on it.

Prosecutors must prove that the defendant engaged in a "scheme to defraud" by using the mails or wires to make material misstatements or omissions, which then resulted in the victim's loss of money or property.[41] Because nearly every organization in the United States uses the mails or wires in the course of conducting business, almost any health care fraud violates the federal mail and wire fraud statutes. Furthermore, it is not necessary for the primary fraudulent statement itself (e.g., "These vitamins cure cancer") to be transmitted by mail or wire. The fraudulent scheme needs only to be advanced in some fashion by the use of the U.S. mail or the wires. As with conspiracy, prosecutors can obtain a conviction for mail and wire fraud even if the object crime was not committed. But inaccurately predicting future events, failing to fulfill a promise, breaching a contract, or using fine-print disclaimers do not necessarily constitute fraud.[42] Mail and wire fraud are both predicate acts under the RICO Act. According to one attorney:

> The RICO Act is almost single-handedly responsible for the small print disclaimers that appear on every newspaper and T.V. advertisement and for the fast-talking and whispered disclaimers that we hear on the radio. All of those disclaimers essentially say that all the statements made in the advertisement are opinions or are based upon assumptions that may or may not apply to the circumstances of any individual consumer. So, the next time you're squinting to read the fine-print or waiting for the radio announcer to run out of breath, you can thank the RICO Act.[43]

Despite its broad application, the mail and wire fraud statutes stipulate that a fraudulent act must cause harm. Not all prosecutions falling under the broad umbrella of mail fraud, however, meet this test.

Consider the case of a Kansas psychologist. He operated a private outpatient psychology practice where he supervised as many as fifteen psychologists and counselors. By extracting payments for patient referrals from a nearby Kansas City hospital, he found himself in trouble with the federal government. The hospital agreed to pay him $1,000 a month for referrals, calling them "marketing" services. No evidence surfaced, however, that the psychologist ever proffered such services. Nonetheless, between July 1989 and October 1990, the Kansas City hospital paid him $40,500. A hospital administrator testified that the psychologist threatened to refer patients to other hospitals if the payments were not increased, and he allegedly confronted the administrator with a letter from another hospital offering him a monthly payment of $2,500 per patient referral.

The psychologist was convicted in a federal district court of violating both the mail fraud and Medicare antikickback statutes. On appeal, his Medicare kickback conviction was upheld, but his mail fraud conviction was thrown out by the U.S. Court of Appeals (8th Circuit). The opinion states:

> The mail fraud statute prohibits use of the mails to execute "any scheme or artifice to defraud." Essential to a scheme to defraud is fraudulent intent....The scheme to defraud need not have been successful or complete. Therefore, the victims of the scheme need not have been injured. However, the government must show that some actual harm or injury was contemplated by the schemer....The essence of a scheme to defraud is an intent to harm the victim. When there has been no actual harm, "the government must produce evidence independent of the alleged scheme to show the defendant's fraudulent intent." Here, all the evidence suggests that [the psychologist] intended to provide and did in fact provide his patients with the highest quality psychological services. While he also extracted undisclosed, unethical referral fees from an interested third party provider, there is no independent evidence proving that he thereby intended to defraud his patients. True, [he] did not disclose the referral fees, but a fiduciary's nondisclosure must be material to constitute a criminal scheme to defraud. There is no evidence that any patient would have considered [the psychologist's] relationship with [the hospital] material if it did not affect the quality or cost of his services to that patient.[44]

Money Laundering

Health care frauds, especially those involving bribes and kickbacks, may generate large amounts of cash. This embarrassment of riches poses two problems for criminals. First, moving large sums of cash through the U.S. banking system attracts the attention of law enforcement agencies and the IRS. Second, criminals must find places to deposit their wealth that are both secret and safe. That is where money laundering comes in.

Money laundering is the process of converting proceeds derived from criminal activities ("dirty" money) to proceeds that can be spent or invested safely ("clean" money). Money launderers prefer Caribbean nations or other politically stable countries with modern banking systems that are beyond the reach of U.S. authorities. Furthermore, money launderers want to maintain easy access to their funds.

Unlike the nineteenth-century mail and wire fraud statutes, money-laundering statutes are of recent vintage. Over the past two decades, leveling money-laundering charges against white-collar criminals has become increasingly popular with federal prosecutors. Many people regard money launderers with a special disdain, not only because their activities support lucrative criminal enterprises, but also because they evade income taxes.[45] If I make $1 million legitimately, I am entitled to take whatever deductions are allowable under income tax law, but I must still pay my fair share of taxes. Health care crooks who launder money, on the other hand, will pay no taxes on their ill-gotten gains.

Money launderers employ a variety of methods. Cash from illegal endeavors may be transferred electronically to foreign accounts or converted to money orders, U.S. Treasury notes, cashier's checks, or traveler's checks. Some ingenious money launderers convert U.S. currency to gold, jewelry, or expensive merchandise. These items are shipped to other countries and reconverted to cash through legal or black market sales. Other money launderers use foreign currency exchanges, check-cashing services, stored-value cards, shell companies, trusts, gambling casinos, and fake invoices to obfuscate their financial transactions.

Even eBay scams have been used to launder money. An unsuspecting California medical researcher was hired by a European and, supposedly, nonprofit health care organization to forward charitable donations through her bank account to Western Union offices in Germany and Romania. She was told by those who hired her that the money was to be used for AIDS research. In reality, she had been pulled into an international money-laundering scheme. When police showed up at her door, she learned that at least some of the "donations" she received were actually payments from eBay customers. Customers notified the authorities when they paid for merchandise they never received. Although this well-intentioned and trusting intermediary avoided prosecution, she was saddled with having to repay $25,000 to the swindled eBay customers.[46]

In 2007 twelve defendants entered pleas or were convicted in South Florida Federal District Court in connection with a $12.5 million health care fraud and money-laundering operation. The defendants and their thirty-four-year-old ringleader laundered illicit Medicare proceeds through a series of shell corporations and a phony medical clinic. The defendants' fraudulent claims involved medical equipment and expensive HIV treatments and related medications. One distasteful aspect of these crimes was the operation of an HIV clinic that recruited and paid patients to receive injections of a saline solution from recycled medication bottles. In reality, these individuals appeared to be "rent-a-patients" who knowingly received treatments—in this case injections—that they did not need. The defendants were also charged with conspiracy as well as perjury and obstruction of justice for lying about their knowledge of the shell companies and for encouraging witnesses to lie to federal agents and to a federal grand jury.[47]

Under the Bank Secrecy Act of 1970 bank officials must file a currency transaction report when customers make cash deposits or withdrawals in excess of

$10,000 per transaction as well as when customers purchase money orders, cashier's checks, or traveler's checks in excess of $3,000 per transaction.[48] This requirement is supposed to help track illegal transactions. Of course, all good thieves learn quickly how to outsmart the latest legislation so, in response, money launderers quickly developed tactics known as "structuring" to avoid detection under the Bank Secrecy Act. For example, by making multiple deposits of slightly less than $10,000 among several local banks, money launderers structure their transactions to avoid triggering a currency transaction report.

In 1986 Congress countered by passing the Money Laundering Control Act, which makes it a crime to structure cash transactions to sidestep filing a currency transaction report. Under the Money Laundering Control Act, banks are expected to file a suspicious activity report if officials believe an individual or group is laundering money. The IRS provides the following examples of situations that might trigger the filing of a suspicious activity report: "A customer pays for products or services using musty bills having an unusual chemical-like odor"; "A 16-year old, riding a bicycle, brings bags of cash to a money transmitter to transfer [funds] from New York to Miami"; "A customer, a retired CPA, frequently sends and receives money transfers of more than $2,000 to and from many different people"; and "A customer conducting an $11,000 cash transaction attempts to bribe an MSB [money services business] employee not to file a Currency Transaction Report."[49] Bank personnel who willfully fail to file reports in compliance with these laws may face felony charges.

The George W. Bush administration passed additional anti–money-laundering legislation directed primarily at terrorist and drug-trafficking activities. But these measures will also hamstring white-collar criminals. Unfortunately, cyber-laundering will probably continue to grow because of the ubiquity of electronic banking and because of the growth of multinational enterprises, international travel and migration, and transnational criminal organizations.

Tax Crimes

Money-laundering schemes are developed, in part, to help criminals evade taxes, so it is hardly surprising that tax crimes go hand in hand with money laundering. Individuals being investigated for object crimes such as health care fraud may also be subject to prosecution for tax crimes. Conversely, when tax crimes are the object of investigators, evidence may surface that the suspect has committed other white-collar crimes such as health care fraud.

The three categories of tax offenses are tax evasion, filing a false income tax return, and failure to file a tax return.[50] Evading taxes is a felony, and federal prosecutors use charges of tax evasion as a favorite weapon in their fight against white-collar crime.[51] A general practitioner in a small town who is participating in a Medicare fraud conspiracy or a pharmacist who is part of a pill-mill scheme might be hard-pressed to explain their high incomes to the IRS or FBI, so they fail to report it, which means they are tax evaders.

White-collar criminals also frequently evade taxes by shifting income and expense deductions between their personal and business endeavors. Health care professionals with separate businesses may take illegal deductions on their corporate tax returns for personal business trips or for home renovations. In addition to income tax evasion, white-collar offenders may be charged with evading sales or property taxes on expensive items purchased with the proceeds from criminal activities.

A person may be charged with filing a false tax return even though the falsification creates no financial loss to the government. A health care provider may pay her fair share of taxes but conceal illegal business interests by misidentifying sources of income on her tax return. Making false statements on a tax return and misleading the government in its taxation efforts is a felony.

Failure to file a federal tax return is a misdemeanor. Such cases usually entail failing to file and pay taxes in a timely fashion, maintaining inadequate tax records, or missing a tax deadline. Some people who fail to file income tax returns are tax protesters. Misdemeanor charges carry a jail sentence of no more than one year. The fines for failing to file a timely tax return, however, may be substantial. These fines include failure-to-file penalties of up to 25 percent of unpaid taxes as well as the loss of any refunds due.[52]

White-collar criminals who engage in health care fraud may appear respectable, but they may call attention to themselves by living beyond their apparent means (e.g., a general practitioner who practices medicine in a small Midwestern town, lives in a $15 million home, owns luxury European automobiles, and takes frequent vacations to posh resorts). Other white-collar criminals may be deviously deft at maintaining a low profile by hiding major assets such as airplanes, boats, or real estate. As their frauds begin to unravel, however, law enforcement or the tax authorities may use forensic accountants to dig into a criminal's financial affairs.

The goal of forensic accounting is to determine what portion of a person's income came from legal sources and what portion came from illegal sources.[53] Forensic accountants have the tedious job of sifting through bank statements, checkbooks, investment portfolios, credit card receipts, and other documents as they try to reconstruct the suspect's financial transactions. The amount of income deemed by forensic accountants to have been derived from illegal sources may then be used as the basis for RICO Act and tax-evasion charges.

When separating legal from illegal income, forensic accountants take one of two approaches. Using what is known as the net worth method, they may track shifts in a person's net worth by measuring changes in their assets and liabilities. Net worth increases are measured against the suspect's income from legal sources to estimate income from illegal sources. This method is applied to suspects whose lifestyles appear to be stable (e.g., they have a permanent address, bank and credit card accounts, memberships in church or civic organizations—often pillars in their communities). Many, if not most, health care fraud perpetrators—hospital executives, physicians, attorneys, and pharmacists—fall into the "stable" category.

A second approach—the expenditure method—tracks a suspect's cash expenditures over a period of time, and it is directed at transient individuals who have few family or community ties and live "fast and loose," spending their illegal proceeds quickly and carelessly. With the expenditure method, forensic accountants compare a suspect's income from known legal sources with his or her total expenditures. When the suspect's expenditures exceed income from legal sources, the difference is assumed to be income from illegal sources.

Lying, Perjury, and Obstruction of Justice

When law enforcement officers arrive at the door, many perpetrators initially deny knowledge or responsibility for criminal acts. Later, during the investigation or during court proceedings, a defendant may mislead investigators, intimidate potential witnesses, or lie under oath. By trying to cover up their crimes, persons accused of health care fraud may face additional criminal charges.

If someone "knowingly and willfully" lies about material matters made within the jurisdiction of the U.S. federal government, then they have committed a criminal offense under the False Statements Accountability Act (1996).[54] The term "material" refers to any statement having the potential to influence the decision of a government official. This statute has been broadly defined to include both lies of commission (e.g., lying about the treatment provided to a patient) and lies of omission (e.g., concealing the fact one has been banned from a federal health care program).

Anyone who has ever watched *Law and Order* or other television crime shows knows that you risk perjury charges when you lie under oath during a court, grand jury, or ancillary proceeding.[55] Prosecutors often find it difficult to make a perjury charge stick because the defendant must knowingly and willfully make a false statement about a material fact. Lying under oath about one's age, for example, is not perjury unless age is material to the testimony. Similarly, absent proof of an intentional deception, a mistaken answer or a lapse of memory during testimony does not constitute perjury. To support a perjury conviction, one witness along with corroborating evidence must show that the testimony was intentionally false and deceptive (the two-witness rule).[56] In some instances, a witness may recant a statement to avoid charges of perjury. Furthermore, an individual can be charged with subornation of perjury if he or she tries to persuade another person to commit perjury.[57]

Obstruction of justice occurs when a defendant interferes with the administration of a judicial, legislative, or administrative proceeding.[58] It might include a perpetrator's altering, defacing, or falsifying records, creating false documents to support a fraudulent activity, withholding or destroying documents, denying the existence of documents, or erasing computer files. Obstruction of justice might also include interfering with an agency investigation or a federal audit, threatening or intimidating witnesses, retaliating against witnesses or informants, or attempting to influence jurors or other court officials.[59] As an inchoate crime, there is no requirement for the obstruction to have actually taken place.

One tragic instance of obstruction of justice was the murder of an Illinois grand jury witness days before she was scheduled to testify against an Evanston, Illinois, podiatrist. The podiatrist was accused of billing Medicare for foot surgeries he never performed (over six thousand surgeries, netting him over $1.2 million). His ludicrous Medicare billings included 117 phony foot surgeries on a seventy-four-year-old woman who, on learning of this fraud at his trial, remarked: "One hundred seventeen? Wow. I wouldn't be able to walk." The podiatrist also paid kickbacks to patients and their families in exchange for allowing him to use their Social Security numbers to file false claims.

The podiatrist was sentenced to seventy-eight months in prison for health care fraud, ordered to pay $1.8 million in restitution, and sentenced to death for the woman's murder.[60] At his capital murder sentencing, the fifty-seven-year-old fraudster and murderer, who had remained silent throughout the legal proceedings against him, said in a strong voice to U.S. Federal District Court Judge Ronald Guzman that he did not kill the woman who was scheduled to testify against him. But he was found guilty of invading the disabled nurse's residence and, at point-blank range, shooting her to death as she sat in her garden. The podiatrist then tried to pin the murder on a gang that frequented the woman's neighborhood.[61] Citing the doctor's mental health problems and drug abuse, his attorneys argued that his death sentence was too severe. He remains, however, on death row at a federal prison in Terre Haute, Indiana.[62]

The facilitating crimes described here often take center stage in white-collar criminal proceedings. These crimes—conspiracy, mail and wire fraud, money laundering, tax evasion, and perjury—are important prosecutorial weapons in health care fraud cases. In cases where health care fraudsters are habitual criminals, the RICO Act may be used by prosecutors.

The next chapter deals with federal laws—the antikickback, self-referral, HIPAA, and food and drug laws—that were enacted specifically to attack health care fraud and abuse. The false-claims statutes, resurrected after decades of disuse, are also discussed.

THE MAJOR HEALTH CARE FRAUD LAWS

Kickbacks, Self-Referrals, and False Claims

The current and former owners of a Miami hospital agreed to pay $15.4 million to settle federal and state civil suits over kickbacks paid to physicians for patient admissions. Other patients—some of whom were from assisted-living facilities owned by the perpetrators—were admitted to the hospital for unnecessary treatments.[1]

An Atlanta hospital and two physician-owned businesses agreed to pay $6.37 million after being accused of violating the physician self-referral statute as a way of increasing their Medicare reimbursements. The government claimed that the hospital had purchased platelet products from one of the businesses at an inflated price and had paid the other business fees that exceeded fair market value.[2]

A hospital group based in South Texas agreed to pay the U.S. government $27.5 million to settle violations of the federal antikickback, self-referral, and false claims acts. Between 1999 and 2006, the group paid doctors for patient referrals—in violation of the antikickback law—and disguised this arrangement through a series of sham contracts, medical directorships, and lease agreements—in violation of the antireferral law. Because this case also involved Medicare billings, the hospital group violated the federal false claims act. A former employee turned whistle-blower received $5.5 million for reporting the false claims and assisting federal prosecutors.[3]

These cases involve violations of two major federal laws—the antikickback statute and the Stark Law—both of which prohibit certain conflicting business relationships in the health care field—and the false claims acts, which punish those filing false or fraudulent claims against the government. In this chapter I discuss these laws as well as several other major laws that have a direct impact on health care in the United States.

Federal Fraud Laws and Health Care

When criminals commit fraud, they usually also commit the facilitating crimes— conspiracy, mail and wire fraud, money laundering, tax evasion, lying to federal officials, perjury, and obstruction of justice—described in the previous chapter. There are, however, five laws that are specific to health care fraud: the antikickback statute, the Stark Law prohibiting self-referrals by physicians, the false claims statutes, the Health Insurance Portability and Accountability Act, and the Federal Food, Drug and Cosmetic Act.

With the establishment of the Medicare and Medicaid programs in 1965 and the fee-for-service emphasis of these programs, perpetrators of health care fraud turned their attention to the deep pockets of the federal and state governments. Simultaneously, Congress, state legislatures, the health care professions, and health insurers began to pay serious attention to health care fraud and abuse. By the mid-1980s, the U.S. Department of Health and Human Services, Office of the Inspector General had become the primary enforcement agency in the battle to abate health care fraud. The OIG has the authority to investigate and enforce Medicare and Medicaid fraud and abuse laws through administrative agency proceedings. Other federal agencies, including the U.S. Department of Justice, U.S. Department of Defense, and the FBI also become involved in specific fraud cases. Since Medicaid is jointly administered by the federal and state governments, most states have Medicaid fraud units.

The Antikickback Statute

Practices long regarded as unethical among health care providers were made illegal under the 1972 antikickback law.[4] This statute prohibits the solicitation or receipt of payments (kickbacks) in return for referring patients to purchase products or services paid for by Medicare, Medicaid, or other federally funded health care programs.[5] A hospital that offers kickbacks to an ambulance company for transporting accident victims to their hospital instead of to a more conveniently located or better equipped one violates the antikickback statute as does a laboratory that offers payments to doctors in exchange for directing blood work to their labs instead of to a competitor's lab.

Kickbacks for referrals have the potential to compromise the quality of patient care by giving doctors, podiatrists, or whoever is involved, an incentive to deliver treatment that is not needed, to prescribe drugs that are unproven for a particular illness, or to charge for services that may have not been delivered. Patients are at risk for harm when their treatments are based not on their efficacy but on the amount of money these treatments funnel into their doctor's back account. Moreover, kickbacks drive up the cost of operating federal health care and private insurance programs.

Violations of the antikickback statute constitute a felony punishable by a maximum fine of $25,000, five years in prison, or both. Under the Balanced Budget Act of 1997, the OIG may impose an additional penalty of up to $50,000 per illegal kickback and damages of up to three times the amount of the kickback.[6]

On the surface, the antikickback law appears to be straightforward: a violation of the statute occurs, for example, when a person extracts or accepts a fee for patient referrals or when a doctor gets money under the table for purchasing medical equipment. A typical case arose in 2009 when four medical-device firms were accused of paying kickbacks to heart surgeons and hospitals for buying surgical products used to correct irregular heartbeats. These kickbacks were illegal because they resulted in excessive charges to the Medicare program.[7] In *U.S. v. Hancock*, the U.S. Court of Appeals (7th Circuit) rejected an earlier district court opinion, favoring instead a broad definition of kickbacks, bribes, and rebates. *Hancock* upheld the conviction of a group of chiropractors who had received "handling fees" for referring blood and tissue samples to a laboratory.[8] The antikickback statute was again amended in 1980 to require a conviction only if the perpetrator "knowingly and willfully" violated the law.

Defining what constitutes a kickback, bribe, or rebate, however, has posed a problem for the courts. Giving a physician a hundred bucks per referral is obviously a kickback. But is it a kickback for a pharmaceutical sales representative to take a physician to dinner at a fancy restaurant as part of a sales campaign to promote a recently approved drug? What if dinner is not enough to convince the physician to prescribe the drug to her patients? Is it legal to pay her way to an exclusive resort in the Bahamas for a week-long "educational" session on its benefits? What about university medical school faculty having lucrative consulting arrangements with major pharmaceutical and medical equipment firms? Is it a form of kickback for them to skew the results of their research in favor of the corporation that pays their consulting fee if such dishonesty ultimately affects Medicare or Medicaid expenditures?

The Medicare and Medicaid Antifraud and Abuse Amendments (1977) expanded the antikickback statute by including any remuneration—cash or any other object of value—given directly, indirectly, overtly, or covertly.[9] Items of value may include free trips to medical conferences, free training for medical office staff, frequent-flier miles, and consulting fees designed to hide kickbacks.

Doctors have argued that they are not influenced by such gifts. Federal legislation, however, is based on the well-known psychological and anthropological insight that gift giving involves an obligation to reciprocate. We seem hard-wired to reciprocate when we receive a "gift"—no matter how small. That is why wine stores give tastings on Saturday afternoons. Wine store managers know that someone who receives the equivalent of an eight-ounce glass of wine will feel somewhat obliged to buy a bottle to return the favor. The gift-exchange phenomenon is found in nearly all sales-customer relationships, including the dealings between physicians and medical equipment or pharmaceutical sales representatives.[10] According to a study of 352 third- and fourth-year students at two medical schools, even giving someone an item of little value, such as a clipboard or a notepad emblazoned with a pharmaceutical brand, can alter one's preference for a particular product. (In this study the favored product was the anticholesterol drug, Lipitor).[11] If gifts such as a coffee mug or a pen-and-pencil set are enough to sway at least some physicians to prefer one brand over another, one can only imagine the loyalty that a physician might show if given a "free" trip to a Caribbean resort or a set of "complimentary" tickets to a major sporting event.

For this reason, states such as Minnesota, Massachusetts, and Vermont enacted laws that restrict physicians from receiving gifts from pharmaceutical and medical-equipment manufacturers. Many medical schools have also imposed similar prohibitions on their faculty. Impressed with the effectiveness of these state laws, the federal government followed suit by passing the Physician Payments Sunshine Act that goes in to effect in 2012. The federal law provides transparency by requiring companies to record and report any payment to a physician in excess of $10. A searchable database of physician payments is supposed to be available by fall 2013.[12]

An example of a kickback scheme involves the ringleader of one of the largest illegal patient-brokering networks in the United States. Patient brokering is simple. Brokers round up patients, often those who are elderly or indigent, and they receive a bounty (or kickback) from health care providers who want to make a fast buck from Medicare or Medicaid. The provider who pays the bounty treats the patient—or pretends to do so—and then submits a claim to a public or private insurer. Prosecutors claim that the ringleader and his partners used bribes, phony employment contracts, and false promises to clients to run their New Jersey patient-brokering business. This criminal enterprise sold referrals to treatment centers—mostly in Florida—for up to three thousand dollars per patient, and the patients often received inappropriate and unnecessary treatments. Between 1989 and 1997, the scheme generated $32 million in illegal kickbacks to the broker. The ringleader was also charged with conspiracy, mail and wire fraud, and obstruction of justice (because he shredded incriminating records that had been subpoenaed by a grand jury). But by assisting in the prosecution of thirty other Medicare fraud cases, however, he received a light, sixteen-month, federal prison sentence. He was also ordered to pay a fine of $250,000 and make restitution of $1.5 million to settle the government's civil claims against him.[13]

Another patient-brokering case, this one from the Tampa, Florida, area, is also illustrative.

> [The broker] was a pitiful sight Thursday in the center of a quiet federal courtroom. The 60-year-old grandmother wept after testifying about being broke, unemployed, afflicted with chronic health problems and the sole caregiver for her frail, 95-year-old mother.... It has been a rapid descent for the Spring Hill woman. Just a few years ago [she was] a well-traveled entrepreneur in a health care cottage industry that raked in millions by matching patients with treatment facilities.... But [her] pitches to patients were often as phony as her Ph.D., a $150 certificate from a California diploma mill.... Her business was brokering patients into treatment for bounties as high as $3,000 a head.... When she collected on patients insured by Medicare or Medicaid, the brokering became a federal crime, one that put the FBI and federal prosecutors in Tampa on the track of one of the largest health care scams in U.S. history.[14]

Kickbacks often come with a disguise. A fraudster may attempt to hide funds obtained from illegal kickbacks by combining them with funds earned from a legal business. In *United States v. Greber,* the U.S. Court of Appeals (3rd Circuit) held that "if one purpose of the payment was to induce future referrals, the Medicare statute has been violated."[15] The defendant, an osteopathic physician, was the president and founder of a diagnostic services firm. One device sold by the company was a monitor used for recording a patient's cardiac activity on a computer-monitored tape. Medicare was billed for the monitoring services, and, when reimbursements were received, the company forwarded 40 percent of the Medicare payment (not to exceed $65 per patient) to the referring physician. These payments represented an "interpretation fee" paid to physicians for their initial consultation and for explaining test results to patients. Physicians, however, received these fees even when they did not evaluate the monitoring data. But the fixed percentage paid to the referring physician was more than Medicare allowed for such services. During the trial, the defendant testified that "if the doctor didn't get his consulting fee, he wouldn't be using our service. So the doctor got a consulting fee." Based on the company's billing practices, the indictment charged the defendant with giving kickbacks to the referring physicians in violation of the federal antikickback statute. The *Greber* case established what has become known as the "one-purpose test." This test, according to the court, stipulates that "if the payments were intended to induce the physician to use [the company's] services, the statute was violated, even if the payments were also intended to compensate for professional services."

Other court rulings indicate that expected future payments, in order to be deemed illegal kickbacks, must be fairly specific and not based merely on an uncertain expectation of remuneration. In *United States v. McClatchey* a federal district court jury found that a group of hospital administrators and physicians had conspired to sell hospitals "batches of nursing home patients." One of the defendants served as chief operating officer and senior vice president of a medical center, and later as a senior vice president of its parent corporation. Two doctors who operated a medical practice that provided care to patients in nursing homes were also involved. In January 1985, the medical center entered into a one-year contract with the two doctors, paying them a total of $150,000 to serve as "codirectors of gerontology services." The financial officer of the medical center testified that the negotiations for the 1985 contract had been "backwards," first setting the fee with the doctors and only then agreeing to the services they were expected to provide. As it turned out, the doctors began referring large numbers of their patients to the medical center. In June 1986, the center entered into a second one-year agreement with the doctors that paid them a combined $150,000. The medical center continued the $150,000 salary each year through 1993, with the exception of 1990, when each doctor received only $68,750. Although the hospital tried to shelter this arrangement with a sham contract for services, it was established that the two physicians did not provide the services.

Health care fraud and abuse cases often involve complex medical arrangements that must be evaluated through a proliferating array of complex laws. In *McClatchey* the federal district court judge was unfamiliar with the relevant laws and did his best to give the defendants the benefit of the doubt during evidentiary rulings and jury instructions. The federal district court granted a motion for acquittal on the basis that no reasonable jury could have concluded beyond a reasonable doubt—the standard for criminal trials—that the defendant intended to violate the antikickback law.

On appeal, the 10th Circuit Court disagreed with the lower court's decision, but said that "defendants…cannot be convicted merely because they hoped or expected or believed that referrals may ensue from remuneration that was designed wholly for other purposes. Likewise, mere oral encouragement to refer patients or the mere creation of an attractive place to which patients can be referred does not violate the law. There must be an offer or payment of remuneration to induce."[16] Still, defining what amounts to an intentional violation of the antikickback law remains uncertain. As *McClatchey* and other court rulings indicate, each case will have to be examined in light of its specific facts, circumstances, transaction structure, and financial impact.[17]

Complicating matters further is the fact that Congress has established a number of exceptions to the antikickback statute, known as "safe harbors."[18] Safe harbors encompass business practices such as investments in medically underserved areas, price discounts, referral services, bona fide employment relationships, deductible and coinsurance waivers, investments in ambulatory surgical centers, and certain equipment rentals. For example, it is permissible to pay recruitment fees to physicians as a means of attracting them to medically underserved areas. The physician must earn at least 75 percent of his or her revenues by serving patients in the underserved area, and the safe harbor is limited to three years.

Another safe harbor that has been the target of criticism pertains to group-purchasing organizations—known as GPOs. GPOs are used by networks of health care providers, such as a group of hospitals, to make bulk purchases of supplies. Large-volume purchases—at least in theory—should lower unit costs and save health institutions, consumers, and taxpayers substantial sums of money. The antikickback law comes into play because the expenses associated with GPOs are covered by the vendors who supply them with products. This arrangement might be regarded as a kickback of sorts—except for the fact that these purchasing arrangements have been protected by a safe harbor. Several members of Congress, however, have questioned the legality of the GPOs and are threatening to rescind the safe harbor—a devastating turn of events for medical-supply vendors.[19]

Because of the complexity and uncertain application of the laws regulating federal health care programs, physicians may be fearful of making an illegal kickback by mistake.[20] As one observer noted, "The myriad, cumbersome rules governing state and federal health care programs are not a model of clarity. At times prudent health care providers will attempt in good faith to comply fully with the rules, but because of the inherent ambiguity in the rules, will act in accordance with an incorrect interpretation of the law."[21]

Going back to *McClatchey,* it is hard to know whether the former administrator, who was released from federal prison in March 2004, was the perpetrator of a felony or the victim of his own inability to decipher the antikickback statute. The judicial system claimed he was the first, but another observer views him as the victim.

> The world of health care is no longer real. From [his] perspective, it's not even close. Although he wakes up every morning and falls asleep every night thinking of nothing else, he still can scarcely believe what has happened to him. Were it not for the emotional support of his family and friends, and the financial and legal support of [his former employer], he would have been utterly destroyed, not merely devastated as he is now. And he is still not sure why any of this happened....His own descent into criminality is as confusing to him as it is to the casual observer. Let's see, he helped set up a model program for the sickest of the sick; one that was carefully drafted by the best attorneys in the field to comply with an absurdly vague law; one that cost Medicare no more than it ought to have; one that profited [him] not a dime; one that did little in the way of revenue or glory for his highly respected, not-for-profit employer; one that is being defended vigorously by just about every thinking person in the health care field.

Still, this was all "bad," claimed the prosecutor, Tanya Treadway ("not available for comment"), because "the defendants got together and treated the patients like commodities." But if the truth be told, it was the Medicare program that insisted on the notion of paying "per head," of "capitizing" in healthcare-speak, of treating patients like mindless commodities and not like the independent, thinking customers they once used to be.[22]

A reading of the federal regulations suggests why gaining a clear understanding of the safe harbor provisions can be a challenge, especially for health care professionals with limited legal knowledge. The practice of ambulance replenishing is an example of a simple arrangement between an emergency room and an ambulance operator that has been made exceedingly complex by detailed federal regulations. Ambulance companies may provide patients with drugs and supplies during transport to a hospital. Hospitals, in turn, often agree to replace these items after the ambulance has arrived, a practice that prepares operators for their next trip. Although replenishment appears to be a commonsense practice, it may also be a source of criminal liability under the antikickback statute. Problems arise when a hospital gives something of value (drugs or supplies) to a business (the ambulance company) when that business is a source of federal program revenue (because the ambulance operator makes a decision to bring Medicare or Medicaid patients to Hospital A instead of to Hospital B). In late 2004, the OIG issued the final safe harbors rule addressing the ambulance replenishing issue.[23] A reading of these sometimes arcane provisions makes one wonder how even the most honest health care provider can avoid running afoul of the law.

The Stark Law

The Stark Law is a federal statute regulating the self-referral activities of physicians.[24] Unlike the criminal antikickback law, the Stark Law imposes only civil damages.

The origins of the Stark Law can be traced to the late 1980s when the OIG and other parties began to study the expanding array of physician business interests. These studies revealed that doctors were referring patients to health care businesses (e.g., laboratories, nursing homes, ambulatory surgical centers) in which the doctors also had a financial interest.[25] The growing concern over these conflicts of interest led to legislative proposals by California Congressman Fortney "Pete" Stark and to the passage of the Stark Law in December 1989. The ensuing two decades have been marked by a series of revisions to this complex law.

In its most basic form, the Stark Law prohibits physicians from referring Medicare or Medicaid patients who require designated health services to a business in which the physician (or the physician's immediate family member) has a financial relationship. The statute is complex because the lists of designated health services, financial relationships, and exceptions are broad.

The statute is also controversial. Proponents of the Stark Law claim that physician self-referrals—as with kickbacks—lead to corrupt medical judgments, diminishing the quality of patient care. Opponents of the law claim that self-referrals by physicians can improve working relationships among a network of health care providers, hospitals, clinics, pharmacies, therapists, laboratories, and equipment dealers. These efficiencies, they argue, enhance the quality of patient care.

The Stark Law addresses three fundamental questions. First, is the physician referring a Medicare or Medicaid patient for a "designated health service"? If the referral involves neither a Medicare nor a Medicaid patient, or if the referral does not involve a designated health service, then the Stark Law is not applicable. That is, the Stark Law is not concerned with reimbursements for referrals that are paid for by private insurers, although some states have enacted mini Stark Laws that do prohibit such reimbursements.

The original Stark Law applied only to clinical laboratory services, but the list of designated health services has since been expanded to include inpatient and outpatient hospital services, radiology services, durable medical equipment and supplies, physical and occupation therapies, home health services, prosthetics, and outpatient prescription drugs. Any physician request for a treatment, service, prescription, consultation, or product payable under Medicare or Medicaid may constitute a referral. Referrals within a physician group are also covered by the statute.

The second question pertaining to the Stark Law is whether the physician (or an immediate family member) has a financial interest in the business furnishing the designated health service. If the referral involves no personal or family financial interest, then the Stark Law does not prohibit it. Financial interests include any direct or indirect ownership or investment relationship. Stock ownerships, partnership interests, compensation arrangements, rental contracts, personal-service arrangements, salary payments, gifts, or gratuities all represent potential financial interests under the Stark Law.

The third question relates to Stark Law exceptions. As it turns out, dozens of permissible financial relationships exist between physicians and the businesses receiving their designated health service referrals. Physician compensation is at the heart of the Stark Law. Compensation paid to a referring physician must be set in advance, reflect market value, and must not take into account the volume or value of referrals made by the physician. The Stark Law also gives group practices greater autonomy when allocating or dividing revenues among physicians. Some common, but limited, exceptions to the Stark Law include those for managed-care plans, academic medical centers, in-office ancillary services, bona fide employment relationships, physician recruitment, and physicians practicing in locations designated as health-professional shortage areas.

But the safe harbor hatches have been tightened. The Stark Law was amended because of concerns by the Centers for Medicare and Medicaid Services (CMS) over improper referral arrangements that could lead to abusive overutilization. As of October 2009, additional restrictions were placed on physician-hospital business relationships—known as "under arrangements"—in which hospitals have contracts with physician-owned entities to provide a wide range of laboratory, imaging, or other ancillary services. Restrictions were also placed on the leasing arrangements of property owned by doctors in which the lease payments—known as "per use" or "per click" payments—were based on the amount of designated health services rendered at that location.[26]

The Stark Law is a strict liability statute, meaning that the physician's liability does not depend on actual negligence or on intentional harm. Civil monetary penalties may be imposed up to $15,000 for each knowing violation, or $100,000 per arrangement, depending on the seriousness of the violation. Under both the antikickback and self-referral provisions, the OIG may exclude a provider from future participation in federal programs such as Medicare or Medicaid.

Although Stark Law prosecutions are rare, the settlements have been large. In May 2006, one of the nation's largest durable medical equipment suppliers entered into an agreement with the OIG, under which the supplier agreed to pay $10 million. The settlement resolved allegations that it used a nationwide scheme to pay physicians kickbacks for patient referrals. It claimed that the company gave referring physicians items such as sporting and entertainment tickets, gift certificates, sporting goods and fishing trips, meals, advertising expenses, office equipment, and medical equipment. The illegal kickbacks also came disguised as payments for consulting agreements. Furthermore, the OIG also claimed the DME supplier violated the Stark Law by accepting referrals from parties to the illegal consulting agreements. "This significant settlement is an important example of OIG's continuing effort to eliminate illegal kickback practices and violations of the Self-Referral Law," said Inspector General Daniel R. Levinson. He added, "[The] OIG will continue to pursue aggressively those who undermine the integrity of the Medicare program."[27] Given the complex provisions and exceptions of the Stark Law, its strict liability provisions, and its potentially large monetary penalties, health care providers must be extremely careful to ensure they are in compliance.

False Claims Statutes

When it comes to the military, stories abound of the seven hundred dollar toilet seats, the exorbitant development costs that led to the B-2 bomber being "worth five times its weight in gold," and the abuses of cost-plus contractors and their runaway expenses.[28] But now it is the health care industry that has taken center stage in false claims cases. The term "false claim" is broad. It pertains to the filing of a claim seeking funds or the reimbursement of funds from the federal government under false pretenses. Such claims include charging outrageous prices for products or services, billing for substandard products or services, or billing for products or services not provided.

Under the criminal false claims act, a person or an organization filing a false claim to obtain money from the United States government may face criminal prosecution or a civil suit. The criminal statute encompasses both false and fraudulent claims.[29] The former might be charges for a medical service or product that was not provided and the latter might be charges for an unnecessary medical service or product.

The criminal false claims statute is popular among federal prosecutors, easily understood by juries, and backed with ample case precedent.[30] It also contains its own conspiracy provision that carries heavier penalties (twice the maximum sentence) than the federal conspiracy statute discussed earlier.[31]

The False Claims Act (FCA) is a civil statute regarded as the U.S. government's primary antifraud law.[32] As they go about their daily business, employees of a dishonest government contractor may suspect that the federal government is being cheated and billed fraudulently for products or services. Under the FCA, individuals with insider knowledge (known in legalese as "relators") may bring civil action against those who knowingly submit (or cause the submission of) fraudulent claims against the federal government. Such actions are known as whistle-blower or *qui tam* suits.

In some cases, the U.S. Department of Justice (DOJ) assumes primary responsibility for prosecution. In most cases, however, the DOJ declines to prosecute, leaving the individual whistle-blower free to pursue the case without DOJ assistance. If the suit is successful and damages are recovered, whistle-blowers may receive a monetary reward—usually between 15 and 25 percent of the total recovery. To qualify for a reward, insiders must base their allegations against the defendant on information not otherwise available to the government.[33] If this "inside information" is already known to government investigators—often a contentious issue—then it becomes part of the public domain and the whistle-blower is not eligible for a portion of the settlement.

The FCA (also known as the Lincoln Law) was enacted during the Civil War in response to the Union Army's problems with unscrupulous suppliers. It fell into disuse until 1986 when Congress revamped the FCA to make it a more potent weapon against crooked defense contractors.

By the 1990s, health care fraud became the most prominent of the FCA suits. From fiscal years 1987 through 2005, the DOJ received 8,869 cases, 5,129 of which were whistle-blower cases filed in ninety-two U.S. district courts. The HHS agencies were named in 54 percent of the cases compared to 29 percent for the Department of Defense. A total of $15 billion was recovered in these cases, and whistle-blowers garnered $1.6 billion in settlement rewards. (The distribution of awards is skewed, with the average settlement being $1.7 million and the median settlement $123,885.) Health care fraud cases constituted about 46 percent (1,145 out of 2,490) of all whistle-blower cases. The largest health care whistle-blower recovery during this period was $568 million, and the largest award to a whistle-blower was almost $96.6 million.[34] Health care fraud recoveries under the FCA were $2.2 billion in 2006, $1.5 billion in 2007, $1.1 billion in 2008, and $1.6 billion in 2009.[35]

The FCA recognizes two categories of "falsity."[36] "Literal falsity" arises when a person submits inaccurate or misleading information to the federal government to obtain payment. A health care provider who bills Medicare or Medicaid for services not provided to a patient has committed a literal falsity.[37] A Washington, D.C.–area ambulance company owner was charged with filing $1.6 million in false Medicaid claims. The owner sought reimbursement from Medicaid for transportation services that, according to at least eleven patients, were never provided. Investigators also discovered that three patients were deceased at the time the defendant claimed to have transported them.[38]

To prove literal falsity, a definable gap must exist between the services or products billed to Medicare or Medicaid and the services or products actually proffered by the health care provider. A psychiatrist, for example, who bills Medicare for ten hours of counseling when she provided only seven hours of counseling has created a literal falsity. As the definable gap widens, the likelihood of a FCA violation also increases.

Interpreting unclear regulations in an advantageous light, however, is not necessarily a violation of the FCA. An air-ambulance service billed a federal program for mileage based on statute rather than on nautical miles. Billings based on statute miles gave the air-ambulance operator an additional 15 percent in billable miles. Since the law did not prohibit the use of statute miles in air-ambulance billings, the operator did not violate the FCA.[39]

Some health care providers, on the other hand, may deliberately file a false claim because of a disagreement with a government policy. An ophthalmologist might feel entitled to file a Medicare claim for a routine eye examination (not covered by Medicare) when that examination was performed in preparation for a patient's cataract surgery (which is covered by Medicare). But by "pulling a fast one" and slipping an uncovered procedure into a claim with a covered procedure, the ophthalmologist has committed Medicare fraud. Such claims may also arise if a health care provider disputes the government's interpretation of a regulation and, instead, files a claim based on his or her personal interpretation of the regulation. As noted by the court in *Visiting Nurses Ass'n. of Brooklyn v. Thompson,* however, "the FCA would be rendered toothless overnight if parties claiming federal funds were permitted to rely on any reasonable interpretation they might prefer, even if it directly conflicted with an agency's official interpretation of the same law."[40]

"Falsity by implicit certification" arises when a business omits information from a claim or fails to adhere to regulatory guidelines or standards.[41] The federal government has brought a series of civil actions against nursing home operators for violations of the federal False Claims Act. According to government prosecutors, if a nursing home submits Medicare or Medicaid claims for care that the government later finds to be substandard, then the claims are false for that reason alone.[42] Substandard care fails to achieve a professionally recognized level of quality.[43] Care may be regarded as conforming to an accepted standard, however, even if it does not always achieve its intended result (e.g., a patient dies despite receiving excellent care).

This category of falsity occurred in *Covington v. Sisters of the Third Order of St. Dominic of Hanford.* Auditors for Blue Cross of California, the fiscal administrators of the Medicare program in that state, applied an incorrect geographical adjustment to compute Medicare reimbursements to a California hospital. Although the hospital was located in a rural area, it received the higher reimbursement rates paid to urban hospitals. Hospital personnel knew for several years of the incorrect overpayments, yet they continued to accept and use the funds in violation of the FCA.[44]

A major requirement of the FCA is that the health care provider must "knowingly" submit a false claim. In most instances, health care providers, such as a corrupt nursing home manager, are aware of the aforementioned gap between the services actually provided and the services described on the billings. Cases exist, however, in which poor administrative practices lead to erroneous Medicare or Medicaid claims and FCA violations.

A health care provider may file bogus claims because of his or her "reckless disregard" for the truth. Consider, for example, a psychiatrist who operated a practice in the Washington, D.C., area. The federal authorities accused him of violating the FCA when he delegated the task of patient and insurance billings to his wife and a hired clerk. Their poor record keeping and slipshod billing practices led to federal program reimbursement claims that were frequently ludicrous. Many billings were made for an unrealistically high number of hours. On three separate occasions, bills were submitted for the impossible feat of providing more than twenty-four hours of services in a single day.[45] The government originally sued the psychiatrist and his wife for $81 million. After a three-week trial and extensive appeals, they were ordered to pay over $250,000 in penalties. Whether they deliberately violated the law or whether they were guilty only of sloppy billing is hard to know. The case, however, became an albatross around the doctor's neck and it plagued him until, due to health reasons, he had to close his practice.[46]

The U.S. Supreme Court in a June 2008 opinion may have narrowed—at least temporarily—the application of the False Claims Act to health care fraud cases. In

Allison Engine Co. v. United States, the Court was asked to decide whether persons or businesses not billing the federal government directly for services or products can be held liable for fraud under the FCA. The justices clarified that the whistle-blowers bringing a FCA action must show the defendant intended to defraud the United States and not just an intermediate business. According to the Court:

> It is insufficient for a plaintiff asserting a ... claim to show merely that the false statement's use resulted in payment or approval of the claim or that Government money was used to pay the false or fraudulent claim. Instead, such a plaintiff must prove that the defendant intended that the false statement be material to the Government's decision to pay or approve the false claim.... Similarly, it is not enough ... for a plaintiff to show that the alleged conspirators agreed upon a fraud scheme that had the effect of causing a private entity to make payments using money obtained from the Government. Instead, it must be shown that they intended" to defraud the Government." Where their alleged conduct involved the making of a false statement, it need not be shown that they intended the statement to be presented directly to the Government, but it must be established that they agreed that the statement would have a material effect on the Government's decision to pay the false or fraudulent claim.[47]

Allison Engine involved Navy shipbuilders and subcontractors, not health care organizations. But the Supreme Court's decision could discourage FCA whistle-blower cases against health care defendants who were not involved directly in defrauding the federal government. Congress, however, has introduced the False Claims Correction Act that, if enacted, could negate the Supreme Court's decision in *Allison Engine* and increase the power of FCA whistle-blowers.[48]

Health Insurance Portability and Accountability Act of 1996

Mention the acronym "HIPAA" in a hospital or health care institution and you will hear the most amazing—often wrong-headed—assertions about what the law does and does not allow. The Health Insurance Portability and Accountability Act of 1996—a difficult-to-fathom law—is probably best known for its safeguarding the privacy of patient medical information. Even in this area, it is often misunderstood. How many people know or understand, however, that the law also targets people who commit health care fraud?[49] Most important, the HIPAA and the Medicare Integrity Program are used to review and investigate Medicare expenditures and to safeguard these expenditures against fraud, abuse, and waste. The HIPAA prohibits health care frauds against public insurers (Medicare and Medicaid) as well as frauds against private insurers affecting interstate commerce. The Act targets the embezzlement, theft, or misappropriation of the money, property, or other assets of a health care benefit program. It also makes it a federal offense for a person to achieve eligibility for Medicaid benefits by disposing of their personal assets.

Concealing material facts or making false statements regarding health care delivery and insurance claims is also a HIPAA violation. The HIPPA's long reach is illustrated by the conviction of three individuals who staged automobile accidents to take advantage of the New York Comprehensive Motor Vehicle Insurance Reparations Act.[50] The defendants arranged for passengers in these accidents to sign their claims over to health care providers or to the defendants. On appeal, the defendants claimed the HIPAA applied only to health care professionals and that the New York state no-fault automobile insurance program is not a health care benefit within the meaning of the federal law. Citing the language and legislative history of the HIPAA, the U.S. Court of Appeals (2nd Circuit) rejected both contentions and affirmed the federal district court's health care fraud convictions. By receiving medical benefits in conjunction with the feigned injuries, the appeals court said that the no-fault insurance contracts of vehicle owners in New York qualify as a "health care benefit program" under the HIPAA:

> In sum, the federal health care fraud statute applies to defendants' participation as passengers in staged automobile accidents designed to profit from New York's no-fault automobile insurance regime. We recognize that this holding authorizes the application of the federal health care fraud statute to circumstances that are atypical of the health care fraud case law, which to date has concerned itself more exclusively with conduct within the medical community. Despite this factual twist, it is clear that defendants' conduct falls squarely within the unambiguous terms of the statute and therefore the statute applies in the circumstances presented by this case.

The HIPAA also links health care fraud specifically to the facilitative crimes of obstruction of justice and money laundering, and it expands antikickback provisions to other federal programs such as the military TRICARE program. As with the antikickback and Stark laws, the HIPAA provides exceptions and safe harbors, most notably for managed-care arrangements. People committing frauds under HIPAA are subject to fines as well as to imprisonment for up to ten years. If a HIPAA violation results in serious bodily injury, the defendant may be imprisoned for up to twenty years. Defendants engaging in frauds resulting in death are subject to life imprisonment.

In 1972 Congress enacted federal fraud enforcement provisions in the Social Security Act. This act, which HIPAA broadened considerably in 1996, encompasses a variety of previously discussed crimes and statutes directed at all federal health care programs, not just the prominent Medicare, Medicaid, TRICARE, Veterans Affairs, or the federal employee-benefits programs.[51] The statute covers false statements, misrepresentations, kickbacks, false statements with respect to the operation of a health care institution, illegal patient admittance and retention practices, and the wrongful disclosure of individually identifiable health information.

The Federal Food, Drug, and Cosmetic Act

In 1937 doctors in fifteen states had, in good faith, prescribed a drug called Elixir Sulfanilamide to patients. One hundred and five of these patients, mostly children, died. It was later discovered that the drug, in tablet form, worked well against streptococcal infections. But an unscrupulous Tennessee firm had processed it in liquid form using diethylene glycol, a highly toxic chemical analogue of antifreeze. As one of the prescribing doctors, A. S. Calhoun, wrote at the time:

> Nobody but Almighty God and I know what I have been through these past few days. I have been familiar with death in the years since I received my M.D. from Tulane University School of Medicine with the rest of my class of 1911. Covington County has been my home. I have practiced here for years. Any doctor who has practiced more than a quarter of a century has seen his share of death.
>
> But to realize that six human beings, all of them my patients, one of them my best friend, are dead because they took medicine that I prescribed for them innocently, and to realize that the medicine which I had used for years in such cases suddenly had become a deadly poison in its newest and most modern form, as recommended by a great and reputable pharmaceutical firm in Tennessee: well, that realization has given me such days and nights of mental and spiritual agony as I did not believe a human being could undergo and survive. I have known hours when death for me would be a welcome relief from this agony. (Letter by Dr. A. S. Calhoun, October 22, 1937)[52]

Also during the 1930s, journalists were giving a great deal of press to dangerous medical products such as Banbar, a worthless "cure" for diabetes; Lash-Lure, an eyelash dye that blinded some women; Radithor, a radium-containing tonic that caused a slow and painful death for its users; and Wilhide Exhaler, a fake cure for tuberculosis and other pulmonary diseases.[53] The public outcry over these scandals resulted in the passage of the Federal Food, Drug, and Cosmetic Act of 1938 (FDCA).[54]

Prior to the passage of the FDCA, drug regulations did not control the premarket toxicity testing of drugs. The FDCA changed the focus of the Food and Drug Administration from a policing agency confiscating adulterated drugs to a regulatory agency evaluating new drugs.[55] Today the FDCA—which still comes under attack for not doing enough to protect patients—is supposed to protect the public from harmful drugs or medical devices through its regulation of the testing, manufacturing, and labeling of drugs and medical devices.[56]

To ensure new drugs are safe and effective for their intended use, the FDA has mandated a highly structured three-phase clinical-investigation process requiring extensive documentation and record keeping.[57] FDA approval is also required when the testing process involves the use of human subjects. Fraud in the testing stage is a primary concern of the FDA, and violations occur when manufacturers or their representatives deviate from rigorous research protocols or falsify data and other relevant information associated with the testing process (a criminal offense). Although generic drugs are subjected to less-extensive testing than new drugs, generic manufacturers have been prosecuted for falsifying information on the FDA application and for making unapproved changes in the manufacturing process. In fact, any change in the manufacturing process, composition, or expiration date of a generic drug requires FDA approval. For example, personnel working in the manufacturing of drugs often must wear special protective clothing; any deviation from this requirement requires the consent of the FDA.

A drug must be manufactured exactly as it was approved by the FDA. To ensure that the composition of a drug has not been altered, the FDA inspects the entire manufacturing operation, including the machines used in each stage of production (e.g., the maintenance and calibration of the machinery), the training programs for employees, the design and construction of the production plant, and the manufacturing environment. If the manufacturing process results in an adulterated product, the product no longer earns FDA approval and its distribution for human consumption is illegal. Fraud in the production process includes altering or falsifying production records to conceal the improper storage or contamination of drugs, to hide unfavorable test results or process failures, to destroy information of interest to inspectors, or to mislabel products.

A drug or device approved by the FDA must be affixed with a label defining its specific use. Promotion by the manufacturer for an off-label use of the drug or device violates the FDCA—although physicians may prescribe a drug for off-label use. A drug is considered misbranded when its label is in any way false or misleading, when it contains inadequate directions for using the drug, or when the dosage or use of the drug as prescribed is dangerous to the patient's health. Information on labels is directed primarily at the health care professional. Based on their training and experience, they are expected to exercise prudence and to avoid being deceived by misbranded or erroneously labeled pharmaceuticals.

Finally, the FDCA prohibits the sale, purchase, or trade—including offers to do so—of a prescription drug sample. Pharmaceutical manufacturers may distribute drug samples only to physicians and designated health care providers.

Other administrative and record-keeping regulations are also associated with the distribution of drug samples. A sales representative cannot, for example, distribute a drug sample without a written request from a physician.

Manufacturers of medical devices are required to meet FDCA standards similar to those imposed on drug manufacturers. Although drugs are lumped into a single category because of their invasiveness, medical devices vary widely in terms of their design and function. For these reasons, medical devices are categorized into three classes. Class I devices (e.g., crutches and coverings for minor wounds) present minimal potential harm to the user and are subject to the least regulatory control. Those requiring more general controls to assure safety and effectiveness (e.g., wheelchairs and tampons) are Class II devices. The most stringent regulatory category for devices, Class III, includes artificial heart valves and pacemakers that support or sustain human life, prevent impairments to human health, or present an unreasonable risk of illness or injury.[58]

Federal programs such as Medicare and Medicaid, as well as private insurers, do not usually reimburse health care providers or patients for drugs, medical devices, or medical procedures that the FDA has not approved. Physicians may, under some circumstances, prescribe unapproved drugs, although reputable pharmacists may be reluctant to stock such pharmaceuticals. Since Medicare and other programs pay only for "reasonable and necessary" drugs and equipment, providers billing federal programs for unapproved, adulterated, or misbranded drugs may face federal false claims charges. The combination of FDCA and Medicare policy may cut off hope for terminally ill patients who are desperate for a last-ditch, but unapproved, treatment.[59] These patients may seek therapies outside the United States, often in Mexico.

The illegal distribution of prescription drugs has become a growing concern. Physicians who write illicit prescriptions, online drug trafficking, pill-mill schemes that divert drugs from their intended use, and doctor-shopping drug abusers have infiltrated health care systems both in the United States and elsewhere. It is difficult, however, to judge when a physician has overprescribed a drug. And pharmacists are not subject to criminal liability as long as they dispense controlled substances within the course of their duties. A pharmacist who is part of a conspiracy to distribute controlled substances illegally or one who turns a blind eye to patently unrealistic medical practices, however, may be subject to criminal prosecution.

Nearly every segment of the vast U.S. health care system is now subject to fraud, antikickback, self-referral, false claims, and food and drug litigation. The laws and accompanying regulations available for fighting health care fraud are lengthy, complex, overlapping, and confusing to honest health care providers who are trying to chart their course through this maze of legislation and regulation.

From the mid-1960s to 2010, the federal government has enacted several major antifraud laws, and it has enhanced its enforcement measures to combat health care fraud and abuse. Despite the expansion and stiff civil and criminal penalties, the payoffs are still too high and the risks of apprehension are still too low to deter the thousands of fraudsters who have both the interest and the skill to steal large sums of money from the treasure chests of Medicare, Medicaid, and private insurance programs. The next chapter illustrates the variety and ever-expanding array of health care fraud and abuse cases.

FRAUD IN FEE-FOR-SERVICE AND MANAGED CARE

Different Sides of the Same Coin

Fee-for-Service Shenanigans

After a four-week trial, a former Florida dermatologist was sentenced to twenty-two years in prison, ordered to pay $3.7 million and to forfeit an additional $3.7 million, and slapped with a $25,000 fine for performing 3,086 unnecessary invasive surgeries on 865 Medicare beneficiaries. Between 1998 and 2004, the doctor used faked biopsy results to generate diagnoses of skin cancer. Some of the specimens were actually slides containing chewing gum, Styrofoam, or skin tissue from the dermatologist's employees. By performing five surgeries a day and billing Medicare between $1,500 and $2,000 per procedure, the doctor's crooked business resembled a gigantic ATM machine with a huge cash-withdrawal limit.[1]

Take one health care provider. Add a fee-for-service system. Then mix. What you have here is a perfect prescription for health care fraud and abuse. The reality is simple. Under fee-for-service, the more care or services a health care provider delivers, the more revenue the provider generates. It is really no surprise then that fee-for-service arrangements encourage a variety of money-generating frauds and abuses. Here is a partial list: making false diagnoses, upcoding insurance claims, ordering bogus laboratory tests, committing home health care frauds, submitting false billings for psychological and psychiatric services, and selling unnecessary or substandard durable medical equipment. These schemes are used in every imaginable way. Not only are they used to cheat public and private health insurers, but they are also used to fleece the most vulnerable and needy—such as elderly and low-income persons.

Probably the most common health care fraud that is linked directly to fee-for-service is the submission of fraudulent claims to the Medicare program. The following two cases reported by the Department of Health and Human Services are typical of what occurred in the Miami area, a major center for health care fraud.

> Eight individuals who owned two home health care centers were indicted and their company and personal assets frozen in June of 2009 after they were accused of engineering a $22 million Medicare fraud scheme. Federal prosecutors claimed that the defendants recruited beneficiaries and paid kickbacks and bribes to them in exchange for their Medicare beneficiary numbers. The numbers were then used by the defendants to file phony Medicare claims for home health care services. One defendant, a medical assistant, also falsified medical tests and records to make it appear that the services were needed.[2]

> A 54-year old Miami physician was sentenced on June 29, 2009 by U.S. District Judge Paul C. Huck to 97 months in prison for a Medicare fraud. A month earlier, the doctor pleaded guilty before Judge Huck to conspiracy to commit healthcare fraud. He was a co-owner and practicing physician of a Miami HIV clinic where he and his co-conspirators routinely billed the Medicare program for services that were either medically unnecessary or were never provided. The doctor admitted further that he purchased only a small fraction of the drugs that were administered to patients at the clinic.

> Most of the services billed to the Medicare program were treatments for thrombocytopenia, a disorder involving a low blood platelet count. According to the court documents, none of the patients treated for this condition actually had low counts. But, to fake the results, he employed chemists to alter the patients' blood samples before they were sent to a laboratory.

> The doctor also admitted that he had engaged in similar criminal activities between October 2003 and February 2005 while working as a medical director and practicing physician at five other Miami area HIV infusion clinics. He admitted to billing the Medicare program for phony HIV infusion services, claiming he was directly responsible for more than $20 million in false Medicare claims.[3]

Since both honest and dishonest fee-for-service arrangements have produced ever-escalating health care costs, efforts to rein in costs were initiated in the 1990s with the introduction of more and more managed-care plans that tended to micromanage hospitals, doctors, and other health care providers. So, is it fair to say that replacing fee-for-service health care with managed care will mark the end of health care fraud and abuse? Definitely not.

Managed care encourages money-saving frauds that impose fees on patients and insurers for *little or no* service. Money-saving frauds typically involve pre-paid services such as health maintenance organizations (HMOs). The fraudulent health care provider accepts payments from patients and then shortchanges them by cutting corners or by spending as little money as possible on their care. Of course, many health care frauds combine both money-generating and money-saving strategies. Moreover, as I discuss later, the second fraud—shortchanging patients on care—is particularly complex and raises many vexing questions. For example, is it fraud or a highly unethical practice when an HMO picks subscribers—using advertising schemes to try to find the healthiest people and trying to discourage the sickest—in the hope that it will have to provide as few services as possible? What if an insurer routinely denies 10 percent of all customer claims, expecting that many of those people will not fight the denial? Is using a technicality to deny payments to patients an act of fraud? If not, why not? Changing the methods of health care delivery will not eliminate fraud, although it may change the tactics used by perpetrators to commit such frauds.

The Major U.S. Public Insurance Programs: A Criminal's Favorite Target

The public insurance programs Medicare and Medicaid (including the State Children's Health Insurance Program) are primary targets for criminals bent on committing health care fraud. Perpetrators of fraud have learned three things about these programs. The first thing that attracts them is the sheer size of the pot they can poach from. Public health insurance programs have claims budgets amounting to hundreds of billions of dollars. Medicare and Medicaid together financed some $755.2 billion in health care services in 2007.[4] And an aging population and higher unemployment rates are driving up both Medicare and Medicaid expenditures. Medicare expenditures are projected to be $528 billion in 2010, up 6 percent from 2009. By 2020 annual Medicare expenditures are expected to exceed $1 trillion.[5]

Furthermore, health care providers, patients, and regulators expect Medicare, Medicaid, TRICARE, or other insurance claims to be processed quickly. Expediting payments for claims usually takes priority over fraud detection.

Finally, the antifraud measures of these programs have been aimed mainly at stopping the blatant, high-dollar frauds. The more mundane, low-dollar frauds, however, may be slipping undetected through the reimbursement process.

Later, in chapter six, I discuss the often inadequate detection and preventive methods used by these public programs to deter and reduce health care fraud and abuse. A perpetrator's imagination seems to be the only limit when it comes to planning and committing health care fraud, however. Such imaginations come in both big and small packages. Those who commit health care fraud and abuse may be as small time as a street hoodlum or as big time as a preeminent professor at an elite medical school. Whether big or small, however, health care fraud cases prosecuted by the federal or state governments usually involve one or more of the following schemes.

Intentional False Diagnoses and Unnecessary Treatments

For physicians, nurses, or other health care providers, the diagnosis is the starting point for any treatment. It is also one of the starting points for health care fraud. False diagnoses—as opposed to erroneous diagnoses—enable a health care provider to obtain payments from patients or insurers for unnecessary medical treatments, pharmaceuticals, or durable medical equipment. Here are just a few examples of how these scams work.

- A regional medical center in Louisiana agreed to pay $3.8 million to the federal government to settle allegations of Medicare fraud. The center submitted claims for medically unnecessary angioplasty and stent procedures performed between 1999 and 2003.[6]
- A Kansas ear, nose, and throat specialist had his medical license suspended and was sentenced to six years in prison for performing unnecessary sinus and ear surgeries. The government's expert witness found 40 percent of the 105 sinus surgeries and all but one of the 40 mastoid ear surgeries performed by the defendant were unnecessary.[7] And these are not benign procedures. In an article posted on the website of the American Rhinologic Society, Jay M. Dutton, M.D., of the Rush–Presbyterian–St. Luke's Medical Center in Chicago, lists nine complications of nasal and sinus surgery. These include leakage of cerebrospinal fluid, meningitis, and, in rare cases, blindness, not to mention voice changes, nasal obstruction, numbness, and infection.[8] Thus, more than 80 patients were anesthetized and subjected to significant and painful side effects for no clinical reason at all.
- A provider of anatomic and clinical pathology services, patient information, and business-practice solutions for physicians paid $4.8 million in conjunction with Medicare and TRICARE billing frauds. The company billed for medically unnecessary DNA tests and for second-opinion consultations and reports that it failed to provide.[9]
- Two chiropractors were convicted of conspiracy and health care fraud against Medicare for using marketing techniques to attract customers with "good" health insurance policies and then tailoring patient treatments to their insurance coverage rather than to their medical needs.[10]

As noted earlier, false diagnoses can lead to unnecessary and dangerous treatments as well as to pain, suffering, and psychological damage. An Ohio physician was sentenced to life in prison for administering unnecessary and painful "trigger point" injections of the UN's Single Convention on Narcotic Drugs Schedule II and III narcotics, causing the deaths of two patients. He was also ordered to pay $14.3 million in restitution for false billings to Medicare, Medicaid, and the Ohio Bureau of Workers' Compensation. A Manhattan dermatologist was ordered to repay $880,000 for billing public and private insurers for services not provided to patients. The doctor lured patients back for more office visits by providing them with prescriptions for addictive drugs. This scam led to the death of one individual.[11]

Another form of unnecessary service is the practice of "ping-ponging." A network of health care providers may refer a patient to other providers in the network for bogus examinations or treatments. These reciprocal referrals generate illicit revenues as the patient bounces as a ping-pong ball from one health care provider to another with each provider collecting a fee for providing services the patient did not need.

Medical Identity Theft

The 1995 movie *The Net* is about Angela Bennett (played by Sandra Bullock), a computer analyst vacationing in Mexico who meets computer hacker and scoundrel Jack Devin (played by Jeremy Northam). Over the course of the film's ninety minutes, viewers watch a nefarious group of criminals who are intent on gaining access to secret government files, stealing Bennett's identity, and wrecking havoc. The group hacks into medical records, and they seem bent on destroying the lives of their victims before Bennett finally uses her considerable computer skills to foil their plot and reestablish her stolen life. *The Net*'s plot was far-fetched by 1995 standards. Today, however, such plots in real life are anything but. Many forms of identity theft are becoming increasingly common, with plots more insidious and convoluted than even the most creative screenwriter could have imagined. And, unlike Angela Bennett, people who are victims of identity theft suffer its consequences for months, or even years. Now, added to other forms of identity theft, we have the medical version, which occurs when one person (the perpetrator) uses the identity of another person (the victim) to obtain health care services from a provider or reimbursement from an insurer.

Anyone who peruses a patient's medical records will find a treasure trove of information—name and address, Social Security number, driver's license number, insurance information (e.g., Medicare number), and other documentation. And health care institutions have begun to store more and more confidential information on computers. Thieves can steal the computers, often with the help of insiders, and then circumvent security barriers, decode the data (if the data was encrypted), and either sell it to other criminals or use the data to file phony insurance claims. Unauthorized access may range from health care personnel who want to pry into the personal affairs of celebrity patients, as was the case with hospital workers who snooped through the medical files of the Britney Spears, George Clooney, Maria Shriver, and the late Farrah Fawcett—possibly selling information about their medical treatments and prognoses to tabloids—to scams leading to tens of thousands of dollars in fraudulent billings.[12] At least eight employees at a California hospital breached the records of Nadya Suleman, the publicity seeking "octomom" (and mother of fourteen). A total of $437,500 in fines was levied against the hospital under a California privacy law that went into effect at the beginning of 2009. The law also imposes fines on individual health care workers.[13] In a bizarre case at a Miami hospital, an ultrasound technician pleaded guilty to selling patient medical records to a so-called medical records broker who, in turn, sold them to a personal injury attorney. The attorney used the patient information to find clients, sharing any money he earned with the broker.[14]

Fraudulent billings caused by acts of identity theft have forced victims to deal with harassment by health care institution billing firms, collection agencies, and attorneys.

- A fifty-six-year-old retired teacher in Florida received a $66,000 surgical bill for the amputation of her right foot. She told a Federal Trade Commission workshop that her troubles started after someone stole her daughter's wallet, which contained the family's health insurance card. The thief even managed to get her blood type changed, something that could have been a disaster had she ever required emergency health care. Even after sending photographs to the hospital to prove that both of her feet were intact, the woman soon discovered that straightening out the fraudulent billings and correcting the errors in her medical records was a full-time job.[15]
- A Colorado victim had his medical identity stolen by a man who received multiple surgeries in his name. The victim was uninsured and lost property and a business due to the theft. Two years after being victimized, the man was so destitute that he had difficulty even paying his cell phone bill.[16]
- A twenty-two-year-old Marine first realized something was amiss in 2005 when his mother called to tell him he was a lead suspect in a car theft in South Carolina. He had lost his wallet more than a year earlier while celebrating with friends after completing boot camp at Parris Island, near Beaufort, South Carolina. An imposter used his military ID and driver's license to not only test-drive new cars and then steal them, but also to receive treatments for kidney stones and an injured hand. The identity thief ran up nearly twenty thousand dollars in medical charges, destroying the young soldier's credit. "It was horrible," he said. "And what made it worse is that

no one really knew what to do when it first started happening." Although the imposter was eventually arrested, the soldier's identity theft problems persisted, even while he was serving a tour of duty in Iraq. His tax refund money was confiscated by the state as he continued to try to clean up his credit. If the Marine ever needs medical attention—his records, now possibly contaminated with errors—could put him in danger. And if those medical records someday become linked electronically to a nationwide health information network, correcting the errors could be even more difficult.[17]

In a nutshell, medical identity theft is even worse than its counterpart, financial identity theft. And its victims find no easy solutions. Although the Federal Trade Commission is well aware of the plight of identity theft victims, and although tougher laws have been enacted to deter criminals from committing identity theft and to help victims repair their credit ratings, the effects of this crime can plague its victims for months and even years. No central office exists where one can go for a quick repair job on his or her credit history or medical information. Adverse credit information connected to victims of identity theft has a way of staying stubbornly in the computers of the major credit bureaus. And if these battles are not punishment enough, medical identity theft can also damage the employment prospects and future insurability of someone whose medical records contain erroneous data about a physical or mental impairment.[18] As is the case with other forms of health care fraud, medical identity theft may consume a victim's health benefits, possibly reducing or exhausting his or her lifetime coverage limits.[19]

Medical identity theft can also damage a victim's family life and reputation. A woman answered a knock on her door and was horrified to see law enforcement officers standing on the threshold. They accused her of being an unfit mother because she had given birth to a drug-addicted baby. The real mother, who was the perpetrator in this fraud, had used the woman's identity to receive labor and delivery services from a hospital. Nevertheless, authorities threatened to take custody of the innocent woman's four children, and she was saddled with a $10,000 hospital bill.

A similar incident occurred to a woman who was informed by hospital personnel that her newborn had tested positive for illegal drugs. The woman, however, had not given birth in years. She was the victim of a drug-abusing mother who had stolen her driver's license and used it as an ID to obtain admission to the hospital.[20] These cases illustrate how a moment of inattention and a stolen wallet may subject the victim to a seemingly never-ending stream of nightmarish hassles. Health care institutions want to settle past-due accounts, the police and social agencies want to ensure the safety of children, credit bureaus want to keep their huge databanks up to date, and collection agencies want to harass "deadbeat" consumers into paying their bills. If you are accused of a crime, the legal system assumes you are innocent until proven guilty, and it goes to great lengths to ensure that you receive due process. If your identity and credit are stolen, however, the "court of commerce" seems to say that you, the victim, are assumed guilty until you can somehow produce strong evidence of your innocence. Obtaining such evidence, however, is a herculean task.

Perpetrators of medical identity fraud not only leave a wake of financial destruction and psychological trauma behind them, but their schemes often place erroneous information in a victim's medical records. If the victim and the identity thief have different blood types, for example, posting the wrong blood type in her medical records could be life threatening. One industry expert posed the hypothetical situation of a medical identity theft victim with an acute case of appendicitis. On entering the hospital, medical personnel note all of the symptoms of acute appendicitis, but the patient's records indicate he has already undergone an appendectomy. Of course, it is the imposter patient, not the current patient, who has undergone the earlier surgery. The victim, in the meantime, is placed at risk as medical personnel look elsewhere for the source of his abdominal pain.[21] This scenario sounds eerily similar to the plot of *The Net*.

Overbilling for Services and Equipment

When you leave the doctor's office, you often pay your health insurance deductible or copayment. Later, you may receive additional statements from your provider or insurer that lists the services you received along with a summary of payments and outstanding charges.

Now the fun begins as you try to decipher the exact billings for these services, how much you will be required to pay, and how much your insurer will pay on your behalf. Reading hieroglyphics is probably easier. And the process becomes almost impossible when the fees are spread among multiple health care providers—doctors, hospitals, labs, therapists, medical equipment firms, and so forth. The paperwork produced by health care providers and insurers—paperwork that is seemingly shrouded in secrecy—is unlike that of any other purchase, with the possible exception of real estate. But at least with real estate buying and selling, an attorney is usually present at the point of sale (closing) to guide you through the legal mumbo jumbo. We are usually on our own, however, to make sense of the obfuscated charges, the arcane insurance policy provisions, and the price haggling between providers and insurers. In this byzantine system, the left hand often does not know—or care—what the right hand is doing. So, we have a system that is ripe for fraud, especially when the right hand is up to no good.

One of the frauds that is encouraged by our current system is the practice of double billing—that is, submitting duplicate (or multiple) invoices to a patient or to an insurer for the same service. The double billings may be made by one or by more than one provider. A Tennessee physician pleaded guilty to overbilling insurers by nearly $117,000 for submitting duplicate claims for ear tests. Instead of billing for the standard two-ear test, he doubled his charges by submitting separate claims for each ear. The doctor, whose medical license was revoked, was also accused of sexual assault, subornation of perjury, and other improper practices.[22]

Another form of duplicate billing is for two providers to bill for the same service. A family physician might submit a bill to Medicare for the analysis of X-rays even though a radiologist has already performed and billed Medicare for the same service.[23] In other cases, a single X-ray is taken, but the insurer is billed for multiple X-rays. Unless the patient receives billing information from each source and recognizes that a double or multiple billing has taken place, the fraud—or error—may go undetected.

It is not only the small providers that practice this scam. The big providers do it too. A New York hospital agreed to pay $2.3 million to resolve civil charges of defrauding the federal government by double billing Medicare for outpatient services between January 1992 and June 2001. According to the complaint, the hospital "submitted these duplicate claims for payment even though it knew, or acted with deliberate ignorance or reckless disregard of the fact, that it had already been paid for the very same services, and thus its claims for payment were false." The complaint also indicated that Empire Medical Services, the government's Medicare claims processing intermediary, notified the hospital of the double billings and directed them to stop. These warnings were ignored.[24]

How, one wonders, can people get away with this practice? Is no one watching the store? The answer seems to be that some providers, such as the Tennessee doctor described above, have such an inflated sense of self-worth that they believe they are above the law. Health care providers work far from the view of regulators, and they may assume boldly—and often correctly—that their patients are either too naive or too afraid to blow the whistle. The Tennessee doctor worked in a small town where it was probably difficult to attract and retain physicians. He was probably a revered figure among the townspeople, and it took a set of extremely brash, irresponsible, and dangerous acts on his part before a public outcry arose. When his license was revoked in November 2004, the Notice of Charges accused him of working on patients while he was intoxicated and engaging in sexual acts with female staff, at times "in full view of patients." This doctor also allowed patients and his staff to reuse prescription medicines, and he allowed untrained and unlicensed staff to diagnose, prescribe, and administer medicines.[25] The seemingly incomprehensible audacity exhibited by the likes of this "loose cannon" of a physician is a sure-fire recipe for abominable fraud.

The more modest offenders may believe, and rightfully so, that they can fly under the radar and avoid detection. They bank on the fact that their treatments and billings will not come to the attention of the authorities as long as they resist becoming too greedy and careless and stick to filing false claims only for ordinary treatments and services.

Some health care fraud perpetrators use hard-to-track multiple billings scattered over a wide geographic area, organizations with multiple names, or multiple provider addresses. A psychiatrist billed Medicare for services he provided in seven different states. His scheme entailed duplicate billings through two separate businesses that used twenty-four different mailing addresses, twenty-three different telephone numbers, and at least twelve different provider numbers.[26]

University teaching hospitals have been a source of concern regarding double billing in possible violation of the False Claims Act. The Physicians at Teaching Hospitals (PATH) initiative was initiated in June 1996 by the U.S Department of Health and Human Services, OIG. The initiative focuses on double payments made to faculty teaching physicians and resident physicians under their supervision. A teaching physician is allowed to receive payment for a service only if he or she personally provided the service or was present when the resident furnished the treatment. If the resident alone provided the treatment, the teaching physician cannot submit a claim for the same service without violating the FCA.

One of the nation's most respected medical schools entered into an $800,000 settlement with the OIG over allegations of false Medicare claims by faculty physicians. The university had no documentation to prove these physicians were personally involved in services delivered by interns or residents at the teaching hospital.[27]

A northeastern medical school agreed to pay a $2 million false claims settlement over charges that it double billed Medicaid. Between 1993 and 2004, the university's hospital charged Medicaid for outpatient services that were also billed by faculty working at its outpatient clinics.[28] Similar settlements for disputed Medicare billings were reached earlier at other prominent medical schools. The settlements in these cases ranged from $8.6 million to $30 million.[29] Again, in our health care system, these respectable players seem to do whatever they think they can get away with to increase their revenues, even though they are ostensibly not-for-profit institutions.

Overcharging for treatments or products is another ubiquitous health care fraud.

- An Ohio podiatrist was sentenced to a seventy-eight-month stretch in prison for (in part) providing only nail-trimming services but billing Medicare for more complex procedures.[30]
- A supplier of lymphedema pumps billed Medicare $4,500 each for pumps worth only $600 apiece.
- A psychological service billed Medicare for patient sessions reputedly lasting 45 to 50 minutes when, in reality, the sessions lasted only 20 to 30 minutes.[31]

- A large health care system in New Jersey paid $265 million to resolve allegations of overcharging Medicare for inpatient and outpatient services at nine of the system's hospitals.[32]
- A Connecticut hospital provided outpatient surgical services for kidney dialysis patients, a procedure earning a $1,500 Medicare reimbursement. But by admitting the patients and keeping them overnight, the hospital obtained a $13,000 reimbursement. The hospital settled the civil suit with the federal government for $632,000.[33]
- A provider of kyphoplasties, an orthopedic procedure for controlling pain, agreed to pay the federal government $75 million to settle a suit that accused one of its recently acquired companies of engaging in a seven-year scheme to defrauded Medicare. Rather than submitting bills to Medicare for the less costly clinically appropriate kyphoplasties, the company submitted bills for the more expensive inpatient kyphoplasties. This whistle-blower case was initiated by two former employees who shared $14.9 million of the recovery. The employees' attorney said, "A big, inpatient price tag allowed [the company] to make thousands of dollars each time it sold a kyphoplasty kit. Because of its scheme, the Medicare program paid many millions of dollars more than it needed to pay."[34]
- The state of Alabama filed suit against seventy-nine drug companies for overcharging Medicaid. One of the defendants charged $928 dollars for a unit of sodium chloride (table salt) worth only $1.71.[35]
- A major pharmaceutical company agreed to pay $671 million to settle claims of overcharging the government and bribing physicians to prescribe its pharmaceuticals. The nationwide scandal centered on four of the company's most popular drugs.[36]
- A university health center reached a $475,000 settlement with the federal government after being accused of overcharging Medicare for cancer treatments between 2002 and 2004. The government charged the center's hospital with billing Medicare for the number of hours it spent on patient care rather than for the services it provided to each patient. This billing practice inflated charges by two to seven times the normal Medicare payment limits.[37]
- The CMS accused twenty California hospitals of overcharging Medicare after evidence indicated Medicare had overpaid these hospitals by as much as $2 billion a year over a three-year period.[38]

Hospitals have prematurely billed federal programs for outpatient services even though the patient still occupied a hospital bed. In this scheme, a hospital discharges the patient "on paper," and Medicare is billed a flat diagnosis-related group (DRG) amount for the hospital stay (rather than billing Medicare based on the length of the stay). The hospital can then begin to bill Medicare for the more lucrative outpatient services, even though the patient remains in a hospital bed. A related scam is to hold a patient under observation for several days rather than admitting him or her to the hospital. Since hospital observation charges under Medicare Part B are usually higher than inpatient stay charges under Medicare Part A, the hospital receives a larger reimbursement.[39]

It is sometimes difficult to distinguish between fraud and billing errors. Health care billings can be complicated, and the staff responsible for such billings are often pressed for time and overworked. This situation leads both to fraud and to honest mistakes. Common errors include duplicate billings, overcharging the patient for the number of days spent in a hospital room (e.g., charging for both the day of admission *and* the day of discharge), incorrect hospital room charges (e.g., billing the patient for a private room when he or she stayed in a semiprivate room), overstating the amount of time a patient spent in the operating room, charging patients for work that was scheduled but then cancelled, and simple keystroke errors.[40]

Although random errors are possible, a pattern of such errors may be a sign of fraud. According to the CMS, Medicare recovered more than $1 billion through its Recovery Audit Contractor (RAC) program between 2005 and 2008. About 85 percent of the recoveries were from hospitals. Most claims were the result of billing and coding errors resulting in duplicate billings. Health care providers appealed 14 percent of RAC overpayment decisions, but fewer than 5 percent of the appeals were reversed.[41]

Upcoding, Unbundling, and Billing for Uninsured and Bogus Services

A prevalent and vexing problem for insurers is a scam called "upcoding." Medicare and Medicaid billings use a standardized system of codes, known as CPT (current procedural terminology) codes, for various diagnoses and procedures. The coding system tells the claims processor what services or equipment have been provided to the patient. For example, a therapist for a fifteen-minute span of treatment cannot bill certain pairs of CPT codes for outpatient therapy services.[42] Software is available to speed claims processing, to reduce errors, and to calculate the amount to be reimbursed to the health care provider.[43]

When providers are "upcoding" (also known as "upcharging" or "DRG drift"), they are, in fact, providing a less expensive service and then submitting an insurance claim using the code for a similar, but more expensive, service. Different codes or code combinations can produce significantly different reimbursements from Medicare or Medicaid. These claims might include billing for surgical assistants when none were required during a specific procedure, charging for life-support transportation when only wheelchair transportation was provided by an ambulance operator, billing for physician services when the services were performed by medical technicians, and submitting claims for critically ill kidney dialysis patients when only routine dialyses were provided to patients who were not critically ill.[44]

A Baltimore medical center agreed to pay $2.75 million to settle false claims charges pertaining to upcoding. Two hospital employees claimed that between July 1, 2005, and February 28, 2007, they were told to review charts and upcode the severity of two secondary diagnoses—malnutrition and acute respiratory failure—even if the patients neither had nor were treated for these conditions.[45]

Dartmouth College medical researchers Elaine Silverman and Jonathan S. Skinner investigated the problem of upcoding. They zeroed in on hospital admissions that were for pneumonia and respiratory infections. As they point out, it is sometimes difficult to tell the two apart, except for one very clear thing—respiratory infections net the hospital about $2,000 more. Silverman and Skinner found the incidence of the most expensive DRG for pneumonia and respiratory infections increased by 10 percentage points among stable not-for-profit hospitals and by 37 percentage points among hospitals converting to for-profit status.[46] Although not-for-profit institutions are not guiltless, this study points out that for-profits are especially tempted to use upcoding with more regularity. The researchers made an additional observation: "Upcoding behavior exhibits a close correspondence with tax evasion, where disputed tax returns are often settled quietly (with penalties), litigated, and only rarely the subject of criminal proceedings."[47]

Upcoding can be done by individual doctors or it can be a group effort. A physician billing service used an automatic coding software system that "routinely upcoded emergency room visits." The company agreed to a $15 million settlement with the federal government, and the whistle-blower received $2.4 million.[48] Similarly, one of the largest hospital chains serving small towns and rural areas in the United States entered into a $31.8 million settlement for widespread upcoding of diagnostic codes. The company initiated an aggressive coding procedure, encouraging its hospitals to meet unrealistically high coding-volume goals.[49]

Several emergency-physician groups agreed to reimburse the government for over $2.6 million in conjunction with overpayments received from upcoded claims. A former employee of an Oklahoma billing company launched the case, and, for this, her estate was awarded $443,502 as part of the whistle-blower settlement.[50]

Some especially daring health care providers may recode and resubmit a rejected insurance claim. A geriatric hospital paid $800,000 to settle charges it defrauded Medicare. Claims denied by Medicare for room and board were resubmitted by the hospital as claims for supplies, laboratory work, and other covered services.[51]

Not content to up the ante, some criminals may "unbundle" it. That is, they may take services typically offered as a group or bundle and disentangle them so that they can bill each one separately to obtain a higher insurance reimbursement. A Florida ophthalmology service agreed to a $2.85 million payment as settlement for the fraudulent Medicare billings made by its billing company. The billing service fragmented claims for surgical procedures that Medicare had already reimbursed the provider for as part of a global payment. The company, seemingly a chronic offender, had previously paid several million dollars in other fraud settlements.[52]

Laboratories are among the most frequent perpetrators of unbundling. Blood chemistry tests performed using a multichannel analyzer, for example, measure twenty different tests on the same specimen. These tests include cholesterol, total protein, and various electrolytes (including sodium, potassium, chlorine, and others). Medicare typically bundles a daily blood test under a single reimbursement rate. An unscrupulous laboratory operator, however, may inflate Medicare or Medicaid claims by charging separately for some of the tests. Bundling and duplicate payments can also be combined by submitting a claim for a bundled set of procedures and then unbundling the same procedures and billing the insurer again.

During the 1990s and into the early years of the twenty-first century, the Departments of Justice and Health and Human Service's Operation LABSCAM targeted laboratory unbundling practices. The federal government recovered more than $850 million from the nation's largest clinical laboratories as a result of its LABSCAM and related investigations.[53]

So why do laboratories unbundle tests, and how do they get away with it? The answer probably lies in the huge volume of work they perform. The profit added by unbundling just one lab test is small. But when a laboratory performs hundreds of thousands of tests, that margin becomes highly significant. The sheer number of tests performed and the claims submitted to public and private insurers also makes it easier to hide the unbundling activities. But as the federal authorities begin to scrutinize this illicit practice, it may diminish. Although the unbundling of services was a major problem in the 1990s, it has once again become an investigative priority for the U.S. Department of Health and Human Services, possibly making this fraud a less attractive option for dishonest providers.

Public and private insurers may be defrauded by being billed for services or items not covered by their plans. Doctors and other health care providers commit fraud when they knowingly provide their patient with an uninsured treatment but file a claim for an insured treatment. The costs of cosmetic surgeries are not reimbursable under Medicare, Medicaid, or most private health insurance plans. Uncovered services, however, may be billed falsely as covered procedures. Performing a liposuction but billing for a hernia repair, removing unsightly spider veins but billing for varicose vein surgery, or performing cosmetic nose surgery but billing for surgery to correct a deviated septum (and to relieve a patient's breathing problems) are all examples of insurance fraud. The operators of a Seattle acupuncture center pleaded guilty to falsifying Medicare and Medicaid claims when they provided patients with $375,000 in uncovered acupuncture treatments, but disguised the claims as covered physical therapy services.[54]

In some cases, a patient has no idea whether his or her health insurance covers a particular medical procedure and accepts the provider's word that the claim is legitimate. In other cases, a patient may never see the claim documents that are submitted to the health insurer and, as a result, will know nothing of the fraud committed on his or her behalf. In still other cases, however, the health care provider and the patient may conspire to submit a false claim covering a nonreimbursable service, making both parties liable for fraud charges. Because public and private insurers were not in the room when the treatments were delivered, they must depend on auditors or whistle-blowers to bring the fraud to light. Obviously, the chance of a single fraud being revealed is small.

Michael F. Mangano, a principal deputy inspector general for HHS, testified before the Senate Committee on Governmental Affairs, Permanent Subcommittee on Investigations regarding deceptive Medicare billings. According to Mangano, one medical supplier agreed to plead guilty to conspiracy to defraud Medicare of more than $70 million. The supplier sold adult diapers to nursing homes (not reimbursable by Medicare) but billed the program for urinary collection pouches (reimbursable by Medicare). In another case, a group of sales people were charged with recruiting Medicare beneficiaries by giving them nonreimbursable items, such as microwave ovens and air conditioners, but billing Medicare for reimbursable items, such as hospital beds and wheelchairs.[55] Again, the beneficiaries just took the microwaves and had no idea that Medicare was being dunned for the more expensive items.

As in the case my father encountered, ambulance companies also run afoul of the law by billing Medicare for nonallowable services.[56] The fraudulent schemes ambulance operators have perpetrated include overstating the miles traveled, double billing patients and insurance companies for the same services, billing for oxygen and advanced life support services not provided to a patient, and billing for emergency ambulance trips when a taxi cab or nonemergency vehicle was used.[57] One form of ambulance fraud, for example, involves transporting dialysis patients.[58] In most cases, these patients do not require ambulance services, and they can travel at significantly less expense to a dialysis treatment center using personal or public transportation. Patients have been filmed, however, walking to the vehicle, riding in the front passenger seat of the ambulance, and being transported in an automobile with Medicare being billed for ambulance services. Patients may not realize—or not care—how they are being transported if Medicare or their private insurer is footing the bill. In other instances, the patients may assume that sitting in a passenger seat instead of being transported in a supine position is "standard operating procedure." Ambulance operators also take advantage of unsuspecting patients when they transport two or three patients on a single trip and then bill Medicare for separate trips.[59]

Billing insurers for services not provided is yet another major health care fraud. A Beverly Hills physician defrauded Medicare of more than $216,000 by billing for treatments to patients who were dead, incarcerated, or living in distant locations where the doctor could not have possibly seen them on the dates in question.[60]

In Delaware, a physician specializing in pain management was convicted of submitting bills to insurance companies for services she did not perform. She duplicated test results, used cut-and-paste or white-out techniques to replace one patient's name with another, and sent these documents to insurance companies. In over one hundred cases, test results for two patients matched perfectly, something that is almost a statistical impossibility. This ham-handed attempt at fraud is one that even an ineffective fraud-detection system should be able to uncover. It is no surprise then that the scam was revealed and that—for her dishonesty and ineptness—the doctor received a six-and-one-half-year prison sentence.[61]

Medical laboratories have billed for services that were neither ordered nor provided. In a sixty-day period, one lab submitted 717 claims to Medicare amounting to $330,000 for 416 beneficiaries (some of whom were deceased). Even more incredible, one of the physicians who had allegedly made a referral had also been dead for two years.[62]

Medical school graduates are normally at the top of the IQ scale. Such was obviously not the case with a Texas doctor who conspired with his attorney (and brother) as well as with a certified public accountant, a physician's assistant, office managers, patients, and staff members. This diverse group of conspirators devised a large cross-referral scheme to commit automobile accident, personal injury, and workers' compensation fraud. Telemarketers hired by the group solicited and referred accident victims to the attorney and to the doctor. They provided trumped up services to the clients and made phony claims to insurance carriers.

When the FBI conducted a computer analysis of the group's billing records, it revealed widespread upcoding, falsified medical reports, and multiple billings for the same service. According to claims records, the doctor would have had to work ninety hours a day to generate the $34 million in office visits he billed to insurers. Much of the money from this scam was laundered through Central American and Caribbean banks. The brothers and their accomplices were required to pay steep fines and restitution. They were also forced to forfeit assets derived from their criminal activities and faced lengthy prison terms.[63]

Nursing Home Fraud and Abuse

As baby boomers age, nursing homes will become a rapidly growing part of the health care system. Once a person is admitted to a nursing home, he or she is out of the daily sight of regulators and insurers. And even the patient's family may know little about their loved one's care and treatment regimes, especially for patients suffering from dementia. They are unable to judge the quality of their care or to report incidents of fraud and abuse.

Some nursing home administrators take advantage of the fact that their patients are "dual eligible," being covered under both Medicare and Medicaid. More fortunate patients may be entitled to benefits under Medicare as well as benefits under a private long-term care plan or a retirement program. Dual coverage enables administrators to submit duplicate claims to both programs, knowing that the likelihood of their being caught is low.

Nursing homes also commit durable medical equipment fraud by supplying inexpensive items to a patient, such as a seat cushion, but billing Medicare for a more expensive item, such as a "custom-fitted orthotic body jacket" that is designed to protect and immobilize the patient's spine. Similarly, unscrupulous providers may bill the Medicare program for more-costly hospice care, but provide terminally ill patients with less-costly standard nursing home services.

Another area rife with fraud is the provision of mental health services to nursing home patients. Psychologists who conduct group counseling sessions for nursing home residents—sometimes referred to as "coffee, cookies, and conversation"—have fraudulently billed Medicare for individual patient sessions. Weight reduction programs, taking residents on shopping trips, listening to music, and other recreational activities have also been billed to Medicare as psychological services. Similarly, "gang visits" result in fraud when practitioners such as physical therapists, optometrists, or podiatrists "stop by" and visit with nursing home residents as a group but bill Medicare for individual services. Some nursing homes have also been prosecuted for employing unlicensed or unqualified staff.[64]

As noted earlier, substandard nursing home care billed to Medicare or Medicaid is automatically regarded as fraudulent. Patient neglect and abuse has long been a critical nursing home problem. Nursing home employees who physically abuse patients are subject to criminal prosecution. A joint federal-state investigation revealed an appalling quality of care at a Connecticut nursing home because of inadequate staffing and patient-care plans. One obviously neglected resident had died of septic infection allegedly caused by bed sores, and others suffered from severe pressure sores and ulcers, dehydration, and weight loss.[65] In some cases, patients suffer from being physically or chemically restrained in violation of federal or state law.

Lewis Morris, chief counsel for OIG, testified in May 2008 before the U.S. House of Representatives Subcommittee on Oversight and Investigation on Energy and Commerce about the substandard care still found in many nursing homes despite the threat of severe sanctions by the government. Morris cited examples of serious cases, such as failing to attend to patient medical needs, neglecting to supervise patients who fell repeatedly, ignoring patients suffering from malnutrition and dehydration, and allowing patients to go for extended periods of time without being cleaned or bathed. One particularly horrible example of patient neglect involved a Georgia nursing home patient who had maggots in her mouth and died of larvae infestation because staff failed to provide her with basic oral hygiene care.[66]

Abuse also becomes fraud when nursing home management denies allegations or conceals evidence of patient mistreatment. A question that has not been answered fully is at what point do frauds that are born out of a desire to maximize profits lead to charges of reckless endangerment, manslaughter, or even murder? An analysis of eighty-two studies of U.S. and Canadian nursing homes conducted between 1965 and 2003 indicates that nonprofit nursing homes provide better care than for-profit ones.[67] Nevertheless, it takes a special breed of provider to place the financial bottom line of a nursing home business over the welfare, dignity, and basic comfort of its patients. It seems, however, that this "special breed" is becoming more commonplace.

Home Health Care Fraud and Abuse

The introduction of for-profit health care has also increased the problem of fraud and abuse in the home care setting. Home health care enables elderly, chronically ill, or disabled persons to remain self-sufficient by receiving the care they need in the familiar surroundings of their own homes. This form of care also offers a useful transition for patients who have been discharged from the hospital but who still need medical supervision. Furthermore, home health care is significantly less expensive than nursing home or hospital care. Over 70 percent of home health care patients are age seventy or older, and they frequently require care for heart problems, diabetes, and cerebral vascular diseases.

Home health care services include in-home skilled nursing services, counseling, physical and occupational therapy, equipment and supplies, pharmaceutical services, homemaker and companion services, social services, dietary and nutritional services, intravenous therapy, speech therapy, audiology, and even twenty-four-hour home care. The home health care industry is highly fragmented, consisting of over twenty thousand small companies that primarily serve local markets. The top-performing home health care companies, on the average, in 2007 had been in business for more than sixteen years, employed about 217 workers, and had revenues of $17.3 million—up by over 30 percent from the previous three years.[68] Not surprisingly, these companies depend heavily on revenues from the Medicare and Medicaid programs. In 2008 the Medicare program spent $16.5 billion on home health care, an amount that will probably increase in the years ahead.

Regulation of the home health care industry is uneven at best. Although it is among the fastest-growing occupations in the United States, home health care workers are often poorly paid, which may lead to the hiring of persons who are unreliable, dishonest, or lacking in critical skills. Because of the vulnerability of their clients, home health workers must, in most states, be screened for criminal backgrounds. In nineteen states, however, these workers can be hired without a criminal background check. And even in states requiring such checks, persons with criminal records may slip through the cracks and pose a danger to elderly homebound patients.

In most instances, dishonest home health care workers commit property crimes—pilfering items from their clients' homes or stealing money from their clients' checking or credit card accounts. Direct violence, although rare, is always a possibility. An eighty-five-year-old bedridden California woman, for example, was murdered by a home health care worker. Indirect violence, a hallmark of white-collar criminals, is also possible.[69] According to the *Boston Globe,* a personal care attendant was accused of leaving a quadriplegic with cerebral palsy undressed, with no water, and without stockings that were supposed to help prevent blood clots.[70]

Because of the irresistible temptation to unscrupulous entrepreneurs, the rise in the number of for-profit home health care patients means a concomitant rise in home health care fraud. A Los Angeles man was sentenced to 120 months in prison and ordered to pay over $7 million in restitution to Medicare after he pleaded guilty in July 2007 to health care fraud. He admitted that during an eighteen-month period he defrauded Medicare by recruiting beneficiaries who were neither homebound nor in need of skilled nursing services. The beneficiaries were paid anywhere from one hundred to four hundred dollars in cash. This fraudulent patient recruiter profited handsomely from the scheme; he received kickbacks from the home health care service, ranging from $1,200 to $4,800 per patient. The case also involved conspiracy charges because the fraudster had an accomplice, the owner of the home health care service. The owner was sentenced to forty-six months in prison for his part in the scheme. Money-laundering charges were also levied because the fraud artist tried to cover his tracks by having the kickback checks made payable to other businesses.

In March 2008, a St. Louis woman was sentenced to forty-eight months in prison and ordered to pay $545,713 in restitution for health care fraud, failure to pay employment taxes, and the misuse of a Social Security number in a banking transaction. She operated a homemaker and personal-care service business for homebound elderly and disabled clients. The woman lied about the training and certification of her employees, and she submitted claims for home-care services that were never rendered. She also failed to pay more than $73,000 in employee federal withholding taxes. In addition to requiring restitution, the court also placed her company on probation for five years.[71]

To qualify for Medicare reimbursement, a patient must be homebound (i.e., unable to leave his or her residence without undergoing considerable hardship).

According to the 2009 document on Medicare and home health care from the Centers for Medicare and Medicaid Services, "you must be homebound or normally unable to leave home unassisted. To be homebound means that leaving home takes considerable and taxing effort. A person may leave home for medical treatment or short, infrequent absences for non-medical reasons, such as a trip to attend religious services. You can still get home health care if you attend adult day care."[72] Yet Medicare is often faced with billings for patients who do not meet the definition of "homebound." A similar problem occurs among hospice patients who are ineligible for Medicare benefits because they are not terminally ill.[73]

For these reasons, the issue of home care fraud and abuse is a complex one that may force us to rethink how we define fraud and abuse in the first place. Medicare demands that patients meet the definition of "homebound" described above. Perhaps nurses or social workers, not doctors, have a more realistic idea of the issues confronting the homebound. For example, homebound patients are often capable of making short excursions from their living quarters. A homebound elderly woman may have just enough energy to walk down the block to socialize with neighbors. Another might be able to make it to the grocery store to pick up a few basic necessities. Getting out of the house for a short walk can have healthful benefits, but these individuals may still desperately need home health care services to maintain their fragile conditions. According to Medicare's eligibility requirements, however, such a patient may not be considered "homebound." A visiting nurse or therapist who is paid by Medicare for providing services to this patient could conceivably be charged with fraud.

And sometimes the patient is the culprit. California's In-Home Supportive Services (IHSS) program had a $5.42 billion budget in 2009 to help 440,000 low-income and elderly residents avoid more expensive nursing home stays. But the program became a target for fraud because beneficiaries were allowed to hire services from anyone they choose, including relatives. A man who claimed he was disabled to the point of being bedridden cheated the IHSS program out of $150,000. As it turned out, this "bedridden patient" spent eight to ten hours a day working on an ice cream truck. Investigators watched him stock the truck and, despite his "severe disability," were amazed to see him muster the strength to drag a washing machine across his driveway. According to Michael Ramsey, the district attorney in Butte County, California, "this program is very easy to abuse. It invites chicanery and fraud."[74] Apparently the program has a backlog of fraud cases and few investigators to pursue them. As a result, Governor Arnold Schwarzenegger has threatened to cut IHSS's budget. This case could be another example in which the actions of a fraudulent few make life difficult for thousands of law-abiding elderly who need home-care services.

But for crooked providers, home health care is a gold mine. As with corrupt nursing home managers and workers, corrupt home health care workers bank on the fact that their clients are often elderly, suffering from dementia, and easily confused. They also know that regulators cannot directly observe what they do inside a patient's home. Unfair marketing practices, billing for more visits than are actually made, performing housekeeping and custodial services but submitting claims for skilled nursing or therapy services, kickbacks to physicians for referrals, physician self-referrals, and other frauds discussed in this book are also common among home health providers. More and more Americans will need home health care services in the decades ahead, and more money will be directed toward this industry. Distinguishing between the honest and dishonest uses of home health care will be essential to controlling health care costs as the population ages.

Rent-a-Patient Schemes

Rent-a-patient schemes depend on two things: greedy health care providers who want to make a quick buck and "patients" with health insurance coverage—Medicare, Medicaid, or private insurance—who are willing to undergo painful medical procedures in exchange for under-the-table cash payments. In this scheme, the patients are taken by "associates," also known as "recruiters" or "runners," to health care facilities that are operated by fraudulent health care providers—usually doctors. The patients may be told to complain about or exaggerate certain symptoms. They may also be coached on how to fill out a patient questionnaire. Once inside the clinic, the rent-a-patients are asked to sign an "informed consent" form promising to turn over all insurance claim checks to the crooked health care provider. The patients, who usually understand that their health is of no concern to those providing the "care," receive examinations, treatments, and durable medical equipment referrals. Then either a public or private insurer is billed for the bogus services and products. Recruiters, in turn, are paid for each patient they lure into the scheme, and the patients are paid a fee for their participation.

Sometimes the rent-a-patient scheme becomes a nightmare, as this Phoenix, Arizona, newspaper story illustrates:

> Julio Hernandez says he felt "healthy as a horse" before he agreed to use his body as an instrument for insurance fraud. But during a five-month stretch last year, the 36-year-old Phoenix resident endured the following medical procedures: A circumcision. Removal of his sweat glands. A nose operation. A colonoscopy. An endoscopy. Hernandez admits he needed none of these procedures. But, he says, a work associate persuaded him to travel to Southern California for the operations, again and again. The associate…moonlights as a health-care coyote—a ubiquitous middleman for…surgical clinics that are performing unnecessary, sometimes

> risky medical procedures on "rent-a-patients" such as Hernandez.... In
> return for using their bodies as mini-cottage industries, they are getting
> paid cash in under-the-table payments.

Mr. Hernandez, looking for quick cash, received eight hundred dollars for each
medical procedure he underwent. The perpetrators made millions of dollars
from this scam.[75]

In a bizarre variation, a South Carolina doctor recruited friends and family
to serve as rent-a-patients. With the aid of an accomplice, he filed $2 million in
billings for unnecessary nerve and vascular tests.[76] An Indiana dentist operating
out of a mobile office was sentenced to fifty-seven months in prison for Medicaid
fraud. By offering free gift cards and CD players, the dentist induced parents to
bring their children to his office for unnecessary treatments. He used this scheme
to obtain over $2.4 million.[77]

Rent-a-patient schemes have several common elements. Fraudulent health
care providers often target working-class minority groups. The patients are often
factory workers with employer-sponsored health insurance who are recruited by
runners from the same ethnic background. Although not destitute, these patients
may regard several hundred dollars in tax-free cash as a small fortune. Then they
are pleasantly surprised to learn that they can up the amount to several thousand
dollars by enticing their family members, including children, to participate in the
scam. Many of these scams are centered in Southern California, although greedy
health care providers there have been known to transport patients from as far
away as Florida. One such example was a California physician who was sentenced
in late 2007 to fifty-eight months in prison after he billed insurance companies for
unnecessary surgical procedures as part of a broad-based rent-a-patient scam.[78]

In another Southern California case, top executives at a medical center in Los
Angeles were charged with a rent-a-patient operation that stole $4.1 million from
Medicare and Medi-Cal coffers. (Medi-Cal is California's Medicaid program.)
Three persons all entered guilty pleas—a former center co-owner and board
chair, a former CEO, and a recruiter who had been paid $500,000 to entice home-
less people into the scam. Patients were typically paid twenty to thirty dollars to
participate, and the recruiter received forty dollars for bringing in a Medicaid-
eligible patient and twenty dollars for bringing in a Medi-Cal–eligible patient.[79]
On January 25, 2010, the United States obtained a $10 million dollar consent
judgment against the former co-owner and the former CEO for Medicare and
Medi-Cal fraud. According to Tony West, assistant attorney general for the Civil
Division of the Department of Justice, "Performing unnecessary medical procedures just to take money from taxpayers' pockets is bad enough, but to prey on
homeless people struggling to survive day to day is particularly reprehensible."
The pair, at this writing, was also awaiting sentencing on criminal charges.[80]

Rent-a-patient scam artists—whose audacity seemingly knows no boundaries—often submit exaggerated claims, stating falsely that their services were provided on an emergency basis in an attempt to obtain a higher reimbursement.[81] These so-called health care providers also have a thorough understanding of insurance policies and claims procedures. They may first target employed patients with comprehensive insurance plans before shifting to those with more restrictive plans. Once their claims are submitted, these scam artists often pursue collections aggressively. According to Steven E. Skwara, director of fraud investigation for Blue Cross Blue Shield of Massachusetts, "They'd call constantly, they write nasty letters, they write nasty letters to your boss."[82]

So how do "patients" fall prey to these schemes? For the indigent covered by Medicaid, it is their desperate need for quick, but not easy, cash—cash that provides them with the basic necessities or, in some cases, drugs. For the working class covered by an employer-sponsored health plan, it is the prospect of extra money that can be used to pay past-due bills or to purchase otherwise unattainable items, such as a new car or a much-wanted flat-screen television. For the elderly covered by Medicare, cash may also be the primary attraction. It is probable, however, that some elderly victims are misled into believing that they need medical attention when, in fact, they do not.

The perpetrators of these schemes are aware that many of their low-income Medicaid-eligible victims may be difficult to locate, especially if they have been transported to the clinics from distant locations. These same perpetrators also know that the elderly, if suffering from dementia, are easily confused and either will not make reliable witnesses or will be easily discredited by defense attorneys. Many of the culprits are caught, but only after they have bilked public and private insurance programs out of millions of dollars.

Some might get a dark sense of satisfaction from knowing that some rent-a-patients cheat the cheaters. Rather than signing over their insurance checks to the clinics as they agreed to do at the outset, they cut the dishonest providers out of the loop by cashing the checks and keeping the proceeds for themselves.

Pill-Mill Schemes

A fifty-three-year-old Brooklyn pharmacist was sentenced from one to three years in prison for his part in a scheme that funneled tens of thousands of pills, including powerful narcotics and barbiturates, to street-level drug dealers. His accomplice, a fifty-eight-year-old Brooklyn internist, supported the pharmacist by writing phony prescriptions for the painkiller Percocet and the sleeping pills Seconal and Tuinal. The physician received five years of probation, a $40,000 fine, and community service.[83]

The pharmacist and doctor were running what is known as a "pill-mill." Pill-mill schemes involve the fraudulent prescribing, buying, and selling of prescription drugs. They invariably involve a "patient finder" who directs patients to designated medical clinics for unnecessary physical examinations and laboratory tests. Based on the bogus or perfunctory examinations and tests, the corrupt physician writes a prescription for the patient. Medicare, Medicaid, or other insurers are then billed for the phony services and prescriptions. Once the prescription is filled, the patient turns the drugs over to a pill buyer in exchange for cash, merchandise, or illegal drugs. The pill buyer then resells the drugs to a corrupt pharmacist at lower-than-wholesale prices. This cycle is repeated as the same drugs are bought and sold several times.

If the diverted drugs have a high value to street users, they may be sold to drug traffickers. The term "pill-mill" has also been used to describe doctors who prescribe drugs freely to patients whose medical condition does not warrant their use. A federal jury found a Naples, Florida, physician guilty of overprescribing powerful painkillers to patients. According to undercover agents, the doctor's prescriptions were written after she gave patients a cursory medical examination by checking their blood pressure and knee reflexes and by having them extend their arms outward in front of their bodies.[84]

A Kansas grand jury returned a thirty-four-count indictment against a physician and his wife for conspiracy, unlawful distribution of a controlled substance, health care fraud, illegal monetary transactions, and money laundering. They allegedly wrote illicit prescriptions for painkillers, muscle relaxants, and other drugs. According to prosecutors, this scheme caused the deaths of at least four patients. The doctor's wife also bragged to job applicants that their clinic, with its pain-management patients, prescribed more painkillers than any clinic in the state. With the monikers "the pill man" and "the candy man," the doctor kept his clinic open eleven hours a day, scheduling patients ten minutes apart. The clinic generated $4 million in billings to health-benefit programs.[85]

According to a July 2010 report released by the Office of Applied Studies, Substance Abuse and Mental Health Services Administration, "the proportion of all substance abuse treatment admissions aged 12 or older that reported any pain reliever abuse increased more than fourfold between 1998 and 2008, from 2.2 to 9.8 percent."[86] The Department of Health and Human Services has become suspicious of the growing number of small clinics that have been dispensing an unusually high volume of pain medication. Tipped off by an anonymous caller, a ring of doctors at a clinic in West Virginia was discovered to be attracting patients by writing prescriptions for an inordinate amount of pain medications. The prescriptions were funneled through two local pharmacies under common ownership. In 2006 one pharmacy sold about 3.2 million hydrocodone pills—or about one prescription per minute—an amount that was well above the national dispensing rate of 97,431 hydrocodone pills per pharmacy. One cardiology resident, working on behalf of the clinic, earned more than $250,000 by signing prescriptions for pain medications.[87]

Illegal drugs may also be dispensed through the practice of "doctor shopping." These shoppers visit the offices of numerous practitioners within a short amount of time to obtain more prescription medications than are clinically necessary.[88] If the shopper is a drug abuser, he takes the drugs for nonmedical reasons. If the shopper is a drug trafficker, he sells the drugs to pill buyers or street traffickers. An Arizona resident obtained more than 27,000 pills (primarily Percocet and oxycodone) from fifty-one Tucson-area pharmacies. He was charged with, among other things, possession of a controlled substance with the intent to distribute.[89]

Pill-mill schemes impose several costs on society. Because prescription drugs are a major portion of health care expenditures, these scams inflate health care and insurance costs. Pill-mill schemes also foster illegal drug trafficking. Painkillers are among the most common drugs used in pill-mill schemes. But recycling and trafficking prescription drugs poses a major health hazard to unwary users. The generic pain medication oxycodone is in high demand by drug abusers and addicts because it generates a euphoric state similar to that of heroin. The drug also has been abused extensively and blamed for hundreds of deaths.[90]

Pill-mill schemes have also created a problem for physicians and their patients who have a legitimate need for pain medications. Physicians have become increasingly concerned that they will be arrested, lose their license to practice medicine, and face incarceration. Prosecutors even threatened one outspoken doctor, who believed in the liberal prescribing of pain medication, with the death penalty. The dilemma is in knowing where to draw the line between the legitimate management of pain and the illegal prescription of painkillers.

The defendants in the Kansas case described above appear to land squarely on the wrong side of the law. People have an enormous capacity for adjusting to life-changing circumstances, but pain is something that one never gets used to. When pain cannot be alleviated, it takes its toll on the victim's physical and mental health.

But patients have different thresholds for pain. For these reasons, doctors are hard put to know whether a patient's complaints about pain are legitimate or whether their complaints are motivated by their addiction to a painkiller. How responsible should a doctor be if his or her patient becomes addicted to a controlled substance? Some doctors take the approach of let's cure your source of pain and we will worry about your addiction to the painkiller later. Others are concerned about the legal ramifications of overprescribing pain medication. What is the doctor's liability if the patient suffers harm or dies after mixing prescribed painkillers with illegal drugs? What is the doctor's culpability if the patient sells his or her drugs to someone else? To answer these queries and more, the University of Wisconsin, in conjunction with the Drug Enforcement Administration (DEA), drafted a forty-eight-page report for physicians and law enforcement personnel that addressed frequently asked questions about the medical and legal ramifications of prescribing opioid analgesics and other painkillers.[91] Shortly after the guidelines were published, however, the DEA withdrew its support—a sign that the controversy over pain management will continue.[92]

The Emerging Drug Frauds in Medicare Part D

The Medicare Prescription Drug, Improvement, and Modernization Act of 2003 (MMA) established a prescription-drug plan known as Medicare Part D (effective January 1, 2006). The plan is a decentralized, voluntary outpatient prescription-drug program relying heavily on the cooperation and integrity of private insurance companies, pharmacy benefit managers, retail pharmacies, and pharmaceutical firms (manufacturers).

Providers of prescription drugs, known as "sponsors," are private insurers under contract with the Centers for Medicare and Medicaid Services. Sponsors, in turn, develop contracts with pharmacy benefit managers, and the pharmacy benefit managers are expected to negotiate with pharmaceutical manufacturers and retail pharmacies to control prescription-drug costs. Medicare beneficiaries have the option of selecting from among a number of stand-alone drug plans or from plans that are affiliated with a managed-care organization (Medicare Part C).

The Medicare Part D program pits the quality health care and cost-control interests of the Medicare program and its beneficiaries against the profit-seeking interests of the health care providers, insurance companies, pharmacies, and pharmaceutical manufacturers. Its decentralized structure, however, has created a fertile environment for fraud and abuse. Fraudulent actions may arise with regard to marketing and beneficiary enrollments, kickbacks and rebates on pharmaceuticals, manipulation of covered services, and claims processing.[93]

The MMA antifraud provisions are directed primarily at the sponsors (private insurers). Sponsors must develop antifraud and abuse programs tailored to their operations. Furthermore, the OIG develops an annual "work plan" targeting designated forms of fraud and abuse. Knowledge of the work plan emphasis areas provides guidance to sponsors and other entities doing business with the Medicare program. The OIG's 2008 work plan, for example, identified audit priorities such as diagnostic Medicare Part D duplicate claims and the ability of pharmacies to purchase drugs at the average manufacturer price.[94] Sponsors must also submit to the CMS detailed quarterly reports on their program operations. Special attention is paid to the calculation of a sponsor's pharmaceutical costs and reimbursement rates, marketing strategies, drug formulary, and management structures. A lengthy, but possibly incomplete, list of frauds directed at the Medicare Part D program is provided in table 3.1.

Persons outside the health care industry, most notably crooked telemarketers, have also taken advantage of the complex and, for many beneficiaries, seemingly incomprehensible provisions of Medicare Part D. In the "299 scam," telemarketers posing as Medicare sponsors with legitimate-sounding names such as the "National Medical Office" call Medicare beneficiaries. Some callers may already have personal information on their targeted elderly victims, further enhancing their credibility. Typically, the caller offers to help the victim select the best deal on a Medicare Part D plan for a one-time fee of $299—hence the name "299 scam."[95] The caller uses this subterfuge to obtain the beneficiary's Medicare or Social Security number as well as information about his or her bank or credit card accounts. This tactic opens the door to a variety of scams, including Medicare fraud, identity theft, and credit card fraud.

The CMS may impose several sanctions on sponsors who fail to comply with Medicare Part D antifraud provisions. The most severe penalties include termination of the sponsor's Medicare contract and civil monetary penalties ranging from $10,000 to $100,000. Errant sponsors and others are also subject to prosecution under the False Claims Act, the antikickback statute, and the Stark Law.

Durable Medical Equipment Frauds

Durable medical equipment frauds have recently received a great deal of attention from Congress and the CMS. DME includes wheelchairs, scooters, walkers, hospital beds, prosthetics, special seating cushions, urinary-collection devices, surgical dressings, airway-pressure machines, breathing aids, oxygen equipment, orthopedic devices, and nutritional supplies such as milk supplements.

To receive reimbursement under Medicare or Medicaid for durable medical equipment, patients must obtain a certificate of medical necessity completed jointly by a physician and the equipment provider. The CMS contracts with the National Supplier Clearinghouse to verify that suppliers meet twenty-one standards before they are permitted to bill federal programs. Unfortunately, there has been inadequate oversight of DME suppliers, a condition that has enabled the proliferation of disreputable firms and massive frauds. A September 2005 Government Accounting Office report revealed $900 million in overpayments out of the total $8.8 billion paid for durable medical equipment by Medicare in 2004.[96] DME fraud operations are especially prevalent in South Florida and in Southern California. An OIG investigation discovered over half of the 1,581 South Florida DME suppliers do not meet HHS's minimum standards. When federal agents made surprise visits to these companies, 491 of them (31%) either had no facilities or maintained no staff or operating hours. Yet, during 2006, these phantom DME supply firms managed to collect $97 million from Medicare.[97]

On July 2, 2007, then Department of Health and Human Services (HHS) secretary Mike Leavitt announced a two-year plan directed at fighting DME fraud in South Florida and Southern California. All DME suppliers in these locations were asked to reapply for certification in the Medicare program.[98] In previous testimony, Secretary Leavitt described a visit that he made to DME suppliers in South Florida.

> Just to give you a sense of this, during the time I spent there, we visited several locations. You'd walk up to a strip mall, and there would be what looked to be a business. You'd look inside and there was no one there, but you could see a chair, a little medical equipment on the wall, and what was established to look like a business.…When you checked the Medicare records, you'd find that—from this essentially vacant business—that sometimes $1 million, $2 million, sometimes $3 million or more would have been billed in a relatively short period of time from this so-called business.…I went to an office building in the Miami area. I would say it was 20,000 square feet, maybe two stories. Inside this office building was a marquee listing probably 60 or 70 companies.…Fifty or so of these companies—my estimate—were durable equipment businesses. You'd walk down long corridors that would remind you of a dorm room, with a door roughly every 15 feet.…On the door would be a marquee that would say XYZ—the name of the durable equipment dealer—the hours and the phone number. Those three things happen to be requirements to get a Medicare billing number.…You'd knock on the door, try to open the door—no one there—door, after door, after door.…When you would find someone there, it would be generally someone caring for small children, and waiting for a Medicare inspector to come help them get their number.…It was a shocking level of fraud to me. This kind of fraud is hard to believe.…And yet, when you realize that every vacant storefront represents tens, hundreds, even thousands of seniors who have been cheated, it is simply intolerable.[99]

DME frauds take several forms. Medicare and Medicaid may be billed for undelivered equipment and supplies. Seven South Florida men were charged on seventy-nine counts, including health care fraud and money laundering, after they created a DME company and billed Medicare for equipment that beneficiaries never received.[100]

Cheap equipment or supplies may be provided to a patient, with Medicare or Medicaid being billed for more expensive items. An Idaho DME dealer provided two-thousand-dollar scooters to his elderly clients but billed Medicare and Medicaid for six-thousand-dollar electric wheelchairs.[101]

Patients may receive items that are of no use to them, with Medicare picking up the tab. For example, Medicare pays for oxygen concentrators if a patient has a documented need for oxygen. Illicit suppliers, however, have colluded

Table 3.1   Major Types of Fraudulent Activities, Medicare Part D

BY SPONSORS (PRIVATE INSURERS WITH CMS CONTRACTS)

- Offering cash to prospective beneficiaries to encourage their enrollment.
- "Cherry-picking" (e.g., targeting beneficiaries from high-income areas only).
- Using bait-and-switch tactics.
- Telling prospective beneficiaries the federal government prefers a particular plan.
- Using a health care provider to distribute brochures touting a preferred plan.
- Failing to provide medically necessary benefits covered by law or contract.
- Reporting improper cost calculations or fraudulent information (e.g., nondisclosure of rebates) to the CMS.
- Paying for excluded drugs or paying for the use of "off-label" drugs (drugs used for something other than their approved purpose).
- Charging excessive or duplicate premium payments or extracting higher than mandated deductibles and copayments from beneficiaries.
- Submitting multiple billings to Medicare.
- Rejecting legitimate claims by beneficiaries, "slow walking" claims, or denying beneficiaries the right to appeal a rejected claim.

BY PHARMACY BENEFIT MANAGERS

- Receiving kickbacks to switch beneficiaries from one drug plan to another.
- Placing a drug on a formulary list because of its low cost rather than because of its clinical efficacy.
- Splitting a prescription (putting one prescription into two bottles) to obtain a higher reimbursement or short-filling a prescription (not providing the beneficiary with the full prescription amount).

BY RETAIL PHARMACIES

- Dispensing generic drugs to patients and billing Medicare for a brand-name drug.
- Drug diversion through a pill-mill scheme.
- Altering or forging a prescription.
- Dispensing expired or adulterated drugs.

BY PHYSICIANS PRESCRIBING DRUGS

- Selling free sample drugs or products provided by pharmaceutical manufacturers.
- Accepting kickbacks or gratuities from pharmaceutical manufacturers in exchange for prescribing the manufacturer's drug.
- Writing a prescription for a patient knowing the drugs will be used by another person (perhaps done by a well-intentioned doctor who wants to help an elderly couple around a deductible or copayment problem).
- Prescribing controlled substances for no medical reason (a variation of the pill-mill scam).
- Providing false prescription information to justify insurance coverage (e.g., filing a claim for a drug covered by Medicare to pay for a substitute drug not covered by Medicare).
- Submitting duplicate bills or manipulating the system by exploiting the differential copayments between Parts B and D.

BY PHARMACEUTICAL MANUFACTURERS

- Reporting false cost and pricing information.
- Paying kickbacks or inducements to pharmacies, PBMs, or doctors to increase sales (e.g., lavish meals, travel and entertainment, or grants for bogus research or teaching activities).
- Concealing price concessions, discounts, or rebates.
- Entering into financial relationships or other conflicts of interest with PBMs or sponsors for formulary placements.
- Promoting drugs for illegal off-label promotions.

BY MEDICARE BENEFICIARIES

- Falsifying personal information to enroll in Medicare.
- Allowing ineligible individuals to use their Medicare card to obtain services or prescription drugs.
- Falsifying out-of-pocket costs to speed movement through Medicare coverage gaps.
- Altering or forging prescriptions.
- Selling drugs to street traffickers.
- Obtaining multiple prescriptions and drug stockpiling.

Sources: Based, in part, on U.S. Department of Health and Human Services, Centers for Medicare and Medicaid Services 2009; Short and Liner 2007 in Baumann 2007; 860–65; and Maruca 2006.

with physicians and laboratories to falsify oximetry test results. Patients are then provided with oxygen concentrators that they do not need.[102] Similarly, suppliers may fail to pick up equipment when it is no longer used by the patient, allowing rental charges to continue. Hospitals have allowed "discharge planners" employed by DME companies to work with patients. With greed-driven flair, the planners try to provide as many pieces of equipment as possible to patients, regardless of their medical needs.[103]

Dishonest DME suppliers may bilk Medicare by offering beneficiaries free services, supplies, food, or health screenings in exchange for their Medicare numbers. Other scam artists, posing as university or health care–institution researchers, trick beneficiaries into revealing their Medicare numbers under the pretext of conducting a survey. A South Florida DME supplier pleaded guilty to Medicare fraud after he obtained 250 Medicare numbers from beneficiaries and ten provider numbers from physicians. He used these numbers to submit 4,000 Medicare claims between January and March 2007, amounting to $2.2 million in false claims for equipment never provided to beneficiaries.[104]

Kickbacks are a major part of DME fraud. A Texas jury convicted a Houston osteopath on thirteen counts of health care fraud. The doctor, who rarely examined the patients, was paid by DME marketers to sign certificates of medical necessity for motorized wheelchairs. The marketers then sold the signed documents to DME suppliers in Texas and elsewhere. In Florida, a licensed orthotist and patient-recruiter provided DME suppliers with signed certificates of medical necessity and prescriptions for orthotic devices—again, without bothering to examine the patients. The DME companies billed Medicare for expensive custom-fitted equipment but provided patients with cheap, prefabricated devices. In another Texas kickback case, the owner of a power wheelchair business, along with the owner's brother, hired recruiters to find Medicare beneficiaries. They paid a crooked physician to falsify certificates of medical necessity on the patients and then submitted fraudulent bills in excess of $12 million to Medicare. The owner was sentenced to nearly thirteen years in prison. The brother received sixty-six months and the physician fifty-four months behind bars.[105]

Health Care Frauds That Save Money

As the title to this chapter suggests, health care fraud can be viewed as a two-sided coin: on one side, money is stolen and, on the other, money is conserved. The most prominent frauds are based on the indemnity approach to health care. That is, the service is provided—or allegedly provided—and a fee is paid to the health care provider by the patient or by the patient's insurer. Fraud arises when the objective becomes one of generating as much money as possible rather than one of providing optimal patient care.

A second and less-publicized fraud occurs primarily in managed-care plans. Health maintenance organizations—a major form of managed care—provide services on a capitation basis. Under this arrangement, members pay a flat monthly premium entitling them to receive health care services as needed. In theory, HMOs should both discourage fraud and encourage the cost-efficient delivery of health care services and products. When health care providers or insurers become too preoccupied with slashing costs, however, patient care can be compromised. The problem is compounded when physicians or other health care providers are offered financial incentives to save money. Medical ethicists Nancy S. Jecker and Clarence H. Braddock III have warned of the dangers of placing too much emphasis on "efficiency" and controlling costs in managed-care settings.

> Most often, efficiency is maximized by increasing productivity while fixing cost. Hence, managed care may create pressure to do more with less: less time per patient, less costly medicines, and fewer costly diagnostic tests and treatments. Monetary incentives are often used to affect physician behavior, and may include rewarding physicians who practice medicine frugally by offering financial rewards, such as bonuses, for those who provide the most cost-efficient care. Those who perform too many procedures or are cost-inefficient in other ways may be penalized,

often by withholding bonuses or portions of income. Nonmonetary inducements to limit care take the form of bringing peer pressure, or pressure from superiors, to bear on those who fail to take into account the financial well being of their employer. These monetary and non-monetary incentives raise the ethical concern that physicians may compromise patient advocacy in order to achieve cost savings.[106]

Dr. Linda Peeno, a physician who worked for a managed-care plan, provided lengthy testimony before the U.S. House of Representatives, Committee on Commerce, Subcommittee on Health and Environment. Her testimony described the pressures she encountered as medical director at a 35,000-member HMO as well as at other health care institutions to use "my medical expertise for the financial benefit of the organization, often at great harm and potentially death, to some patients."

Dr. Peeno identified practices such as using complex benefits restrictions and exclusions to deny treatment, developing marketing practices to attract the "best" patients to the plan but hiding the plan's pitfalls, drafting incomprehensible language in physician contracts, threatening economic sanctions against recalcitrant physicians, rigging patient contracts so that claims could be denied based on technicalities set up by "a maze of rules for authorizations, referrals, and network availability," and devising unorthodox definitions of "medical necessity" to deny treatment to patients.[107]

Because cost containment is essential to the survival and profitability of managed-care plans, some plans employ seemingly standard, but underhanded, tactics to reduce costs. These tactics include accepting only healthy enrollees—a practice known as "cherry picking"—or removing unhealthy patients from the plan (disenrollment fraud). Beneficiaries may be encouraged to leave a managed-care plan for expensive treatments elsewhere only to be reenrolled once the treatments are completed. Additional iniquitous cost-saving tactics include selecting providers with offices in distant or inconvenient locations, using providers with very limited office hours, refusing to pay for covered care such as emergency services, delaying patient referrals to specialists, pressuring providers to cut corners on patient care, using low-cost but incompetent providers, "losing" or refusing to pay claims, and manipulating and inflating Medicare administrative cost data.[108]

Managed-care frauds are often harder to spot and more difficult to prosecute than other health care frauds. This dilemma may be due to the government's focus on detecting and prosecuting money-producing frauds rather than on money-saving ones. As James G. Sheehan, New York's Medicaid inspector general, said, "We're watching by land, and they're coming by sea. The reality is we've been doing (medical) provider fraud for a hundred years; we've been doing managed care fraud for 10 years."[109]

Another way of cheating people enrolled in managed-care programs is to force them to subsidize physician kickbacks and lucrative commissions to insurance agents. Because some plans may require patient referrals to nonplan specialists, a common fraud is for physicians to accept kickbacks for referrals.[110] The specialists cover the costs of the kickback by charging higher rates for treatments, which ultimately come to rest in the laps of their patients in the form of higher managed-care plan premiums.

Federal officials have also become concerned about the lucrative commissions paid by Medicare Advantage plan insurers to their agents and brokers. Agents were making between $500 and $550 in 2008 for enrolling a beneficiary in one of their plans, and they stood to make an additional $500 for each year the beneficiary stayed in the plan. In expressing concern about elderly patients being lured into plans not meeting their medical needs, Senator Max Baucus (D-Montana) remarked, "Medicare Advantage plans that have nearly quadrupled agent commissions are putting profits before patients and that's wrong. We can't let seniors remain at risk of being targeted by predatory sales agents looking to make a quick buck."[111] At this writing, the CMS is promulgating regulations to curb abusive commission practices.[112]

Insurance Companies That Dodge Their Obligations

The insurance mechanism transfers risk from the individual policyholder to the large group of policyholders of a specific insurance company; the risk is then shared by policyholders on some equitable basis. In essence, insurance represents the payment of a small, but certain, premium in exchange for protection against a large, but uncertain, loss. Underwriting by an insurance company entails selecting and classifying risks. The premiums charged to policyholders are a direct reflection of these risks.

Group insurance provides coverage for employees or union members. The underwriting process focuses on the entire group, not on any specific individual within the group. For persons working at companies offering no health insurance or for persons who are unemployed, the only alternatives are Medicare, Medicaid, or an individual health insurance policy. Medicare and Medicaid have age- and income-eligibility requirements, and purchasing a health insurance policy on an individual basis can be prohibitively expensive, or impossible, for persons in poor health.

Injured or unhealthy members of a group health insurance plan are protected from losing their coverage, and their expenses are absorbed by the larger group. Policyholders with individual plans, however, are subject to medical examinations and an underwriting process that has allowed insurance companies to select customers based on their health and preexisting conditions. It is the individual policyholders—not those under a group health insurance plan—who have been targeted for abuse by health insurers.

Health care insurance companies could earn tremendous profits if they were allowed to drop coverage on those suffering from a serious injury or an illness, an illegal practice known as "rescission." Rescission occurs when a health insurance carrier retroactively cancels a policy after the policyholder becomes seriously injured or ill and files expensive medical claims. Unlike a simple cancellation, rescissions treat the coverage as if it had never been approved, and it leaves the confused and distraught policyholder responsible for all medical bills dating back to the starting date of the policy. The insurance companies have justified these rescissions by accusing policyholders of omitting information on the insurance application or of failing to reveal preexisting conditions.

California has been the scene of several cases in which policyholders incurring large medical bills were dumped by health insurance companies. In 2006 one of the state's largest health insurers was the target of thirteen lawsuits filed by former policyholders who were allegedly jilted by the insurer. One plaintiff said he was left with $15,000 in bills when the company retroactively cancelled his son's coverage after a surgery. Policyholders complained they were dropped under the pretext of having trivial or inadvertent omissions on their health care insurance applications.

California insurance commissioner John Garamendi said that "this may be one of the reasons [the company] has such a very, very high profit margin on these products."[113] Less than a year later, Garamendi's successor, insurance commissioner Steve Poizner, commented shortly after taking office, "I am very concerned about the practice of post-claims underwriting. The law does not permit a health insurer to agree to provide coverage and then wait until a claim comes in to decide whether to pay for the medical care a policyholder needs. Specifically, I am concerned about insurers rescinding coverage for small, inadvertent and innocent omissions on applications for coverage."[114] Lawmakers and regulators have accused insurance companies of using confusing applications to trick consumers into making mistakes that could later be used against them. Insurers have also been accused of failing to verify the medical histories of insurance applicants before issuing a policy.[115]

Another large insurer agreed in July 2008 to settle claims from 480 California hospitals for failing to pay the bills of patients whose coverage had been revoked. The $11.8 million settlement was triggered by allegations from scores of patients who were dropped illegally by the company after they received both emergency and authorized care. The insurer said the patients had undisclosed preexisting conditions affecting their insurability. In addition, the insurer was also fined $1 million by the California Department of Managed Care for illegal rescission practices, and it faced even more serious liability after agreeing to pay $13 million and reinstate coverage to 1,770 former policyholders whose coverage had been cancelled.[116]

Another form of health insurance fraud involves companies that either mislead or fail to disclose important coverage limits to prospective policyholders. A health insurance company with some 612,000 policyholders in forty-four states agreed to pay $20 million to settle regulatory violations in thirty-six states. The legal problems were sparked by consumer complaints of denied health care coverage and slow payments of claims. According to *USA Today,* the company sold limited-coverage plans to self-employed individuals. But it was accused of improperly training its agents, who then failed to disclose policy limits to customers.[117]

And some health insurance "plans" are outright frauds. An Oklahoma man purchased coverage from a company called the American Trade Association, and a Colorado man purchased his health insurance through the National Trade Business Alliance. Despite the legitimate-sounding names of these companies, the American Trade Association turned out to be fake, paying nothing when the Oklahoma man filed a claim for medical expenses brought on by a heart problem. The National Trade Association was little better, paying just $250 after the Colorado man was fatally injured in a hit-and-run accident. Many of these plans are classic "fly-by-night" operations that employ aggressive telemarketing, website, and email advertisements offering premiums that are too good to be true. Other phony health insurers use door-to-door sales people who claim to represent the federal government. These imposter agents pressure uninsured victims—often the elderly—into signing up for health insurance that is "required" under the Obama administration's health care reform.[118]

Short-Pilling Consumers and Diluting Drug Therapies

Some unscrupulous pharmacists have engaged in two money-saving, but highly dangerous, practices—"short-pilling" (or "short-filling") patient prescriptions and diluting drug therapies. In the former, retail pharmacies fail to provide patients with a complete prescription, but bill Medicare or Medicaid for the full amount. The OIG has received a number of complaints about retail pharmacies—including several major retail chains—that were accused of billing Medicaid for prescription drugs that were not provided to patients. According to the OIG, this short-pilling fraud resulted in collections of more than $30 million from these pharmacy chains.[119]

A reprehensible health care fraud is the sale of diluted or counterfeit pharmaceuticals. A Tennessee oncologist received a fifteen-year sentence for administering diluted chemotherapies and other medications to patients.[120]

But the worst case of all—possibly the most atrocious health care fraud in history—was the Kansas City–area pharmacist who admitted that he diluted intravenous chemotherapy drugs for as many as 98,000 prescriptions that were written by 400 doctors for 4,200 patients. This astute—but depraved—entrepreneur became one of the first pharmacists in Kansas City to dispense cancer medications in premixed bags, saving doctors the trouble of measuring and mixing the bags themselves. He was accused of diluting Taxol and Gemzar, drugs used to treat a variety of cancers. At least one of the pharmacist's premixed bags contained less than 1 percent of the prescribed measure of Gemzar. In another instance, he provided only 450 milligrams of Gemzar instead of the prescribed 1,900 milligrams, enabling him to pocket an additional $779 profit.

The patients receiving these diluted treatments were pleasantly surprised when they suffered none of the usual side effects of chemotherapy. Their surprise turned to horror, however, when they and their families learned the sordid truth about the pharmacist's diabolical scheme. And the unsuspecting physicians who trusted him and thought their patients were receiving a full measure of chemotherapy were equally devastated.

A son of a minister, this pharmacist-gone-bad was a Sunday school teacher and multimillionaire who pledged huge amounts of money to his church.[121] According to a *New York Times* magazine article about him:

> The sheer voraciousness of his dilutions suggests the compulsion of a pathological shoplifter. At times, [he] diluted conservatively; at others, he reduced medications to trace amounts, seemingly taunting their recipients: Feel anything now? Though [his] highest profits came from diluting expensive chemotherapy medication—a plaintiff's lawyer says he pocketed as much as $50,000 in the treatments of a single cancer patient—[he] adulterated a total of 72 different drugs, including fertility drugs, antibiotics, drugs to prevent nausea and others to improve blood clotting. "Basically," says Judy Lewis, the F.B.I. agent in charge of the…investigation, "if you could mix it or inject it, he diluted it." In addition to shorting prescriptions and buying meds from illegal sources, the pharmacist chiseled whenever an opportunity arose. To one oncologist in the [place] where he worked, [he] dispensed generic drugs while charging them for the more expensive brand-name versions. When customers could not make their $5 or $10 copayments, the kindly pharmacist would let them slide, in exchange for taking back the supposed equivalent portion of their medications to be resold later.[122]

This Midwestern pharmacist's unforgivable fraud began to unravel when a sales representative for Eli Lilly and Company—who harbored a strong personal animosity against the pharmacist for his arrogant and pretentious ways—noted his chemotherapy drug purchases from Lilly were only about one third of the amount he billed to area physicians.[123]

At this writing, the pharmacist is incarcerated at a federal prison hospital in Rochester, Minnesota. Shortly after entering the federal prison system, he petitioned the court for a temporary release to attend his daughter's wedding. In denying his request, a judge noted: "Defendant would be unable to give his daughter away at her wedding while dressed in a prison jumpsuit and wearing leg chains and handcuffs."[124] His release date, according to the Federal Bureau of Prisons inmate locator, is November 20, 2027.

Short-changing consumers by providing diluted or counterfeit drugs obviously poses major health hazards. Cancer patients who fail to get the full measure of their chemotherapy lose valuable time. Instead of forcing their cancer into remission, the diluted medications provided by the Kansas City pharmacist probably allowed the disease to progress to the point where further treatments were ineffective. He banked on his deceptions going undetected because cancer patients undergoing chemotherapy often have uncertain prognoses; some may not survive even when given a full dose of medication. In addition, certain bacteriological disease strains develop immunity to adulterated or diluted drugs. And contagious diseases may spread if ineffective counterfeit or diluted drugs are administered by unwitting or unscrupulous health care providers.[125]

The cases of health care fraud and abuse described here cover a wide spectrum. Although these cases vary widely, they all contain the common elements of illicit transfer of resources, misinformation, manipulation, and—sometimes—bodily harm. The line between legal and illegal health care practices is not always clear, but the cases illustrated here either violated a law or, at a minimum, represented a serious breach of ethics. I now turn my discussion to the marquee health care fraud prosecutions that have resulted in hundreds and millions of dollars in settlements.

FRAUD AT MAJOR HOSPITALS
Profits at Any Cost, Part One

Some Important Questions

During a conversation about health care fraud and abuse, a physician that I have known casually for several years related an incredible story. Now in the twilight of his medical career, he reflected back—telling me that he had always tried to run an honest practice and that he had always tried to do the right thing by his patients. But he still seemed miffed—even several years later—about a minor surgical procedure he had performed at a local hospital. This doctor charged his patient $300 for his services. Shortly after the surgery, his patient called him, puzzled about the size of the bill. The doctor was shocked to learn that the hospital had charged his patient an additional $12,000.[1] Although no one could argue that the hospital was entitled to a fee for making its facilities, equipment, supplies, and staff available for the surgical procedure, many of us might wonder whether the hospital deserved to collect forty times the amount paid to the surgeon.

This incident raises three major questions. On what basis did the hospital calculate these charges? Was it taking advantage of a patient or an insurer with deep pockets? If the insurance company paid the claim with no questions asked— and raised the premiums charged to other insured patients—would anyone have even bothered to complain? These questions are at the heart of the large institutional frauds that have arisen over the past two decades.

This chapter and the next focus on frauds instigated by health care institutions, pharmaceutical firms, and equipment manufacturers. Most of these cases have received extensive media coverage and resulted in settlements in the hundreds of millions of dollars.

Profits at Any Cost

Executives at the Tenet Healthcare Corporation, the Hospital Corporation of America, and HealthSouth put profits on a pedestal. A fixation on financial performance—especially the corporation's bottom-line profits and stock market prices—may not only lead to overcharges, false billings, upcoding, and kickbacks, but also to accounting and financial fraud.

Accounting fraud involves the manipulation of accounting documents and journal entries to hide the embezzlement or the misappropriation of funds. The U.S. Securities and Exchange Commission (SEC), for example, accused California-based Medical Capital Holdings of diverting $77 million to administrative fees after telling investors the money would not be used for that purpose.[2] In another case, the CEO of the bankrupt Granada Hills Community Hospital was held personally liable for unpaid federal payroll taxes—monies he allegedly diverted to other uses.[3]

Accounting fraud also forms the foundation for financial fraud. These were the front-page frauds committed by WorldCom, Enron, Tyco, Adelphia, Global Crossing, and Waste Management. Financial fraud occurs when management exaggerates the financial condition of a health care institution, usually for the sake of misleading investors and regulators or for the sake of enabling executives to inflate their stock options. Financial fraud distorts either the corporation's balance sheet (overstating assets and understating liabilities to inflate corporate net worth—as was the case at Enron) or its income statements (overstating revenues and understating expenses to inflate the corporate profits—as was the case at both Enron and WorldCom). Three Cardinal Health executives agreed to pay $245,000 in civil penalties after their accounting legerdemain inflated revenue reports by 30 percent for the 2002 and 2003 fiscal years.[4] The West Penn Allegheny Health System was the subject of a SEC probe after it made a $73 million write-down of revenues.[5] In a few instances, accounting fraud is also used to falsify cash flow—a difficult feat to achieve unless cash is moved secretly from one place to another and counted more than once.

Tenet Healthcare Corporation

The fraud and abuse at Tenet Healthcare Corporation, one of the nation's largest hospital chains, ranks among the most devastating in U.S. health care history. The scandal implicated top-level executives, physicians, and hospital administrators at facilities throughout the United States, caused massive shareholder losses, and brought needless pain and suffering to thousands of patients.

Founded in 1968 as National Medical Enterprises (NME), the company opened hospitals in California and, soon thereafter, began offering stock to the public. NME employed a simple set of strategies: dominate local markets, raise prices, and slash costs. When implemented with prudence, aggressive revenue-building and cost-controlling strategies can enable a company to sustain a competitive advantage in its industry and earn superior profits. When implemented with carelessness and avarice, as they often were at NME and Tenet, these strategies can precipitate massive frauds.

NME's objective was to build, own, and operate a large collection of profitable hospitals and other health care institutions. In its first decade, the company expanded operations by acquiring acute care hospitals, substance-abuse recovery facilities, nursing homes, and medical-product companies. NME also created an international consulting branch. During the late 1970s, revenues from Medicare and other public programs fueled the growth of investor-owned hospitals nationwide. NME, too, depended heavily on reimbursements from Medicare and Medicaid.

By keeping a sharp eye on changing industry conditions, NME executives were quick to acquire profitable facilities (e.g., substance-abuse centers) and they were equally quick to divest unprofitable ones (e.g., acute-care hospitals and outpatient clinics). The company acquired a number of psychiatric facilities in the early 1980s, providing it with a strong earnings base. The tremendous money-making potential of the psychiatric facilities, however, unmasked NME management's obsession with profits.

In 1991 a lawsuit was brought against NME in Texas, accusing the company of using bounty hunters and psychiatric hotlines to find patients for its facilities. Children admitted to psychiatric hospitals, NME discovered, were especially good sources of income because their insurance coverage often permitted lengthy hospital stays. Doctors who referred patients to NME facilities obtained kickbacks disguised as professional fees. To receive a kickback, a doctor making referrals would appear briefly at a hospital and provide perfunctory care to patients. These services were known factitiously as "howdy rounds" and "wave therapy."[6]

As the number of patient and insurance company lawsuits against NME began to mount, the company's CEO and several top executives resigned. NME also found itself a subject of the Clinton administration's crackdown on health care fraud. In August 1993, six hundred FBI and other federal agents raided NME headquarters in Santa Monica, California, as well as eleven of its psychiatric facilities, seizing documents as evidence of criminal activity by the company executives. NME agreed subsequently to a $379 million settlement with the U.S Department of Justice for paying kickbacks and bribes and for hiring bounty hunters to fill psychiatric hospital beds. Not surprisingly, NME's profits plummeted and its reputation was damaged irreparably. Furthermore, the company faced hundreds of millions of dollars in additional lawsuits and legal expenses, forcing it to divest itself of all but ten of its eighty-one psychiatric facilities and seventy-three rehabilitation hospitals and clinics. All told, these divestitures generated some $460 million.

After acquiring American Medical Holdings for $3 billion, NME changed its name to Tenet Healthcare Corporation in 1995, hoping the new name would divert attention from its tarnished image. Tenet eventually became the second-largest hospital chain in the United States. Unfortunately, the company's reincarnation as a law-abiding corporate citizen did not last. In 2002 Tenet again faced seemingly insurmountable legal difficulties after the hospital chain was charged with overbilling Medicare.

Not only did Tenet enrich itself by gouging public insurance programs, it also overcharged patients and their private insurers. A 2003 study revealed that Tenet operated sixty-four of the one hundred most expensive hospitals in the United States—including the fourteen most expensive hospitals. In California, where their prices were especially exorbitant, a patient receiving coronary bypass surgery at a Tenet hospital would pay $93,829 compared to $32,473 for the same surgery at a non-Tenet hospital. Tenet doctors were also accused of putting profits ahead of quality health care as they performed needless heart surgeries on hundreds of patients.[7]

Senator Grassley, the aforementioned leading fighter against health care fraud and chairman of the Senate Committee on Finance, sent a scathing letter to Tenet's acting CEO, Trevor Fetter, demanding that the company produce an array of documents pertaining to their operations. Senator Grassley's letter of September 5, 2003, contained the following highlights:

> In the annals of corporate fraud, Tenet (formerly National Medical Enterprises (NME)) more than holds its own among the worst corporate wrongdoers. When Mr. Jeffrey Barbakow became president and chief executive of NME in 1993, NME was a scandal-plagued corporation accused of, among other allegations: maintaining a corporate policy at its psychiatric facilities of paying doctors for patient referrals; imprisoning patients for insurance payments; charging insurance companies for treatment and medication that were not provided, provided at grossly inflated prices or provided when unnecessary; and milking insurance until coverage was exhausted....Unfortunately, a change of names did not change the culture of fraud at the corporation. If anything, Tenet's history of defrauding government healthcare programs reached new heights under Mr. Barbakow....According to the Department of Health and Human Services (HHS), Office of Inspector General (OIG), Tenet did not stay on the straight and narrow and has been the subject of at least 53 federal investigations dating back to the 1994 CIA [corporate integrity agreement], including among others, allegations of cost report fraud, upcoding, overbilling, duplicate billing,

kickbacks, providing medically unnecessary services, misrepresenting services, falsifying medical records, billing for services not rendered, providing poor quality of care, and for patient abuse....According to DOJ, many of the allegations took place during the 5-year period Tenet was under a CIA [corporate integrity agreement] with HHS–OIG. DOJ alleged that Tenet falsely certified that it was in compliance with Medicare regulations and the terms of its CIA, when in fact, Tenet knew of a significant number of fraudulent claims that had been submitted and for which Tenet had never, and still has not, made restitution to the Medicare program....Today Tenet is mired in lawsuits that detail horror stories about patient deaths and complications due to unnecessary angioplasties, coronary bypasses, and heart catheterizations at Redding Medical Center (RMC)....No recounting of Tenet's sordid corporate history should fail to note those who have profited most handsomely at Tenet. In 2002, Mr. Barbakow realized over $115 million from stock option exercises, Thomas Mackey (former-chief operating officer) realized over $14 million, and in 2001, Ms. Sulzbach realized $7.25 million from her stock options. Both Mr. Barbakow and Mr. Mackey exercised their options at prices very close to Tenet's all-time high stock value. Unfortunately for Tenet stockholders, in November 2002, Tenet's stock price plummeted on news of the outlier payment scandal and Tenet lost more than $17 billion in market value. Mr. Mackey, who allegedly orchestrated the outlier pricing strategy, is all the richer for Tenet's machinations, while Tenet stockholders are all the poorer....Tenet appears to be a corporation that is ethically and morally bankrupt.[8]

Tenet received undeserved bad publicity in October 2005 when the Louisiana attorney general announced an investigation into the deaths of twenty-four hospice patients at Tenet's Memorial Medical Center in New Orleans. The hospice was located on the seventh floor of Memorial, and it was operated by LifeCare through a rental agreement with Tenet. In the aftermath of Hurricane Katrina, LifeCare employees abandoned the hospital, leaving Tenet employees to care for the hospice patients. With no means of escape and beset by debilitating heat, a lack of running water, and no sewage service, twenty-four patients—many of whom were already critically ill—perished. Because the morgue was filled to capacity, Tenet employees placed the bodies of hospice patients along with their medical records in the hospital chapel. Unsubstantiated reports later surfaced accusing hospital personnel of ending the lives of some patients to spare them the ordeal of dying slowly in the horrible conditions.[9] Tenet had earlier denied culpability for the patients' deaths. A doctor and two nurses were charged with second-degree murder, but a New Orleans grand jury declined to indict the trio.

Other accusations of fraud and abuse continued to plague Tenet between 2002 and 2006. On June 29, 2006, the company—by then headquartered in Dallas—agreed to a settlement of $900 million ($725 million in penalties plus $175 million in forfeited claims) for overbilling Medicare. The agreement at the time was the largest False Claims Act settlement in history, amounting to about one-fourth of Tenet's stock market value. The months of bad publicity and uncertainty preceding the settlement were major reasons for the company's stock price dropping from more than $50 a share in late 2002 to only $7.10 a share on the day of the settlement. (Tenet's stock price subsequently fell even further.)[10] Tenet still faced potentially devastating legal problems for other billing discrepancies and for paying impermissible relocation expenses to physicians.

Of the federal government's $900 million settlement with Tenet, more than $788 million arose from claims regarding the company's receipt of excessive "outlier" payments. These payments are normally made to institutions incurring extraordinary costs for treating severely ill patients. Tenet inflated charges for these patients through a practice known as "turbo-charging." An additional $47 million of the settlement was based on claims that Tenet paid kickbacks to physicians to refer Medicare patients to its facilities. The Department of Justice said Tenet billed Medicare for services ordered by physicians with whom Tenet had an improper financial relationship. Another $46 million of the settlement applied to allegations that Tenet upcoded Medicare claims.[11]

Tenet agreed to pay—in installments—the $725 million plus interest over a period of four years. As noted, the company also agreed to waive its right to receive $175 million in Medicare payments for services already rendered. Tenet also reached an agreement with HHS to enter into a multiyear corporate integrity agreement. The company's board of directors was expected to play a major oversight role to ensure compliance. Tenet was also required to retain an independent review organization to monitor the company's Medicare coding, physician financial relationships, hospital charges, and quality of patient care.[12]

Tenet persevered despite its legal troubles. The company announced plans to divest eleven hospitals and to expand capital investments in its remaining hospitals.[13] By the end of 2009, Tenet had fifty general hospitals and a critical access hospital located in twelve states, mostly in the southeastern United States, Texas, and California, with a total of 13,601 licensed beds and 57,613 employees. During FY 2009, the company had over $9 billion in operating revenues, 128,028 inpatient admissions, and 955,868 million outpatient visits.

Tenet and other private hospitals throughout the United States face many of the same problems. These problems include intense competition among local hospitals, shortages of key personnel, disputes with labor unions, and pressure to comply with a myriad of federal and state laws. During the 1990s, approximately nine hundred hospital mergers and acquisitions took place. Mergers and acquisitions—at least in theory—promote economies of scale and enable hospitals to reduce wasteful duplicate services in locales served by more than one hospital. Private hospitals and hospital chains, however, continued to battle headwinds that cut into their profits. Hospital occupancy rates declined as fewer invasive surgeries were needed and improved pharmaceuticals enabled patients to receive treatments without an overnight hospital stay. Upgraded public and not-for-profit hospitals diverted patients from the more expensive private hospitals. Some doctors, frustrated by the mountain of insurance and other paperwork, defected and opened their own facilities.[14]

Tenet's Security and Exchange Commission Form 10-K for FY 2009 revealed several additional problems plaguing the company, such as uncertainties surrounding health care reform measures and changes in the Medicare and Medicaid programs, vulnerabilities to changes in managed-care arrangements, a high volume of uninsured and underinsured patients, critical shortages of physicians and nurses in certain areas, high amounts of debt, poor financial performance, and unresolved legal issues. The latter included lawsuits by shareholders, litigation over violation of laws on wages and hours, disputes with the IRS, several whistle-blower lawsuits, real property disputes, and malpractice claims. With hospitals located in California and coastal areas, Tenet facilities are vulnerable to natural disasters such as earthquakes, brush fires, and hurricanes. All of these influences squeezed profits and may have encouraged some health care providers to cross the line into fraud and abuse.

By the middle of 2009, Tenet continued to survive by controlling costs and boosting its outpatient businesses, and dealing with bad debts from uninsured patients. "Success" in the minds of Tenet officials seemed to be based on the fact that the corporation's losses—yes, the ones recorded in red ink—were not as bad as financial analysts had predicted.[15]

Tenet Healthcare ranks with the likes of Enron and WorldCom in the rogue's gallery of white-collar crime. The collapse of Enron and WorldCom left investors with stock worth pennies a share. Health care frauds of the scope found at Tenet, however, inflict damage that is even more devastating. Tenet Healthcare endangered the health and life expectancy of trusting patients who placed their well-being in the hands of the company's executives and health care professionals. According to the Tenet Shareholder Committee, "When the health and legal rights of ill patients are compromised to increase the corporate bottom line, it's more than just a story about dollars and cents. No amount of money can compensate the victims who unnecessarily lost their lives, or their loved ones who they left behind, grieving and angry."[16]

The Hospital Corporation of America

The Hospital Corporation of America was created in 1968 by Dr. Thomas Frist Sr., Dr. Thomas Frist Jr., and Jack Massey in conjunction with the purchase of the Park View Hospital in Nashville. The senior Frist assumed the position of HCA president with Massey—one of the Kentucky Fried Chicken founders—as board chairman. Thomas Frist Jr. took responsibility for the acquisition and development of HCA hospitals. In 1969 HCA made its first public stock offering, and, a year later, former Aetna Life Insurance chairman and CEO, John Hill, succeeded Frist Sr. as president of the hospital chain.

The growth path of HCA during the 1970s was similar to that of NME/Tenet. By 1973 HCA had fifty-one hospitals, including one in Saudi Arabia. In 1978 Donald MacNaughton, former CEO and chairman of Prudential, took the reigns as CEO of HCA. Under MacNaughton's leadership, HCA acquired General Care Corporation, General Health Services, Hospital Affiliates International, and the Health Care Corporation. These acquisitions added 133 new facilities, consisting of 55 HCA-owned hospitals and 78 hospitals managed by HCA. In 1984 HCA was named the best-managed company in health care by *Investment Decisions* magazine. It described HCA as a "super company that does everything right." By the late 1980s and early 1990s, HCA had gone through several major changes, spinning off 104 acute-care hospitals (1987), becoming private by buying out investors for $5.1 billion (1989), and then once again going public in 1992. These activities were followed by a merger with the 320-hospital Columbia Hospital System in 1994 followed by another merger with Health Trust a year later. The company became known as Columbia/HCA.

During the mid-1990s, Columbia/HCA grew rapidly, acquiring hospitals at the rate of one every week. By 1997 the company was the largest hospital chain and tenth-largest employer in the United States, with 380 hospitals, 200 home health agencies, and 130 surgery centers.[17] At this time, Columbia/HCA began to shift its business strategies from a national acquisition focus to a local operational focus, suggesting that it wanted to get better rather than bigger. Dr. Thomas Frist Jr. returned to the company as CEO in 1997. In 1998 *Modern Healthcare* magazine ranked 28 Columbia/HCA hospitals among its best 100 hospitals. After selling off two hospital companies, Columbia/HCA operated 190 hospitals at the end of 1999.[18] So what went wrong?

The answer is simple: To improve their financial picture even further, Columbia/HCA had begun to play fast and loose with Medicare, Medicaid, and TRICARE reimbursement rules and to engage in widespread fraud. Storm clouds appeared as early as 1997 when federal investigators turned their attention to Columbia/HCA facilities in El Paso, Texas. The investigation, focusing on Columbia/HCA's Medicare billings and home health operations, quickly widened as five hundred federal agents raided company facilities in seven states.[19] Health care industry analysts also publicly accused the company of placing acquisitions and profits ahead of quality patient care.[20]

A year later, the federal government announced False Claims Act suits against Columbia/HCA and a former subsidiary, the Quorum Health Group, for filing inflated expense claims. The government contended that Columbia/HCA had, over a fourteen-year period, misrepresented costs to increase Medicare reimbursements. Both Columbia/HCA and Quorum were purported to have used separate sets of books, one set for actual costs and another set for Medicare claims that reflected higher-than-actual costs. The companies, for example, represented operating expenses (reimbursable at a lower rate) as capital costs (reimbursable at a higher rate). The lawsuit also claimed the companies manipulated time and square-footage calculations to inflate reimbursements.[21]

In December 2000, HCA—The Healthcare Company (it changed its official name) entered into a plea agreement with the federal government to pay $840 million in criminal fines and civil penalties. The $840 million consisted of $745 million to resolve five charges of improperly billing the U.S. government and the states for health care services. An additional $95 million was levied against the company to resolve civil claims for fraudulent laboratory billing, including billings for unnecessary tests, to Medicare, Medicaid, TRICARE, and the Federal Employees Health Benefits Program.

More than $403 million of the $745 million portion of the settlement (above) was earmarked to remedy civil claims for upcoding pneumonia and other diagnoses. Another $50 million in civil assessments was levied against HCA for misclassifying nonreimbursable marketing and advertising costs as reimbursable public health education costs. HCA agreed to pay an additional $90 million to settle charges accusing the company of billing Medicare for nonreimbursable costs associated with the purchase of home health agencies. The company apparently devised a scheme to convert these costs into reimbursable "management fees" paid to third parties. Finally, HCA agreed to pay $106 million to resolve charges it had billed Medicare, Medicaid, and TRICARE for home health visits that either were not provided to patients or were provided to those who did not qualify for the care.

Two subsidiaries of HCA, Columbia Homecare Group and Columbia Management Companies, entered into a plea agreement to pay $95.3 million in criminal fines for a variety of charges, including conspiracy, false statements, fraudulent cost reporting, fraudulent billings, paying kickbacks, upcoding, and home health fraud.

HCA signed an eight-year corporate integrity agreement requiring compliance policies, procedures, and training for HCA employees. It also mandated immediate restitution of overpayments and a system enabling employees to report misconduct. HCA was forced to divest any subsidiary and to exclude any person that had been banned from participating in a federal health care program or that had been found guilty of Medicare fraud.[22]

HCA's woes continued when, in June 2003, the federal government announced a $631 civil settlement with the hospital company, bringing the total settlement amounts against HCA to $1.7 billion. The settlement was precipitated by nine whistle-blower suits against the company and its affiliated hospitals under the False Claims Act. This settlement required HCA to pay $620 million to resolve eight whistle-blower suits plus an additional $11 million to resolve irregularities in billing practices.

The charges against HCA in the 2003 settlement were similar to those made in 2001. The company was forced to pay $356 million for using hospital cost-reporting schemes to defraud Medicare, Medicaid, and TRICARE. An additional $225.5 million was levied against the company on charges that HCA hospitals and home health agencies had made illegal billings to these programs, including kickbacks for patient referrals. HCA was required to pay $17 million to the government to resolve charges over hospital billings to Medicare for nonreimbursable costs. These costs were incurred by a contractor operating wound-care centers for the company. Part of this $17 million settlement also applied to noncovered drugs manufactured by the contractor and sold to patients. Over $11 million was levied against HCA for overcharges made for transferring patients from one hospital or clinic to another, inflated charges pertaining to indigent patients, and salary and other costs that were shifted improperly. In a separate agreement, HCA paid $1.5 million to settle allegations of paying kickbacks for the referral of diabetes patients to its Atlanta West Paces Medical Center.

A U.S. Justice Department Civil Division Assistant Attorney General said, "We are grateful for the assistance given by the whistleblowers over the course of the past nine years of investigation and litigation…and we are proud of the work of government personnel as well as counsel for the whistleblowers, who together pursued these matters through investigation and strenuous litigation. This result demonstrates the commitment of the Department to the qui tam [whistleblower] statute and that the statute works as Congress intended."[23]

In 2005 then U.S. Senate majority leader Bill Frist, the son of HCA founder Dr. Thomas Frist Sr. and younger brother of Dr. Thomas Frist Jr., was investigated regarding the sale of his HCA stock days before the share price dropped by 9 percent. The senator claimed he sold the shares to avoid any appearance of a conflict of interest in the event he decided to run for the U.S. presidency in 2008. Following an intensive investigation, federal authorities dropped insider trading charges against Frist after documentation revealed he had initiated plans to sell the shares months before the stock price dropped precipitously in July 2005.[24] As a surgeon, former Senate majority leader, and professor of business and medicine at Vanderbilt University Bill Frist began working actively on health care reform.[25]

HCA was acquired for $31.6 billion in July 2006 by three private-equity firms—Bain Capital, Kohlberg Kravis Roberts, and Merrill Lynch—and the family of Bill Frist. The acquisition, at that time, represented the largest leveraged buyout in U.S. business history. It was part of a buying spree by private-equity firms to take advantage of the low cost of capital during that period. The buyout paid $51 a share to HCA shareholders, and it required a $5.5 billion cash outlay with the remainder of the transaction being financed by debt.[26]

By 2010 HCA was still the largest for-profit hospital chain with 170 acute-care psychiatric and rehabilitative hospitals, 100 ambulatory surgery centers, as well as diagnostic imaging, cancer treatment, and outpatient rehabilitative centers in twenty states—mostly in Florida and Texas—as well as in England.[27] At that time, HCA was attempting once again to become a publicly traded company through an initial public offering of approximately $4.6 billion, giving it a market value of around $40 billion.

HealthSouth

When business strategists speak of diversified corporations, they are usually talking about firms that produce or sell a variety of products and services. Health-South, the largest provider of inpatient rehabilitative services in the United States, had an unusual form of diversification. Under its jaded cofounder and former CEO, Richard Scrushy (fired in 2003), HealthSouth's business strategy consisted of both legitimate health care services alongside an array of white-collar crimes that included financial fraud, false billings, and Medicare fraud. The financial frauds made liberal use of cost-accounting machinations.

Scrushy became infamous for his flamboyant lifestyle and his questionable and highly publicized religious conversion as his legal troubles mounted. In November 2003, an eighty-five-count criminal indictment was brought against him for the overstatement of HealthSouth's profits by $2.7 billion between 1996 and 2002.[28] Although Scrushy was acquitted of federal financial fraud charges by a seemingly sympathetic and perhaps naive jury in a Birmingham, Alabama, federal court, he was convicted later of bribery and mail fraud in a separate trial. His punishment on those convictions included an eighty-two-month federal prison sentence and payment of over four hundred thousand dollars in restitution and fines. At this writing, Scrushy is incarcerated at a federal prison in Beaumont, Texas, with a scheduled release date in 2013.[29]

Turning away from financial fraud to the more traditional forms of health care fraud, the U.S. Department of Justice announced a settlement in which Health-South agreed to pay $325 million "to resolve a range of allegations involving outpatient physical therapy services and inpatient rehabilitation admissions." The settlement, announced in late December 2004, included $169 million for submitting claims to Medicare and other federal programs for services lacking a properly certified plan of care, for procedures rendered by persons other than licensed physical therapists, and for the billing of services not provided.

An additional $154.7 million was levied against HealthSouth for submitting hospital and office charges that were not reimbursable under Medicare. The unallowable costs included lavish entertainment and travel costs for HealthSouth's annual administrative meetings at Disney World as well as fees paid to the board of directors, public-information expenses, tax-penalty expenses, and lease claims related to rehabilitation facilities acquired from National Medical Enterprises and NovaCare. This part of the settlement also applied to reimbursements for outlier patient charges, similar to those discussed in the Tenet Healthcare case, and the medically unnecessary admission of patients to HealthSouth inpatient facilities. Finally, HealthSouth paid $1 million to settle charges of unlawfully billing Medicare for the skilled labor used in infusion-therapy services. By misclassifying these services as "ancillary," HealthSouth avoided Medicare limits imposed on services delivered at skilled-nursing facilities.[30]

In 2007 HealthSouth and two company physicians agreed to pay the federal government a total of $14.9 million to settle allegations that the company submitted false claims to the government and paid illegal kickbacks to physicians who referred patients to its hospitals, outpatient-rehabilitation clinics, and ambulatory-surgery centers. HealthSouth agreed to pay $14.2 million, and the two physicians jointly paid $700,000.[31]

By June 2009, despite years of legal wrangling, Richard Scrushy's financial problems were only just beginning. As in the case of the infamous O. J. Simpson, Scrushy escaped the worst of the criminal charges in the HealthSouth financial fraud suit only to be waylaid by what appears to be the biggest judgment ever levied against a single executive. Scrushy was slapped with a $2.88 billion—yes, that is billion with a "b"—civil penalty in a lawsuit brought by angry HealthSouth shareholders.[32]

Scrushy had received as much as $40 million a year in pay and perquisites during his tenure at HealthSouth, money that fueled an ostentatious lifestyle. His conspicuous consumption included six homes and three other pieces of real estate, thirty-seven cars, seven boats, and two airplanes (not counting the twelve HealthSouth business jets he had at his disposal). And one week after his cost-cutting threw a number of HealthSouth employees out of work, Scrushy took delivery of a $6 million Sikorsky helicopter.[33]

By the time he was hit with the huge civil judgment, much of Scrushy's net worth has been consumed by the tens of millions of dollars in legal and settlement expenses. Nevertheless, HealthSouth CEO Jay Grinney believes that Scrushy still has assets, and the company has hired investigators to look within the United States and offshore for hidden trusts, real estate, yachts, and other items of value.[34]

As noted, Scrushy was thought to have hoodwinked a gullible hometown jury into an acquittal during his 2005 criminal-fraud trial. In the civil suit, however, the same evidence brought a very different result. Sans jury, Scrushy faced a lone justice, Jefferson County (Alabama) Circuit Court Judge Allwin E. Horn III, who was anything but gullible. Judge Horn did not believe that Scrushy, a CEO long known for his attention to detail, was unaware of the massive six-year financial fraud at HealthSouth—including a $350 million "budgeting error." To the contrary, Judge Horn referred facetiously to Scrushy and the five CFOs who served during his tenure as "the six testifying felons."[35]

But HealthSouth weathered the damage inflicted by Scrushy and his henchmen. The company continues to operate as the nation's largest provider of in-patient-rehabilitation services, with over 250,000 patients in twenty-six states and Puerto Rico. And, for the first six months of 2009, the company showed a net profit of $39.4 million.[36] The company continued to show strong operating results through June 2010.[37]

Antitrust Problems That Drive Up Costs and Reduce the Quality of Health Care

Noncompetitive or antitrust practices have entered the health care arena. These practices include monopolies—usually as the result of health care institution mergers or joint ventures—as well as practices such as price fixing, collusive bidding among competitors, exclusive buying or dealing arrangements, and predatory pricing.

One antitrust case involved several large hospitals in the Chicago area. The Evanston Northwestern Healthcare Corporation (ENH), consisting of two acute-care hospitals, acquired Highland Park Hospital in 2000. The merger also combined two distinct physician groups. Shortly after the merger, ENH and its associated physician group instituted significant price increases at all three hospitals. ENH also threatened payers (insurers), telling them that their contracts would be terminated if they did not agree to a package contract containing both physician and hospital services. As a result of the merger, competition was reduced and prices were increased for health care plans. ENH was subsequently forced by a Federal Trade Commission administrative law judge to divest itself of its Highland Park Hospital. On appeal, ENH was given a substitute remedy to restore fair competition by establishing separate independent contract-negotiating teams for the Evanston and Glenbrook hospitals and another for Highland Park Hospital, allowing managed-care organizations to negotiate separately with the competing hospitals. The order also contained an arbitration provision for resolving pricing disputes between the payers and ENH.[38]

The ENH case—and others similar to it—does not seem as sinister as the mainstream cases of health care fraud and abuse. But monopolies and other noncompetitive practices dampen competition, remove incentives for providing quality products or services, and result in artificially high prices, all to the detriment of the health care consumer.

Congress first recognized problems associated with noncompetitive practices over a century ago when it passed the Sherman (Antitrust) Act (1890). Section 1 of the act prohibits certain practices such as price fixing, regardless of whether such practices cause economic harm—in legalese, these practices are known as "per se violations." Section 2 of the act prohibits practices such as monopolies that actually cause economic damage—the "rule of reason." Congress widened the scope of the Sherman Act and clarified issues associated with noncompetitive practices through the passage of the Clayton Act (1914) and the Robinson-Patman Act (1936). All of these laws assume that the anticompetitive practice in question affects interstate commerce, and the laws are enforced primarily by the Federal Trade Commission. The FTC also employs thirty-five attorneys to deal solely with health care antitrust issues. Ironically, the Obama administration's attempt at health care reform—which focuses heavily on controlling health care prices—may run afoul of antitrust legislation because of concerns about price-fixing arrangements.[39]

Antitrust litigation is extremely complex, and no bright line separates legal from illegal practices. Furthermore, certain practices may help freely competitive markets at one moment and hinder those same markets at another time. Does the merger of two community hospitals create a monopoly that drives up health care prices, or does that merger create economies of scale and cost savings that benefit consumers? The FTC claims that it will not question hospital mergers in which at least one of the hospitals has fewer than one hundred beds, forty patients per day, and is more than five years old. But are joint ventures among hospitals involving technical, specialized, or expensive clinical services contrary to the antitrust laws? The legality of such ventures, according to the FTC, depends on the number of hospitals involved as well as the weighing of "any anticompetitive effects against any procompetitive efficiencies generated by the venture, and examine whether collateral restraints, if any, are necessary to achieve the efficiencies sought by the venture."[40] How can that vague—actually horrendous—sentence provide clear guidance for hospital boards contemplating such ventures? What about competing hospitals that want to achieve efficiencies and cost savings by pooling resources for information collection and sharing? And what about hospitals participating in wage-and-salary or pricing surveys? Might these practices be regarded as price fixing or illegal collusion? According to the FTC, the devil is once again in the details of the specific sharing arrangement. The FTC says that joint purchasing arrangements among health care institutions are legal as long as they account for fewer than 35 percent of the total market for purchased items.

That rule sounds straightforward, but how does one define the relevant market and how does one know when the 35 percent limit has been exceeded? Furthermore, what potential antitrust law violations do physician and multiprovider networks create? Again, no straightforward answers are available.[41]

Big Partners and Little Partners

We usually think that antitrust issues arise in large organizations. The following case comes from the Boston area—home to some of the world's most venerated educational and health care institutions—and it does, in fact, involve a very large health care institution and a very large insurer.

Partners Healthcare Company and Blue Cross Blue Shield of Massachusetts were accused of making an unwritten agreement in 2000 under which Blue Cross would give Partners a significant increase in payments as long as Partners obtained comparable increases from Blue Cross competitors. During the life of this agreement, Blue Cross boosted—by 78 percent—the rate at which it paid for medical care by Partners doctors and hospitals. This increase far exceeded those made by other Massachusetts hospitals.[42] Here is an example of the differential pricing dilemma caused—at least in part—by this arrangement.

> As his patient lies waiting in an adjacent exam room, Dr. James D. Alderman watches while an assistant reaches into a white envelope and pulls out a piece of paper that will determine where the man will be treated. Big money is on the line....Alderman, an interventional cardiologist plans to open the patient's clogged artery by inserting a flexible tube with a tiny balloon at the tip. Usually he does the procedure, called angioplasty, at MetroWest Medical Center in Framingham. But he sometimes operates in Boston as part of a research program. One time in every four, by the luck of the draw, Alderman and his patient go to a big teaching hospital in the city....If the white slip of paper directs him to do the procedure in Framingham, the insurance company will pay the hospital about $17,000, not counting the physician's fee. If Alderman is sent to Brigham and Women's Hospital in Boston, that hospital will get about $24,550–44 percent more—even though the patient's care will be the same in both places.... "It's the exact same doctor doing the procedure," said Andrei Soran, MetroWest's chief executive. "But the cost? It's unjustifiably higher."[43]

Partners HealthCare Company was created by a 1993 merger between Brigham and Massachusetts General hospitals. The merger and subsequent growth of this nonprofit organization created what some call the proverbial "eight hundred–pound gorilla." Under the cover of deregulation and lax government oversight, Partners Healthcare used its size and bargaining clout—a clout based on its powerful brand name and an elite reputation—to demand higher payments from health insurance companies. The companies, in turn, passed these cost increases to their policyholders in the form of higher premiums. According to Charles Baker, president of Harvard Pilgrim Health Care, the second largest health insurer in Massachusetts after Blue Cross Blue Shield, "The same service delivered the same way with the same outcome can vary in cost from one provider to the next by as much as 300 percent."[44] Over its fifteen-year lifespan Partners became the biggest health care provider and largest private employer in Massachusetts, and it developed the power to drive competitors down with its ambitious expansion programs and to intimidate insurers with its threat to withdraw business.[45]

The seed of Partner HealthCare's tremendous growth was, reportedly, an unwritten and undisclosed—at least to the public—gentleman's pricing agreement between Dr. Samuel O. Thier, then CEO of Partners, and William C. Van Faasen, then CEO of Blue Cross Blue Shield of Massachusetts. Thier has been described as an individual who is "formidable by almost any measure—in intellect, charm, and competitive fire."[46] But Partners justified its pricing based on its reputation, its ambitious expansion plans, and its quality of patient care. Some antitrust experts, however, speculated that the gentleman's agreement between Thier and Van Faasen may have gone too far.[47] Whether the agreement violates the Sherman Act or Massachusetts consumer protection law is uncertain. But the gentlemanly accord between the two CEOs in May 2000 has raised the ire of many Massachusetts health care consumers who believe they are being fleeced.

On April 19, 2010, the U.S. Department of Justice sent letters to Partners and the state's three largest health insurers—Blue Cross Blue Shield of Massachusetts, Harvard Pilgrim Health Care, and Tufts Health Plan–requesting information about contract negotiations, rates, and reimbursement practices. Although the DOJ has requested information as part of its investigation, no antitrust charges had yet been filed.[48] This brewing controversy also illustrates that nonprofit health care organizations can be just as ambitious and aggressive in acquiring market share and making money as their counterparts in the for-profit sector.

Now, I turn to look at a much smaller antitrust case that, by coincidence, has a name similar to that of the big case in Boston.[49] Partners Health Network is a physician-hospital organization (PHO) representing 225 doctors and two hospitals near my home in Pickens County, South Carolina. Far from the urban Northeast, Pickens County is nestled in the foothills of the Blue Ridge Mountains in the northwest corner of the state—not far from where the early 1970s movie *Deliverance* was filmed. Its residents range from the very rich to the very poor.

Partners Health Network PHO claimed to operate as a "messenger model," which allows self-employed physicians to market their services jointly as a network. The messenger model does not, however, give self-employed physicians the right to negotiate fees collectively with health plans or to agree collectively on the fee schedule they will accept.[50] Nevertheless, the members of Partners Health Network agreed to fix prices and other terms on which they would deal with health plans, and they refused to deal with health plans that did not adhere to the fixed-price schedule. The PHO's executive director polled the prices of the network's physicians and then established a fee schedule based on the highest submitted price per procedure from the physician survey. Predictably, many of the health plans were forced to raise the fees paid to Partners' physicians, thereby raising the cost of medical care in the Pickens County area.

To resolve the problem, the FTC and Partners entered into a consent order to stop it from negotiating with health plans on behalf of physicians and to stop threatening health plans if they failed to cooperate or agree to terms with Partners. The Partners Health Network was also obliged, if a payer so requested, to terminate an existing contract without penalty.

Organized Crime's Involvement in Health Care Fraud

Recent media accounts have described how organized crime has begun to infiltrate the U.S. health care system—stealing mainly from the Medicare program. These accounts, however, miss the distinction between the "organized" conspiracies I discuss in this book and the traditional organized crime syndicates that emerged during Prohibition and that continue to exist today.

How is organized crime defined, and how does it differ from organized rent-a-patient schemes, Internet drug trafficking, and bogus laboratories? Organized crime in the United States—at least the way sociologists and criminologists have described it—usually operates within a formal structure. Although not diagramed on paper, the structure has top-down links of communication and formal job duties for the criminal participants, such as the bosses, consiglieri (advisers), caporegimes (crew leaders), and soldiers. Organized criminals also have a strict law of silence with respect to outsiders—especially the police. As with many other participants in health care fraud, organized criminals often use legitimate business "fronts" to hide their illegal activities.

Many of the fraudulent arrangements highlighted in this book have limited life spans. Organized crime groups in the United States, however, have survived for years or even decades. Members of a criminal enterprise may come and go, but the organization itself endures. Also, organized crime is often built on the idea of a territorial monopoly. If members of a crime syndicate encroach on the business territory of a competitor, retaliation is often swift. And, as the television and movies always seem to emphasize, organized criminals are willing to commit acts of violence against those with conflicting business interests as well as against disloyal insiders.

All of the fraud perpetrators discussed here—whether individuals or conspiracies—operated with little or no help from outsiders. Organized crime, on the other hand, depends heavily on groups outside the formal criminal structure. One such group is the "protectors"—corrupt judges, police officers, lawyers, and politicians—who, for a price, have the power to keep crime syndicate members out of trouble with the criminal justice system. Organized criminals also depend on the support of crooked accountants and attorneys. And, most important, organized crime requires a user support group (a criminologist's word for "customers")—drug users, prostitution patrons, and buyers of stolen goods—who are willing to pay for the services offered by a criminal group.

For decades, members of organized crime have made their living through gambling rings, loan sharking, prostitution, pornography, fencing stolen goods, racketeering, extortion, consumer scams, and drug trafficking. Their "lines of business" focus on illegal goods and services that people want to buy repeatedly—say, once a week. But federal investigators now claim that organized crime figures have made the startling discovery that health care fraud is even more lucrative than these traditional crimes. According to Timothy Menke, the head of investigations for HHS–OIG, "They're hitting us and hitting us hard. Organized crime involvement in health care is widespread." In May 2009, eleven men supposedly associated with the New York Bonanno crime family were indicted in South Florida for Medicare fraud along with a number of other crimes.[51]

Although the Bonannos are a well-established, archetypical organized crime family, other organized health care scammers are actually a hybrid between traditional organized crime syndicates and common street thugs. A Russian Armenian crime ring was indicted for stealing $20 million from Medicare through a group of clinics that they operated in the Los Angeles area. Similarly, criminal groups from the former Soviet Union and Nigeria have also been indicted for health care fraud.[52] These crime rings do not always have the same structure as U.S. organized crime. Instead, they work for whoever can make money for them, and they are not shy about engaging in threats of violence, even against the elderly.

Large institutions, whether they are hospital chains or organized crime syndicates, have the wherewithal to commit health care fraud and abuse on a massive scale. A primary concern of these organizations, of course, is not the quality of the patient care they are supposed to deliver. Instead, these rogue corporations care only about making money—trimming costs to the bone, short-changing consumers, maximizing profits, and bolstering stock prices—through any means possible.

The literature on white-collar crime distinguishes between corporate and occupational crimes. Corporate crime—of primary interest in this chapter—benefits the organization, whereas occupational crime benefits the individual perpetrator. This distinction is theoretically appealing, but it is not completely accurate because corporate crimes may also benefit the individual perpetrator, who usually avoids criminal charges.

But the distinction between corporate and occupational crimes does raise the question of who should be held responsible for frauds amounting to hundreds of millions of dollars. Should government officials stick with the tried-and-true strategy of filing civil suits and extracting large settlements from multibillion dollar hospital corporations, or should they bring felony charges against the executives who precipitated these frauds? In the next chapter, I discuss another set of large organizations—pharmaceutical and medical equipment and supply companies. They too have been major players in the arena of health care fraud.

FRAUD IN THE PHARMACEUTICAL, MEDICAL EQUIPMENT, AND SUPPLY INDUSTRIES

Profits at Any Cost, Part Two

Big Pharma Is Big Business

The Reagan administration's "war on drugs" was directed at halting the trafficking of illegal narcotics. During the Obama administration we have a drug problem of a different sort. Americans turn to prescription drugs as a way of medicating the effects of their unhealthy lifestyles. Poor nutrition habits, stress caused by work-family imbalances and personal financial problems, and a lack of physical activity have resulted in an epidemic of obesity, heart disease, diabetes, hypertension, and poor mental health. Rather than eating right, exercising daily, and turning to psychotherapy when necessary, many Americans prefer to medicate and mask their health problems through a plethora of prescription drugs that control cholesterol, acid reflux, heart attacks (antiplatelet agents), high blood pressure, and depression. Not surprisingly, these pharmaceuticals have become staples in the medicine cabinets of many U.S. consumers.

The burgeoning use of prescription drugs is fueled by the aggressive—and sometimes illegal—marketing and pricing tactics of the major pharmaceutical companies. During 2008 total sales for prescription drugs in the United States reached $291.5 billion, a 1.4 percent increase from 2007. And more important, U.S. consumers pay top dollar for their prescription drugs—well above what is paid by consumers in other industrialized countries.[1] In 2008 European drug prices averaged 61 percent of the prices paid by U.S. consumers, and Japanese drug prices averaged 67 percent of the U.S. prices.[2]

It is little wonder that the big pharmaceutical firms are so well-heeled. But every time a member of Big Pharma is accused of a fraudulent practice, the federal government extracts a huge out-of-court settlement and the costs of the legal fees and the settlement amounts are passed on to the consumer in the form of higher drug prices.

Read the Labels Carefully

In its latest round of legal problems, one of the world's largest pharmaceutical firms, Pfizer, was forced to cough up $2.3 billion to settle criminal and civil cases over the illegal, off-label promotion of four pharmaceuticals—the bipolar and schizophrenic treatment drug Geodon, the pain killer Bextra (withdrawn from the market in 2005), the antiepileptic drug Lyrica, and the infection-treatment drug Zyvox. Pfizer boosted its off-label promotions by wining and dining physicians at posh resorts—complete with golf and massages—all expenses paid. In the decade leading up to the record-breaking settlement, Pfizer paid off on three other settlements, including $430 million in off-label settlements in 2004 and $894 million to settle personal injury suits over Bextra and another pain-killer, Celebrex, which plaintiffs claimed caused cardiovascular damage. These settlements—as large as they are—will not bring down a company that had almost $48.3 billion in revenues and $8.1 billion in profits in 2008.[3]

The federal government's second-largest pharmaceutical company settlement is the $1.4 billion dollar settlement imposed on Eli Lilly and Company in January 2009. Lilly agreed to the huge payout after it pleaded guilty to the off-label promotion of Zyprexa, a drug approved only for use by patients suffering from bipolar disorder and schizophrenia. But millions of people, including children in foster care, people having trouble sleeping, and nursing home patients may have also taken the drug. Prosecutors said that Lilly employed thousands of sales representatives in a widespread illegal-marketing campaign. The sales reps were "trained to use the slogan 'five at five,' meaning five milligrams at 5 o'clock at night will keep these elderly patients quiet," said Laurie Magid, acting U.S. Attorney for the Eastern District of Pennsylvania. The drug had also been promoted illegally to treat conditions such as depression, anxiety, irritability, nausea, and gambling addiction. For certain patients, Zyprexa may have severe side effects, something that should have been revealed during the FDA testing and approval process. One patient started taking the drug for bipolar disorder when she was eighteen years old. In a matter of months, she ballooned from 93 pounds to 170 pounds, developed severe diabetes, and endured worsening depression. Although a $1.4 billion forced settlement sounds devastating, Lilly sold about $1.4 billion worth of Zyprexa in the first quarter of 2008 alone.[4]

As these cases illustrate, large-scale frauds occur in the pricing, marketing, and distribution of prescription drugs. Many of these frauds affect the Medicare and Medicaid programs. Lewis Morris, chief counsel to the Inspector General, testified before the House Oversight and Government Reform Committee about waste, fraud, and abuse in the pharmaceutical industry.[5] Between 1995 and 2005, Medicaid expenditures increased more than fourfold—from $8.9 billion to $41 billion. During the same time frame, according to Morris, Medicare drug expenditures increased from $1.4 billion to $10 billion. When Medicare Part D took effect in 2006, it created a spike in Medicare expenditures, temporarily boosting the annual rate of increase to 18.7 percent.[6]

Fraud in prescription drug pricing sometimes involves the underpayment of Medicaid rebates to the states where the drugs are sold. As noted, the Medicaid program spends billions of dollars a year on outpatient prescription drugs. To control the cost of drugs dispensed through Medicaid, the Medicaid Drug Rebate Program was created by the Omnibus Reconciliation Act of 1990. Pharmaceutical manufacturers—about 550 to date—sign rebate agreements with the Secretary of Health and Human Services to sell drugs through the Medicaid program.

Pharmaceutical companies must pay quarterly rebates to state Medicaid programs based on their drug sales, and these rebates are shared with the federal government. Rebates are calculated for every covered prescription drug based on manufacturer-reported pricing data. The two key prices are the "best price"— the lowest price paid to the drug manufacturer by a specific purchaser—and the "average manufacturer's price" (AMP)—the average price wholesalers pay manufacturers for drugs that are sold to retail pharmacies. Rebates are paid on both brand-name drugs (15.1% of AMP) and generic drugs (11.1% of AMP), or on the difference between the AMP and the best price per unit, whichever is greater. The drug prices are submitted by the pharmaceutical firms and posted by the Centers for Medicare and Medicaid Services.[7]

Prices reported to Medicaid must include discounts provided by the manufacturer to health care providers. These discounts, if revealed, lower the actual AMP or best price and increase the amount of rebate that must be paid. Because these rebates amount to millions of dollars per year, pharmaceutical companies may try to avoid payment by concealing or disguising the true prices and rebate amounts. Pharmaceutical companies have disguised discounts to health care providers by structuring them as phony educational grants or as sham data processing fees. Fraud arises when a manufacturer submits an inflated AMP to the CMS that creates a "spread" between the lower purchase price of the drug paid by the provider and the higher amount reimbursed to the provider by the Medicaid program. This inflated, but disguised, spread serves as an effective backdoor marketing tool to encourage physicians to use the dishonest company's drug. As Lewis Morris noted in the aforementioned congressional testimony, "The objective is always the same—the preferred customer gets a drug at a deep discount and the manufacturer avoids additional rebate obligations to the State Medicaid programs."[8]

King Pharmaceuticals was caught manipulating the prices of certain drugs and underpaying its Medicaid rebates to the states. Between 1994 and 2002, the Bristol, Tennessee, company failed to provide accurate reporting of its AMPs and best prices.[9] When an employee expressed his concern to top managers about the company's low-balling of rebates, he was ostracized. Company managers excluded him from meetings and moved his office to a storage room with mold and leaky ceilings.[10] As a result, he turned whistleblower under the False Claims Act. For this fraud, the company paid $124 million plus interest to settle claims with the federal and several state governments.

Fraud in the marketing of drugs may also violate the federal antikickback statute. Physicians often receive free drug samples from pharmaceutical manufacturers. This practice is legal as long as the physician dispenses the samples to patients at no charge. If a physician dispenses the complimentary pharmaceuticals to a patient and then bills Medicare or Medicaid for their cost, an illegal kickback has occurred. The Vaccines for Children program is a joint federal and state effort providing childhood vaccines free of charge to health care providers. Several civil and criminal suits have been settled because providers billed Medicaid for immunizations they had received at no charge. (The provider may, however, recover a small administrative fee for the inoculations.)[11]

Switching drug prescriptions to exploit Medicaid reimbursement rules is another form of pharmaceutical fraud. Drug switching—also known as product conversion—may result in diminishing the efficacy of a patient's treatment or in exposing the patient to undesirable side effects. Omnicare, a nationwide institutional pharmacy serving nursing home patients exclusively, switched from generic Zantac (ranitidine) tablets to generic capsules to avoid both a federal payment upper limit established by the CMS and the "maximum allowable cost" set by state Medicaid programs. This fraud led to a $49.5 million settlement with the OIG.[12] In a similar case, the Walgreen Company agreed to pay $35 million to resolve allegations that it dispensed capsules rather than tablets of generic Zantac and Prozac and brand-name and generic Eldepryl to Medicaid patients without a physician's consent. Forty-six states and Puerto Rico were expected to share the $16.4 million settlement. The federal portion of the settlement was $18.6 million, and the whistle-blower was awarded $5 million.[13]

A pharmaceutical scam of more recent vintage is the growth of Internet pharmaceutical trafficking and abuse. Advances in information technology have made it possible for legitimate health care providers to have prescriptions ordered online, filled, and mailed to patients. Online drug purchases and express delivery are especially useful services for the elderly, the homebound, or those living in rural areas.

Information technology has also made it possible for unscrupulous individuals to establish online pharmacies for the illegal distribution of controlled substances. A Minnesota resident was convicted of using the Internet to distribute more than two million units of Schedule III controlled substances valued at $24 million.[14] Two Iowa doctors who were employed by a corporation that operated Internet pharmacy websites received twenty-month prison sentences for conspiring to dispense Schedule III and Schedule IV controlled substances, primarily pain medications. Although the doctors supposedly reviewed patient questionnaire responses, neither had personally examined any of the patients before prescribing the drugs.[15]

A Texas pharmacist was convicted of being a drug kingpin for his role in conspiring to dispense hydrocodone, a Schedule III controlled substance, through an Internet pharmacy operation. Customers on the websites filled out a medical questionnaire, requested the drug of their choice (usually hydrocodone), and paid a "doctor consultation fee" as well as a fee for the drugs. Three doctors received between forty and a hundred dollars per signed prescription, although they neither examined the patients nor turned down anyone for a prescription. One doctor even admitted he did not review responses to the patient questionnaires. This scheme was linked to the death of a California high school student who overdosed on Vicodin obtained by prescription from the Internet operation.[16]

The federal Drug Enforcement Administration and the FBI, through Operation Cyber Chase, targeted major pharmaceutical traffickers who were selling and shipping controlled substances over the Internet. Using over two hundred known websites, these e-traffickers were selling narcotics, including amphetamines and anabolic steroids, without a physician's prescription. According to FDA official John Taylor, "The medications may be coming from unknown sources, may not be stored or labeled properly, and may not meet quality assurance standards designed to produce safe and effective products. Many of the safeguards for brick and mortar pharmacies do not exist for Internet Pharmacies and the potential for harmful drug interactions is magnified."[17]

Eleven individuals were arrested in China and charged with manufacturing counterfeit Viagra, Cialis, and Lipitor. They had 600,000 counterfeit Viagra labels and packaging and 440,000 counterfeit Viagra and Cialis tablets in their possession, as well as 260 kilograms (about 572 pounds) of ingredients used to manufacture counterfeit pharmaceuticals.[18] In addition to the DEA and FBI enforcement actions, Immigration and Customs Enforcement, the U.S. Postal Service, and Customs and Border Protection have become involved in the fight against rogue online drug dealers.[19]

Major Pharmaceutical Frauds: Deep Pockets and Low-Hanging Fruit

Pharmaceutical firms are among the world's wealthiest corporations. By July 2008, the ten largest pharmaceutical companies in the United States had annual revenues ranging from $20.2 billion (Bristol-Myers Squibb) to $62.3 billion (Johnson & Johnson) and profit margins from approximately 20 percent (AstraZeneca) to 57 percent (Merck & Company).[20] According to the Congressional Budget Office, the pharmaceutical industry spends more on research and development, relative to sales revenue, than almost any other industry. Estimates vary significantly, but R & D expenditures by major pharmaceutical firms may exceed $40 billion annually, with nearly 20 percent of company revenues being used to support the discovery and testing of new drugs. Bringing a new drug to market may require more than $800 million in R & D costs and over twelve years of developmental work.[21] Once a drug passes FDA scrutiny, it is marketed to health care providers and consumers.[22] Pharmaceutical firms often use aggressive sales campaigns to recoup R & D costs and to extract as much profit as possible from a drug before its patent expires and generic or superior drugs erode its market share.

The pharmaceutical firms discussed here provide examples of how the intense competition associated with the development, manufacturing, and marketing of drugs can create a criminogenic industry environment. Nine of the twenty largest False Claims Act settlements have been directed at pharmaceutical companies—although two of these settlements involved products other than drugs.[23] The federal government has demonstrated a willingness to prosecute and impose tough sanctions on pharmaceutical firms.

TAP Pharmaceutical Products: "Marketing the Spread," Bribes, and Kickbacks

TAP Pharmaceutical Products, originally based in Lake Forest, Illinois, was formed in 1977 as a joint venture between Abbott Laboratories, headquartered in Abbott Park, Illinois, and Takeda Chemical Industries of Osaka, Japan. As of July 2008, TAP became Takeda American Holdings with some 5,500 employees. The merger and restructuring activities during 2008 made Takeda one of the fifteen largest pharmaceutical companies in the United States. TAP was best known for Lupron, a drug used to treat prostate cancer, and Prevacid, a drug used to treat heartburn and related problems.[24]

In October 2001, TAP agreed to pay $875 million to resolve criminal charges and civil liabilities arising from its drug-pricing schemes and marketing practices. TAP pleaded guilty and agreed to pay $290 million to settle charges of conspiracy to violate the Prescription Drug Marketing Act.[25] The company also agreed to pay nearly $559.5 million to settle False Claims Act allegations of filing fraudulent Medicare and Medicaid claims. An additional $25.5 million was assessed against the company to compensate state Medicaid programs for losses caused by TAP's deceptive drug-pricing and marketing activities. Furthermore,

TAP agreed to comply with a thirty-three-page corporate integrity agreement that changed the way in which TAP supervised its marketing and sales staff. It also required the company to submit reports on the true prices of its drugs to the Medicare and Medicaid programs.

Prior to the enactment of Medicare Part D, the only drugs subject to reimbursement were those that were injected under the supervision of a physician. Back in those days, Medicare paid patients the lower of either 80 percent of the urologist's charge for Lupron or the average wholesale price of the drug (as set by TAP). Lupron is similar—in terms of its availability and efficacy—to a competing and significantly less expensive prostate cancer drug, Zoladex. Yet, Lupron mysteriously dominated sales and garnered about 80 percent of the market share.[26]

The federal government claimed that TAP and other defendants—using the same deceptive-pricing strategy discussed earlier—concealed the inflated price spread of Lupron. By maximizing the difference between the Medicare reimbursement price and the price charged to physicians—a tactic known as "marketing the spread"—TAP was able to bolster sales by making it extremely profitable for physicians to prescribe the drug. This lucrative deal for physicians, of course, came at the expense of the Medicare program, its beneficiaries, and taxpayers. It also gave companies such as TAP a competitive advantage over pharmaceutical manufacturers that provided truthful pricing information. As noted, the major competing prostate cancer drug was Zoladex, sold by AstraZeneca. Ironically, in 2003, AstraZeneca entered into a $355 million settlement for similar conduct in the marketing and distribution of its prostate cancer drug.[27] One has to wonder—given the timing of the case—whether AstraZeneca was trying to protect its market for Zoladex by fighting fire with fire.

The investigation of TAP began when Douglas Durand, the company's senior sales officer, resigned after becoming concerned about the distribution of free samples of Lupron to physicians. Durand, who has been described as a "straight arrow," tried unsuccessfully during his short tenure at TAP to control the flow of free samples from TAP sales representatives to physicians. Not wanting to get mixed up in wrongdoing, Durand resigned in 1995 and filed a whistle-blower suit against the company in 1996.[28] Also in 1996, Dr. Joseph Gerstein, the medical director for pharmacy programs at the Tufts Associated Health Maintenance Organization in Waltham, Massachusetts, reported to the U.S. Attorney's Office in Boston that he had been offered a generous educational grant if he agreed to include Lupron in the institution's formulary, even though Zoladex cost each patient about $1,200 less per year than the equivalent dosage of Lupron.[29] Dr. Gerstein began working with the FBI and the OIG, and he agreed to participate in a series of secretly taped meetings with two TAP managers from the Boston area.

The criminal and civil investigation of TAP involved several federal agencies, including the FBI, the OIG, the Food and Drug Administration, the Department of Defense, and the Department of Justice. TAP's criminal fine of $290 million was earmarked for the Department of Justice's Crime Victims Fund, which provides services for victims of violent crime. For their roles as whistle-blowers in the case, Durand received $77 million and Gerstein and Tufts shared $17 million.

In a postsettlement statement, Assistant Attorney General Robert D. McCallum Jr., noted:

> The Medicare and Medicaid drug programs are bulwarks against the financial hardship that can be caused by the need for life-saving medical treatments....These programs cannot afford abuses that enrich doctors or drug companies at the expense of taxpayers and patients. This settlement agreement and the compliance steps that TAP has agreed to take will reinforce the government's long-standing objective of paying Medicare and Medicaid providers for the reasonable costs of the drugs they administer.

According to U.S. Attorney Michael J. Sullivan:

> The urologists and the TAP employees who knowingly participated in this broad conspiracy took advantage of older Americans suffering from prostate cancer. The indictment unsealed today alleges that TAP employees sought to influence the doctors' decisions about what drug to prescribe to patients by giving them kickbacks and bribes, from free samples to free consulting services to expensive trips to golf and ski resorts to so-called educational grants. In all instances where the kickbacks worked to ensure the prescription of TAP's product Lupron, the Medicare Program and the elderly Americans suffering from prostate cancer paid more for their care than if the doctor had prescribed the competitor's product....The payment by TAP of nearly $900 million including the highest criminal fine ever imposed on any healthcare company [at that time], and the indictment of the other six TAP employees sends a very strong signal to the pharmaceutical industry that it best police its employees' conduct and deal strongly with those who would gain sales at the expense of the health care programs for the poor and the elderly and the persons insured by those programs.[30]

Thomas Watkins, president of TAP, had a different perspective on the settlement. He said that even though TAP "fundamentally disagreed" with the allegations, the company decided to settle the case because the federal government had threatened to stop all reimbursements for Lupron. At the time, those reimbursements amounted to about $450 million annually. Watkins added: "We could not afford to have this drug denied to our patients."[31]

A federal grand jury also returned indictments against a Massachusetts urologist and six TAP managers for conspiring to pay kickbacks to doctors and other customers, conspiring to defraud state Medicaid programs regarding the best

price of their products, and conspiring to violate the Prescription Drug Marketing Act. The latter charge pertained to billing Medicare for drugs supplied free of
charge to physicians. Hundreds of Medicare beneficiaries were billed for thousands of free samples of Lupron in violation of the Prescription Drug Marketing
Act. Four other physicians, all urologists, had earlier entered guilty pleas in connection with the above practices. The indictment against the seven defendants
also claimed TAP offered kickbacks, free drugs, payments disguised as educational grants, vacations at golf and ski resorts, travel expenses to conferences,
office Christmas parties, medical equipment, forgiveness of debt, free consulting
services, and discounts on Lupron sold to treat endometriosis in women (in addition to its use as a prostate cancer drug).

The trial that began on April 20, 2004, named eleven current and former TAP
officials, who were charged individually with defrauding the government by brib-
ing physicians and hospitals to purchase Lupron. Federal prosecutors amassed
evidence to show that six hospitals, two health plans, twenty-six group practices,
and twenty-five individual doctors were offered or accepted bribes, including
cash, free drugs, and tickets to major league baseball games. The Yale–New Haven
Hospital was accused of accepting $10,000 from TAP to fund a seminar for urol-
ogists and—more to the point—to ensure their continued purchase of Lupron.
A urology practice associated with New England Deaconess Hospital in Boston
supposedly received 111 free doses of Lupron worth over $44,000. Doctors then
billed Medicare for the distribution of these drugs to patients, an arrangement
that was essentially a cash kickback from TAP. A TAP district manager who had
pleaded guilty earlier to conspiracy to commit fraud oversaw an $11,000 write-
off of a physician's debt to the company when he agreed to switch his patients to
Lupron. Another doctor had his debt to TAP expunged, and he also received an
educational grant, a television, and a VCR player from the company.[32]

The trial was expected to last six months, but it was completed in less than
half that time. A federal jury acquitted eight of the eleven named individuals. Two
of the defendants had been acquitted by U.S. District Court Judge Douglas P.
Woodlock before the case went to the jury, and charges against a third defendant
(who was very ill) were dropped by the government.

TAP's defense lawyers argued that the government's confusing drug-marketing
rules made it difficult for the company's sales representatives to know when they
were breaking the law. They also said drug firms often feel compelled to settle out
of court to avoid being driven out of business. A trial and a guilty verdict against
a pharmaceutical firm could result in ruinous criminal and civil payments and
banishment from Medicare, Medicaid, and other federal programs. Another attorney suggested that the government—its confidence soaring after the earlier
settlement with TAP—overreached in prosecuting individual TAP employees.
James Moorman, executive director of Taxpayers Against Fraud, however, called

the verdict a travesty: "The jury has given the big wink to ripping off the old, poor, and sick in this country." Moorman noted, in referring to the earlier settlement, that "at least we got the money back." An attorney who represents pharmaceutical firms opined: "In its instructions to the jury, the court distinguished between improper conduct and cultivating a business relationship with a physician in the hope or expectation that prescriptions might occur." He indicated this verdict could clarify important issues and provide guidance in future cases.[33]

Serono: Extending the Product Life Cycle of an Outmoded Drug

Serono, a Switzerland-based corporation, together with its U.S. subsidiaries agreed to pay $704 million on October 17, 2005, to resolve criminal and civil charges of using illegal methods to promote, market, and sell Serostim, a drug used to treat severe, involuntary weight loss in AIDS victims (a condition known as "AIDS wasting"). The $704 million settlement included a $136.9 million criminal fine and a $567 million payment for civil liabilities. At the time, this case marked the third-largest health care fraud recovery by the U.S. government.[34]

Company officials pleaded guilty to two felony counts—conspiracy to distribute an unapproved and adulterated medical device and conspiracy to pay health care providers to write Serostim prescriptions for Medicaid patients. The civil complaints indicated that Serono sales representatives used a diagnostic test not approved by the FDA and that they manipulated the results of the unapproved test to advance the sales of Serostim. Furthermore, Serono was accused of promoting false and fraudulent claims against Medicaid.

The Serono case was precipitated by the shortened product life cycle of one of its premier drugs, the AIDS-fighting Serostim. Products (and services) follow a life cycle. A product first enters the market and then, if successful, its sales grow. The sales, however, eventually reach a plateau as the market for the product becomes saturated and mature. The demand for the product subsequently declines as its patent expires or as its markets change or as it is rendered obsolete by newer products. A product life cycle may last only a few months—as might be the case for a piece of computer software that quickly becomes outmoded—or it may last for decades—as might be the case with a popular make and model of automobile.[35]

The federal government's investigation of Serono began in 2000 when employees in Massachusetts, Connecticut, and Maryland filed False Claims Act suits against the company. The investigation focused on the company's attempt to preserve its market for Serostim after the drug was rendered largely obsolete by the introduction of protease inhibitor drugs.[36] Protease inhibitor drugs curtailed the progress of the AIDS syndrome to the point where severe weight loss was no longer a major cause of death among patients.

Motivated to recapture their investment in a drug that had once commanded a $21,000 price tag for a six-week treatment regime, the company established a joint venture with RJL Sciences to market a "bioelectrical impedance analysis" computer software package. This venture into uncharted territory created two problems. First, the bioelectrical impedance analysis software had not been approved by the FDA. Second, it redefined what constituted AIDS wasting. Instead of measuring changes in a patient's weight and lean body mass, it defined AIDS wasting based on changes in a patient's body cell mass.

To further promote Serostim sales to physicians, Serono Labs offered them an all-expense paid trip to Cannes on the French Riviera to attend a medical conference on nutrition and HIV infection. Doctors accepting this offer were expected to write thirty new prescriptions for Serostim, generating revenues of $630,000 from each participating physician (i.e., thirty patients at $21,000 per prescription). Serono pressured the company sales representatives to offer financial incentives to high prescribers of Serostim. Under its 6m–6 Day Plan, the representatives were directed to generate $6 million in Serostim sales within six days.[37] According to U.S. Attorney Michael Sullivan in Boston, 85 percent of Serostim prescriptions were unnecessary. These supposedly needless prescriptions amounted to some $615 million in sales for Serono.[38] Sullivan told reporters the medical testing procedure was "almost voodoolike" and that he suspected some patients may have suffered side effects from the drug.[39]

Serono signed a corporate integrity agreement that focused on the company's marketing practices and on the training of its sales representatives. Other provisions included oversight, corporate monitoring, and transparency in communications. The latter provision placed special attention on the relationship between the company's sales representatives and the doctors with whom they did business. Emphasis was also placed on the off-label uses of Serono's products. For example, Serono was required to document all unsolicited requests for information regarding the off-label use of Serostim. The company also had to examine the geographical distribution of these requests to determine whether patterns of suspicious usage existed. One such pattern linked bodybuilders to the illegal use of Serostim; the drug that helped AIDS patients to regain weight also helped bodybuilders gain muscle mass.[40]

The settlement of this case occurred less than four months before Medicare Part D went into effect. The timing of this settlement probably contributed to the federal government's later scrutiny of Medicare drug reimbursements.[41]

"Americans who need medical care depend on health care companies to have their medical devices and drugs thoroughly evaluated and approved before use," said then Attorney General Alberto R. Gonzales. He added, "Serono abused the system of testing and approval, and put its desire to sell more drugs above the interest of patients. Today's settlement will repay with interest the losses to federal and state Medicaid programs incurred by Serono's conduct, and would-be wrongdoers are on notice that we will not tolerate attempts to profit at the expense of the ill and needy in our society."[42]

Assistant Attorney General Peter Keisler of the U.S. Department of Justice Civil Division noted: "This settlement sends the unequivocal message to the health care industry that American taxpayers should not pay for prescriptions induced by unproven medical tests and improper payments to doctors and pharmacies."[43]

Serono was acquired for more than $13 billion in 2006 by Merck KGaA, a German pharmaceutical and chemical company (not to be confused with the American Merck & Company, which became independent of the German company in 1917). In May 2007, four Serono executives were exonerated by a Boston federal district court jury of charges they bribed doctors to prescribe drugs for AIDS patients. This case was eerily similar to the TAP Pharmaceuticals case that resulted in the acquittal of eleven individuals. Attorneys for the four Serono defendants said the federal government had been leaning too hard on the pharmaceutical industry. "The jury's verdict once again says this U.S. Attorney's office has been overreaching on pharmaceutical cases," said Tracy Miner, an attorney who represented one of the former Serono employees and who had previously defended a TAP executive. "It's another case where the office has inappropriately charged employees of a pharma company who did nothing more than their jobs," Miner said. "This is a case that never should have been brought, and the speed of the jury's verdict confirms it," said defense attorney Adam Hoffinger.[44]

The Purdue Frederick Company: The Misbranding of OxyContin

The Purdue Frederick Company and Purdue Pharma (known hereafter as Purdue) are part of a worldwide group of pharmaceutical businesses. The company has been an industry leader in developing sustained-release medications to manage pain.[45] Its zealousness in boosting the sales of pain management products, however, led to problems with the FDA and to allegations of fraud.

On May 10, 2007, the U.S. Attorney for the Western District of Virginia announced that Purdue, along with three of the company's executives, had agreed to pay more than $634.5 million to settle charges that they misbranded Purdue's OxyContin drug. OxyContin is a Schedule II prescription pain relief medication with the highest potential for abuse. It is prescribed primarily for moderate to severe pain. Because of its euphoric effect, OxyContin has also become a favorite drug of narcotics abusers.[46] The drug has been dubbed variously by street users as "Oxy," "OC," "Oxycotton," "Killer," and "Hillbilly Heroin." Its popularity has led to armed robberies of pharmacies, forged prescriptions, and thefts from patients with legal prescriptions for the drug. Abuse of OxyContin has resulted in hundreds of deaths and countless emergency room visits.[47] Multiple prescriptions of OxyContin have also been obtained by doctor-shopping drug abusers.

Between January 1996 and June 2001, federal prosecutors claimed that Purdue's sales supervisors and employees told health care providers that OxyContin was a safe pain medication, even though they knew it was highly addictive and had a strong potential for abuse by users. Company representatives used misleading graphs to exaggerate the differences between blood plasma levels achieved by OxyContin and blood plasma levels of other pain-relief medications. Although the graphs distorted the "peak and trough" blood-level effects of the drugs, they became part of Purdue's sales-training programs.

Purdue also sponsored a study on the use of OxyContin in osteoarthritis patients. The results of the research were published in the March 2000 issue of the *Archives of Internal Medicine*.[48] Eight coauthors contributed to the article: a PhD and seven medical doctors. The PhD was the only contributor, however, who was listed as an employee of Purdue Pharma. The authors noted clearly that oxycodone (the generic form of OxyContin) created side effects in patients: "Common opioid-related side effects were reported during CR [controlled release] oxycodone therapy, several of which decreased in duration as therapy continued. Patients' ability to function was not compromised during short- and long-term treatment with CR oxycodone."[49]

Three months after the article was published, the marketing group at Purdue provided each sales representative with a copy along with a "marketing tip" for using its findings to achieve sales success. According to prosecutors, Purdue sales representatives distributed copies of the *Archives of Internal Medicine* article to health care providers to mislead them into believing that doses smaller than 60 milligrams per day could be terminated abruptly without inducing withdrawal symptoms. Purdue's position was bolstered by citing two sentences from the article: "There were 2 reports of withdrawal symptoms after patients abruptly stopped taking CR oxycodone at doses of 60 or 70 mg/d. Withdrawal syndrome was not reported as an adverse event during scheduled respites, indicating that CR oxycodone at doses below 60 mg/d can be discontinued without tapering the dose if the patient's condition so warrants."[50]

The prosecutors contended that, despite this finding, Purdue representatives knew of other studies that placed OxyContin in a less favorable light. These studies indicated the drug caused patient dependency and withdrawal symptoms. Nevertheless, Purdue decided not to publicize the unfavorable findings. According to the settlement summary issued by the U.S. Department of Justice, Purdue associates "were well aware of the incorrect view held by many physicians that oxycodone was weaker than morphine, they did not want to do anything 'to make physicians think that oxycodone was stronger to [*sic*] or equal to morphine' or to 'take any steps in the form of promotional materials, symposia, clinical, publications, conventions, or communications with the field force that would affect the unique position that OxyContin had in many physicians' minds.'"[51]

Purdue also claimed the drug was less susceptible to intravenous abuse by street users because of the difficulty in extracting oxycodone from an OxyContin tablet. This claim was contradicted by Purdue's own study, which found that a drug abuser could extract approximately 68 percent of oxycodone by crushing a 10 mg. OxyContin tablet, stirring it in water, and drawing the solution through cotton into a syringe. By March 2000, Purdue was aware of OxyContin abuse in various communities, but the company reportedly made no effort to change its marketing strategies in response to that threat.[52]

Purdue and the three executives admitted that the company marketed controlled-release OxyContin by making unsubstantiated claims that it was less euphoric, less addictive, less subject to abuse, and less likely to cause withdrawal symptoms than short-acting opium-based pain medications. Purdue's payments to settle the OxyContin allegations included $276.1 million forfeited to the U.S. government, $160 million paid to the federal and state governments to resolve false claims liabilities against Medicaid and other programs, $130 million allocated to resolve private civil claims, $5.3 million to the Virginia Attorney General's Medicaid fraud control unit to fund further health care fraud investigations, $20 million to fund the Virginia prescription monitoring program, and a criminal fine of $500,000. The three Purdue executives paid a total of $34.5 million, and each was required to pay a $5,000 criminal fine.

"Purdue put its desire to sell OxyContin above the interests of the public," said Assistant Attorney General Peter D. Keisler. "Purdue abused the drug approval process which relies on drug manufacturers to be forthright in reporting clinical data and, instead, misled physicians about the addiction and withdrawal issues involved with Oxycontin."

"Purdue's illegal sales and marketing practices concealed information from patients and many health care providers regarding the potency and abuse potential of OxyContin for corporate profit," said Daniel R. Levinson, Inspector General for the U.S. Department of Health and Human Services.[53]

OxyContin now comes with a black box warning identifying it as a Schedule II substance and cautioning users of its addictive effects. The warning indicates the drug is to be taken only by opioid-tolerant patients. It also contains strict instructions not to break, chew, or crush the tablets. To do so, alters the controlled-release mechanism in the tablets, which could cause a rapid release and potentially fatal absorption of the drug.

Schering-Plough Corporation: Another Repeat Offender

Schering-Plough Corporation (Schering-Plough) is a global health-care company manufacturing prescription, consumer, and animal health products as well as advanced drug therapies. The Kennilworth, New Jersey, company had

$12.7 billion in net sales in 2007, with approximately 55,000 employees doing business in more than 140 countries. As is the case with most pharmaceutical firms, Schering-Plough invests heavily in research and development. In 2007 its R & D investments were $2.9 billion (22.8% of net sales) for research in cardiovascular disease, central nervous system disorders, immunology and infectious diseases, oncology, respiratory disease, and women's health.[54] The first decade of the twenty-first century marked a litigious period in the life of Schering-Plough. In 2002 the company agreed to pay $500 million to the government for failing to comply with federal manufacturing guidelines and for failing to address defects in its drug-manufacturing processes. Problems at Schering-Plough facilities in New Jersey and Puerto Rico included the use of outdated equipment and inadequate controls to identify faulty medicines. Some two hundred pharmaceuticals were involved in the substandard-manufacturing processes, including the allergy medicine Claritin and the lung-development drug Celestone used by infants. Two years earlier, Schering-Plough was forced to recall millions of asthma inhalers because of a possible missing ingredient.[55] According to the FDA:

> The government's action in this case follows 13 inspections at four New Jersey and Puerto Rico facilities since 1998 during which [the] FDA found significant violations of the CGMP [current good manufacturing practice] regulations related to facilities, manufacturing, quality assurance, equipment, laboratories, and packaging and labeling. The decree requires the companies to pay $471,500 to cover the costs of these inspections. The defendants have had a history of failing to comply with CGMP requirements at these plants, which produce about 90 percent of the firm's drug products. The decree affects about 125 different prescription and over-the-counter drugs produced at the Puerto Rico and New Jersey facilities. As part of the decree, the company has agreed to suspend manufacturing 73 other products.[56]

Schering-Plough reached an almost equally devastating settlement in July 2004 after three former employees of one of the company's subsidiaries filed whistle-blower charges. It agreed to pay $345.5 million ($52.5 million in criminal penalties and almost $293 million in civil penalties) to resolve allegations by the government of manipulating prices to overcharge the Medicaid program. The three employees received over $31.6 million as their share of the settlement.

At the center of the case was Claritin, Schering's top-selling allergy drug during the late 1990s. Schering's major competition was Allegra, a significantly less-expensive allergy medication. The company was being pressured by two of its largest managed-care accounts, Cigna Healthcare and Pacificare Health Systems, to reduce its price for Claritin; otherwise, they threatened to drop Claritin from their formularies in favor of Allegra. Schering-Plough, however, faced a major dilemma: if it reduced the price of Claritin to Cigna and Pacificare, it would be forced to report a lower best price to Medicaid and to pay a higher rebate to state Medicaid programs.

Schering-Plough devised a strategy to play both ends of the problem. To retain Cigna's business, Schering provided a $1.8 million "data fee," $3 million worth of deeply discounted Claritin reditabs, below market value health-management services, and prepaid rebates (in essence, an interest-free loan). To retain Pacificare's business, Schering arranged to cover a portion of the managed-care customers' respiratory-drug costs, deep discounts on other Schering products, payment and services for Internet development, and an interest-free loan in the form of prepaid rebates. As noted, a pharmaceutical firm is supposed to include customer discounts when reporting its best price of a drug to Medicaid. By failing to do so, Schering-Plough strengthened its sales of Claritin and short-changed the Medicaid program.

In addition to monetary penalties, Schering-Plough entered into a corporate integrity agreement to monitor its sales and marketing programs. Schering Sales Corporation was also excluded from participation in all federal health care programs for at least five years.[57] A U.S. Attorney described the case as "a very byzantine and complex fraud"; he said the concessions Schering-Plough gave to Cigna amounted to "nothing more than an old-fashioned kickback...a clear payment for nothing."[58]

Even-numbered years seemed to have been especially harsh for Schering-Plough. In 2006 the company once again had to pay a huge settlement—some $435 million—to settle charges for marketing improprieties and for misreporting its best price for drugs to the federal government.[59] The settlement was the culmination of a lengthy investigation by federal agencies. The Department of Justice alleged that Schering-Plough illegally promoted the off-label use of the drugs Temodar and Intron A. Although the company said that such promotions were isolated incidents, the federal government claimed the Schering sales force was trained and paid to sell drugs to physicians for off-label uses.

In exchange for their commitment to prescribe the company's medications, physicians were paid for participating in clinical trials and for serving on sham advisory boards. According to the *New York Times,* one physician received an unsolicited $10,000 check from Schering-Plough and others received remuneration in the six figures. The *Times* described the practice of paying high-prescribing doctors to conduct clinical trials as little more than a thinly disguised marketing effort. One Texas physician said that Schering-Plough "flooded the market with pseudo trials."[60]

Clinical trials performed by working physicians instead of by research laboratories may not adhere to rigorous research protocols. Scientifically sound pharmaceutical trials require blind experimental and control (placebo) groups, proper categorization of patients (e.g., by gender, age, health status, and so forth), correct sampling procedures, regulation of the environment in which the drug is administered, precise measurements of the dosage and the effects of the drug, and meticulous record keeping. Busy—and often overworked—physicians with little or no knowledge of pharmaceutical research are ill-equipped to conduct trials yielding scientifically useful results. As the Texas physician commented, "Science and marketing should not be mixed like that."[61]

Physicians as Consultants: A Money Trail to Fraud and Corruption?

The conflict of interest cultivated by the relationship between pharmaceutical and medical equipment companies and physicians goes well beyond the Schering-Plough case. The *New England Journal of Medicine* published an article in April 2007 that provided survey results from 3,167 physicians across six medical specialties about their relationship with pharmaceutical and medical equipment manufacturers. The survey revealed that approximately 94 percent of practicing physicians in the United States had gift-exchange relationships with pharmaceutical and equipment manufacturers, but the extent of those relationships varied significantly. Most doctors accepted food or prescription samples; one-third of the respondents received reimbursements for professional meetings and educational programs; and more than one-fourth received honoraria for consulting, lecturing, or enrolling patients in clinical trials. Astute sales representatives from pharmaceutical and medical equipment companies clearly understood the need to foster ties with physicians—the so-called opinion leaders—who were especially influential among their colleagues and who had the authority to make major purchasing decisions.

The survey also showed major differences in the closeness of the business-physician relationships by medical specialty and by health care arrangement. Cardiologists appeared to have stronger ties to drug and equipment firms than did pediatricians, anesthesiologists, family practitioners, or surgeons. A physician working in a group practice was three times more likely to receive a gift and four times more likely to receive a consulting fee for professional services than was a physician working in a hospital. Compared to earlier studies, the *New England Journal of Medicine* article suggested that business ties between pharmaceutical companies and physicians were becoming more common.[62]

Another set of ties is the relationship between the pharmaceutical firms and the seven hundred thousand or so physicians practicing in the United States. About 725 accredited providers offer roughly one hundred thousand continuing medical education classes—many of them online—for physicians seeking state-mandated ongoing certification. The key concern, of course, is whether these classes are educational or whether they are a backdoor way of marketing pharmaceuticals. Courses on smoking cessation, premenstrual syndrome, restless legs syndrome, female hypoactive sexuality, and migraine headaches are among those available through pharmaceutical firms. Not surprisingly, accusations have been made that these companies are concerned primarily with promoting their drugs by emphasizing the positive results and downplaying or ignoring the risks they may present to consumers. And, of course, no mention is usually made of the cost or efficacy of competing pharmaceuticals. The University of Wisconsin–Madison, for example, offered a smoke-cessation course to physicians. The course promoted Pfizer's Chantix—a drug that has been linked to serious side effects such as depression, agitation, suicidal behavior, and blackouts. In fact, the FAA has banned its use by pilots and air traffic controllers. But none of these problems were mentioned in the Wisconsin course. Pfizer funded the course to the tune of $12.3 million, with $3.5 million going to the university. "Drug companies have essentially hijacked the highest level of medical education we have in this country," according to Daniel Carlat, an associate clinical professor of psychiatry at Tufts University. Carl Elliott, a professor of bioethics at the University of Minnesota Medical School, said, "American doctors are the best paid doctors in the world. To hear them plead poverty and say they can't pay for their own education is the height of hypocrisy."[63]

Although conflicts of interest are inevitable, it is often difficult to distinguish between business relationships that enhance patient care and those that work against the best interests of patients. A Massachusetts anesthesiologist was the subject of a federal investigation in the spring of 2009 for possibly distorting the results of at least twenty-one studies of painkillers involving three major pharmaceutical firms.[64] Medical-device maker Stryker has been targeted by the New Jersey Attorney General regarding compensation the company paid to doctors for participating in the clinical trials.[65] If the allegations are true, the Massachusetts case seems to be a clear case of fraud. But what about paying doctors to perform research that is potentially beneficial? When does the gift-exchange relationship go too far?

One recent controversy involves questionable consulting relationships between medical school faculty—especially psychiatrists—and pharmaceutical manufacturers. Medical school professors and their associates are involved heavily in research, and they frequently have access to state-of-the-art laboratories and multimillion dollar grants from federal funding sources such as the National Institutes of Health. Researchers in all scientific disciplines are expected to adhere to rigorous methodology and to maintain absolute objectivity in analyzing the results of their work. This objectivity cannot be eclipsed by the personal financial interests of those performing the research.

Potential conflicts of interest between the pharmaceutical industry and the academic community have caught the eye of—once again—Iowa Senator Charles

Grassley. Senator Grassley sent a letter to the American Psychiatric Association questioning its financial links to the pharmaceutical industry and demanding that the APA account for its revenues. According to the *New York Times,* the APA's revenues in 2006 were $62.5 million, and as much as 30 percent of it may have come from the pharmaceutical industry. The key question, of course, is whether psychiatrists at some of the nation's leading universities have developed unethical consulting relationships with drug companies. According to the *Los Angeles Times,* "At issue is the safety and efficacy of the stream of new drugs undergoing clinical trials."[66] And the *New York Times* noted, "Studies have shown that researchers who are paid by a company are more likely to report positive findings when evaluating that company's drugs."[67]

Universities and government agencies providing research grants often require faculty to report income derived from sources outside their institution. But professors at some of the top U.S. medical schools have come under the gun for their failure to disclose payments received from pharmaceutical companies and equipment manufacturers. A University of Minnesota Medical School department head was called on the carpet by Grassley for failing to reveal $1.2 million in consulting fees and honoraria from medical-device maker Medtronic.[68] Grassley aimed another of his mud pies at an Emory University psychiatrist who failed to disclose hundreds of thousands of dollars in payments from pharmaceutical companies. Emory acted decisively and imposed severe sanctions that included removing him from his position as department head, barring him from receiving grants from the National Institutes of Health for two years, and requiring him to report outside income to the school. Grassley said, "Accurate disclosure and transparency are fundamental to the integrity of medical research. Without them, the public trust is violated and public confidence in the system is legitimately shaken."[69]

Concern, for example, has been raised regarding a possible skewing of the clinical trial outcomes of a popular antiseizure drug. But suspecting that something is amiss is one thing, proving it is another. Dr. Steven Nissen, chairman of Cardiovascular Medicine at the Cleveland Foundation, in Ohio, put it this way: "The reality is that a deliberate fraud is extremely difficult to unearth. If scientists and companies agree to report results in a way that wasn't originally intended, unless you have access to original documents, it is extremely difficult to actually figure out what happened and how it happened."[70]

Grassley continued his pursuit of benefactor drug and device makers by sending letters to the American Medical Association (AMA), the American Cancer Society, and thirty-one other medical-advocacy organizations, asking them to provide details on the amount of money they receive from these companies. Earlier, Grassley sent a similar letter to the National Alliance on Mental Illness. The group reported that over two-thirds of its donations came from the pharmaceutical industry, a revelation that prompted one board member to resign.[71]

Stanford University School of Medicine leaders have instituted a policy restricting the drug industry's ability to influence its continuing education programs for physicians. Donations by pharmaceutical firms can no longer be used to finance designated courses at Stanford. Instead, the funds are placed in a schoolwide pool of money and applied to whatever classes the faculty deems appropriate—not the classes supported by a specific company. Stanford's policy is similar to those used at several other medical schools, and it shields faculty from potentially biasing commercial influences.[72] But actions may ultimately speak louder than words. Stanford accepted a fully disclosed, "no strings attached" $3 million grant from the pharmaceutical giant Pfizer to use for whatever purpose the medical school designated. Not surprisingly, the arrangement produced a great deal of skepticism from outsiders. According to Harvard professor emeritus Arnold S. Relman, for example:

> If it is true—a big, big, if—but if it is true that this money is being given without any strings at all and without any obligation on the part of Stanford to please Pfizer, then it's arguable that it's OK. But it's just not a good idea for a profession that says it wants to be independent and trusted, a reliable source of information to the profession and the public about drugs, to take money from the drug company under any conditions.[73]

Pharmaceutical manufacturers have paid physicians to "write" articles promoting the off-label uses of their products when, in reality, these articles were ghostwritten by the manufacturer. Merck & Co. allegedly used ghostwriters to develop an article about its drug Vioxx, which was published in the highly reputable *Journal of the American Medical Association*.[74] These promotions—if based on bad research—not only circumvent the FDA drug-approval process and provide potentially false or misleading information to physicians, but they also pose a danger to patient health and safety.[75] In May 2008, Merck reached a $58 million settlement over allegations that Vioxx advertisements played down the health risks of the drug. As part of the settlement, Merck agreed to stop using ghostwriters to promote the off-label uses of their drugs in medical journals.[76] Similarly, between 1998 and 2005, drug maker Wyeth paid ghostwriters to prepare dozens of journal articles on hormone replacement therapy that were published under physicians' names.[77]

The editors of major medical journals have begun to probe authors' backgrounds to uncover conflicts of interest between writers and corporations. Twelve leading medical journals are requiring authors to complete a disclosure form that reveals things such as board memberships, employment, consulting and expert witness work, grant applications and funding, honoraria and gifts received, patents and royalties, educational and speaking engagements, stock ownership, and travel paid by others. The form was developed, in part, as a response to a 2004 report by the Center for Science in the Public Interest. The report found that 14 percent of scientific-journal articles included unreported financial conflicts of interest.[78]

Pressure is likely to continue for the establishment of a national registry where pharmaceutical and other companies must post payments made to physicians. The previously discussed Physician Payments Sunshine Act and its planned registry is a major step in that direction. Prohibitions on the gift-exchange relationship among pharmaceutical firms, equipment manufacturers, and physicians are also on the horizon. The Wisconsin Medical Society's board voted in favor of banning all gifts to preclude conflicts of interest between physicians and outside commercial interests. The ban forbids Wisconsin doctors from serving on a company's speaker bureau and from serving as authors of articles written by health-product companies.[79] The Association of American Medical Colleges has issued a report, "In the Interest of Patients: Recommendations for Physician Financial Relationships and Clinical Decision Making." The thirty nine–page document provides guidance to academic medical centers on navigating through the maze of conflicts of interest that can arise in clinical care settings.[80] The Harvard Medical School has revised their conflict-of-interest policy into one that might serve as a model for other medical schools, and the University of Michigan Medical School will no longer take money from pharmacuetical and medical equipment manufacturers for the school's continuing medical education programs.[81]

Some Examples of Fraud in the Medical Supply and Equipment Industry

As with the multibillion-dollar pharmaceutical industry, medical supply and equipment companies can be extremely aggressive in the way they price and market their products. Some of these companies not only run afoul of the anti-kickback, false claims, and FDA statutes, but they become entangled in ethical dilemmas with physicians.

Abbott Laboratories, in July 2005, paid $382 million to the federal government and an additional $32 million to the states and Washington, D.C., to settle claims that its Ross Products division defrauded Medicare and Medicaid over a ten-year period. CG Nutritionals, a part of the Ross Products division, pleaded guilty to obstructing a criminal investigation and agreed to pay a $200 million settlement. The case centered on Ross Products' enteral feeding (infusion) devices used to pump special foods into the digestive tracts of patients who cannot ingest foods in a normal manner.

The government accused the company of providing enteral feeding pumps, primarily to nursing homes, at no charge. In return, the buyers agreed to purchase a specific number of pump set components. Ross Products then showed nursing homes and durable medical equipment suppliers how they could bill Medicare and Medicaid for the free pumps.

This fraud was exposed by the federal government's Operation Headwaters, a joint undercover investigation by the FBI, the U.S. Postal Inspection Service, and the OIG that focused on the illegal activities of DME companies. Federal agents used, as part of the undercover operation, a fictitious medical supplier known as Southern Medical Distributors. Various manufacturers, including Ross Products, offered kickbacks to undercover agents for purchasing the products.[82]

The government also claimed that the company made payments to health care providers to convince them to sign long-term contracts for enteral products. Such payments violate the antikickback statute because these items were then billed to Medicare. CG Nutritionals was permanently banned from participating in Medicare and Medicaid. Abbott Labs also agreed to a five-year corporate integrity agreement, requiring them to reform the sales and marketing practices for their enteral feeding products.[83]

Interventional cardiology and cardiovascular surgery are the cash cows of the American health care delivery system, according to Dr. Nortin M. Hadler, a professor at the University of North Carolina School of Medicine and author of *Worried Sick: A Prescription for Health in an Overtreated America*.[84] Not surprisingly, then, possible conflicts of interest between the American College of Cardiology and the Cardiovascular Research Foundation have come under scrutiny. Senator Herb Kohl (D-Wisconsin) has expressed concerns over the relationships between member doctors of the American College of Cardiology and the Cardiovascular Research Foundation, which accepts funding from several medical-device manufacturers. In a prepared statement, Senator Kohl said, "This inquiry is part of a much larger effort to examine the tangled financial relationship between America's physicians and these industries." Dr. David Holmes, a cardiologist at the Mayo Clinic, offered a different view. He claimed the "sole mission is to make sure that we put on the very best scientific meeting that we possibly can that explores the art and science of interventional cardiology."[85]

An aging and overweight U.S. population has created a soaring demand for hip and knee replacements. Although innovations in orthopedic surgery and orthopedic appliances are a boon to patients requiring these replacements, a questionable business relationship has arisen between the orthopedic surgeons and the companies that manufacture devices such as artificial joints. Doctors are being paid as consultants by companies such as Zimmer Holdings, an industry leader in hip and knee products. The question behind these consulting agreements is whether doctors were being paid to conduct training or to assist in product development—both are legal activities—or whether they were being paid kickbacks for using the company's orthopedic products—a violation of the antikickback statute. In September 2007, a criminal investigation put a temporary halt on moonlighting physicians, and the major orthopedic companies paid $311 million and agreed to a monitoring program by the federal government. Payments to doctors, however, have continued as federal authorities try to keep an eye on the new consulting arrangements. Zimmer Holdings, to ensure transparency, posted on their website a list of health care professionals who receive payments from the company as well as a copy of their twenty-three-page deferred prosecution agreement and information on a compliance hotline.[86]

The number of patients with end-stage renal disease is also expected to grow dramatically as U.S. baby boomers age. As the number of kidney dialysis services reimbursed by the federal government grows, so too will their vulnerability to fraud and abuse. Medicare spending for outpatient dialysis was $12 billion in 2000, an amount that was expected to double by 2010.[87]

In December 2004, Gambro Healthcare (Gambro) agreed to pay more than $350 million in criminal fines and civil penalties to settle allegations of health care fraud. The settlement focused on frauds against the Medicare, Medicaid, and TRICARE programs, and it included $25 million in criminal charges and the permanent exclusion of Gambro Supply Corporation from the Medicare program. Gambro Supply was a sham durable medical equipment company owned by Gambro Healthcare. The settlement also required payment of over $310 million to resolve civil liabilities, an additional payment of $15 million for potential state Medicaid program liabilities, and compliance with a comprehensive corporate integrity agreement.

The suit was filed originally in 2001 by Gambro's former chief medical officer, who supervised medical and nursing services at the company's U.S. outpatient dialysis centers. At the time of the case, Gambro was the nation's third-largest owner and operator of renal dialysis clinics. The company used its shell subsidiary, Gambro Supply Corporation, to bill Medicare at the clinical reimbursement rate, which was $500 higher than the home dialysis rate. Gambro Supply, then known as REN Supply Corporation, intentionally left a line blank on Medicare application forms to conceal its connection to the parent company, making it easier to collect the higher reimbursement.[88] Gambro also billed for home dialysis supplies not provided to Medicare beneficiaries. The company used the practice of "hard coding" diagnostic codes to falsify statements and bills submitted for unnecessary services—bone-density studies, nerve-conduction studies, and electrocardiograms, among others. Gambro also violated the antikickback statute by hiring and paying physicians based on the number of patient referrals they made to company clinics.[89]

In an earlier brush with the law (2000), Gambro Healthcare Laboratory Services paid over $53 million to settle similar charges of false claims to Medicare, Medicaid, and TRICARE over laboratory services provided to end-stage renal disease patients. Considering the similarities between the earlier and later violations, the corporate integrity agreement signed by Gambro in 2000 appeared to have had little impact on its subsequent business practices. As one legal observer noted:

> For whatever it's worth, if anything, Gambro was required to sign another "integrity agreement" as part of the December 2004 settlement.... The charges above beg the questions of how many patients received unnecessary testing, medications and equipment, and how many patients went without services that were billed for? Also, how much out-of-pocket money did patients lose in co-payments as a result of bogus billings for services not rendered or for services rendered needlessly?[90]

In 1998 Gambro was also involved in the recall of defective blood tubing after forty patients were hospitalized and four dialysis patients died from hemolysis (the destruction of red blood cells).[91] The FDA later became aware of additional serious injuries and deaths connected with Gambro's Prisma Continuous Renal Replacement Therapy, a system used on critically ill patients. The FDA issued notices in August 2005 and February 2006 regarding safety precautions for renal caregivers.[92]

Fresenius Medical Care of North America agreed to pay $486 million to settle accusations of fraud against its kidney dialysis subsidiary, National Medical Care (NMC). Fresenius acquired NMC in 1996, inheriting some of the problems that led to the settlement in January 2000. Three NMC subsidiaries also pleaded guilty to separate conspiracies and were fined $101 million. The Fresenius and NMC case centered on blood-testing claims by LifeChem, NMC's blood-testing laboratory. Kickbacks were allegedly made to dialysis facilities to obtain blood-testing contracts for LifeChem. Furthermore, fraudulent claims were submitted to Medicare for intradialytic parenteral nutrition, a nutritional therapy provided to dialysis patients. Fresenius was required to enter an eight-year corporate integrity agreement.[93] In a postsettlement press release, Fresenius indicated that, after acquiring NMC, it worked closely with government officials to resolve the case. The company also emphasized that their legal disputes arose over whether Medicare was billed properly for certain products and services; there was never controversy regarding the quality of patient care delivered by Fresenius or NMC.[94]

A Few More Words about Antitrust Violations

In the previous chapter, I discussed antitrust issues involving hospitals and networks of health care providers. A number of cases have also arisen in which pharmaceutical and medical equipment firms have become embroiled in litigation about actions that stifle fair competition. Providers of health care services have been accused of perpetuating monopolies as well as agreements not to compete, price collusion, and the obstruction of innovative forms of health care financing and delivery.

Monopoly concerns arise when competing pharmaceutical or equipment firms merge (horizontal mergers), when a merger is thought to discourage innovation, or when a merger involves a company taking control of a supplier or buyer (vertical merger). As noted, monopolistic arrangements threaten to drive up the cost of health care and drive down its quality and accessibility, placing both consumers and competitors at an unfair advantage.

Some pharmaceutical industry antitrust cases involve collusion. "Pay for delay" occurs when a drug manufacturer pays the manufacturer of a generic drug to postpone introducing a competing product. Bristol-Myers Squibb granted Apotex a license to sell a generic version of Plavix, an anti–blood clotting drug that helps to protect patients against heart attacks and strokes. But Bristol-Myers Squibb agreed not to launch its own generic version of the drug during the first six months of the license. This arrangement gave Apotex a valuable—and unfair—advantage during the six-month period that it was allowed to corner the market.[95]

The FTC charged two generic drug manufacturers, Alpharma and the Perrigo Company, with agreeing to limit competition for over-the-counter children's liquid ibuprofen. Alpharma and Perrigo were the only two manufacturers having FDA approval to manufacture this drug, and they agreed that Perrigo would be the sole distributor of liquid Motrin for seven years. In exchange, Perrigo would pay Alpharma an initial fee plus a sales royalty. Alpharma and Perrigo estimated that this arrangement would raise the price of the drug by 25 percent. A federal district court in Washington, D.C., ordered the companies to forfeit to harmed consumers over $6 million of the illegal profits from the deal and placed limits on the firms' ability to compete.[96]

The Range of Settlements

Between 1990 and 2007, over three hundred health care fraud settlements in the United States resulted in payments of $1 million or more. These settlements yielded almost $15.9 billion to government coffers, including almost $1.8 billion (11% of the total) in criminal fines. Seven settlements were for amounts over $500 million, and twenty settlements exceeded $250 million. More than 83 percent of the individual settlements (253), however, were in the $1 million to $50 million range with most (174) being less than $10 million.

The pharmaceutical industry led the way with $6.2 billion in settlements, an amount that appears to be increasing at a substantial rate. Hospitals and medical devices occupied the second and third positions with hospitals paying $4 billion and medical-device companies $1.1 billion. Various insurance-related businesses had settlements totaling over $1.1 billion. These included insurers, billing services, carriers, and program-eligibility entities. Other health care industry segments with large cumulative settlement amounts between 1990 and 2007 were: kidney dialysis ($943.6 million), laboratory services ($872.7 million), nursing homes ($518.2 million), home health care ($465.3 million), and rehabilitation services ($341.6 million). Physicians and nursing services had small settlement amounts of $85.4 million and $10.3 million. Durable medical equipment businesses had a surprisingly low settlement amount of $158 million over the almost seventeen-year period. Given the federal government's growing concern about this industry segment, DME settlements may rise in the future. Retail pharmacies also had a relatively small cumulative settlement of $93.3 million.[97]

Prosecuting Health Care Fraud Cases Is a Big Business

The high-profile cases discussed here and in the previous chapter, along with their large settlement amounts, illustrate several important points. Health care fraud and abuse involve huge sums of money across a wide range of industry segments. When viewed against the vast size of the U.S. health care system, however, these amounts suggest that the problem is serious but not pandemic—at least not yet. During the four-year period from the beginning of 1999 to the end of 2002, health care fraud settlements amounted to $4.6 billion and U.S. health care expenditures were approximately $5.8 trillion. In the four-year period from the beginning of 2003 until the end of 2006, settlements had increased dramatically to $8.2 billion, but U.S. health care expenditures had also risen significantly to $7.7 trillion.[98] This eight-year trend suggests that the concurrent rise in U.S. health care fraud settlement amounts is greater than the rise in U.S. health care expenditures. It is difficult to know, however, whether this trend is indicative of more health care fraud, more zealous enforcement efforts by federal and state prosecutors, or some combination of the two.

The nearly $15.9 billion in civil and criminal settlements also distorts the magnitude of the problem because the False Claims Act allows federal prosecutors to seek treble damages and penalties against health care providers. That is to say, the economic damage caused by most high-profile frauds is not as bad as the financial settlements suggest. Furthermore, the definition of what constitutes health care fraud and abuse has expanded, possibly overstating the rate at which the problem is growing.

The number of health care providers that are touched by investigations or prosecutions of fraud and abuse is growing. Although only a small number of health care providers have been the target of an investigation, most have known—or have known of—someone who has been a target. Victims, of course, may blow the whistle on those who have defrauded them. Special government investigations and sting operations also play an integral part in nabbing fraud perpetrators. But health care fraud is often revealed by insiders—disgruntled employees, jealous family members, and even former spouses or lovers—who are motivated both by personal revenge and by the prospect of a big payoff under the False Claims Act. Accusations of fraud or abuse against health care providers may also come from consumer advocates, competitors, vendors that have been treated unfairly, disenchanted shareholders, Medicare fiscal intermediaries and carriers, inspectors, auditors, fraud investigators, and professional whistle-blowers who seek employment with the intent of digging up dirt on their employer and, later, filing a lawsuit.

From the 1990s to the present, the federal government has made the prosecution of health care fraud a priority. Two opposing forces are at work with regard to major health care fraud and abuse cases. One is the incessant pressure on health care executives to achieve a strong financial showing. The other is a strong desire by prosecutors to expose and punish large corporations that cheat federal health care programs, consumers, and investors. And based on their postsettlement comments, prosecutors and government officials are not bashful when it comes to bragging about the impact of their legal victories.

Federal prosecutors have followed a strategy of grabbing the low-hanging fruit. The pharmaceutical industry is far and away the federal government's favorite target because pharmaceutical firms are financially well heeled. Prosecuting a hospital chain, medical laboratory, or dialysis equipment manufacturer and obtaining a settlement of several hundred million dollars is a much more efficient use of resources—in terms of the settlement dollars received per the prosecutorial dollar spent—than going after a small group of crooked providers.

The Medicare, Medicaid, and TRICARE programs are similar to a mousetrap: they are an enticing target for fraud perpetrators. But once a perpetrator takes the bait, federal agencies, Medicare fiscal intermediaries and carriers, and state Medicaid agencies have the power to suspend payments temporarily pending the outcome of a fraud investigation. Temporary suspensions, furthermore, are nearly impossible to contest. Even when such suspensions are later found to be without merit, they can have devastating consequences on the cash flow of a hospital, clinic, laboratory, or other provider. For major violators, the HIPAA provides for permanent banishment from the Medicare, Medicaid, or TRICARE programs. And permanent banishment may be the death knell for an outlaw health care organization.[99] For these reasons, hospital chains, pharmaceutical companies, and medical equipment and supply companies often decide to settle on the courthouse steps rather than to risk an adverse verdict in federal court—a verdict that could lead to bankruptcy. The next chapter illustrates the dynamics of prosecuting—and defending—health care fraud and abuse cases.

FIGHTING HEALTH CARE FRAUD AND ABUSE

Bilking Medicare out of $47 Billion

During FY 2009, the federal government reported that it paid more than $47 billion in questionable—and possibly fraudulent—Medicare claims and another $18.1 billion in questionable Medicaid claims. Although this report sounds like a new verse to a song that government auditors have been singing for the past twenty years or so, the over $65 billion in loss estimates far outstrip those of previous years. The Medicare program, for example, estimated "just" $17 billion in losses in FY 2008. So, why the big jump? Is Medicare and Medicaid fraud escalating at a seemingly exponential rate?

The answer is "probably not." Fraud estimates are highly dependent on methodology. From 2005 to 2008, the Bush administration reported an improper payment rate of about 4 percent. But, by using a more exacting methodology in FY 2009, the improper payment rate for Medicare claims jumped to a whopping 12.4 percent. And the Obama administration, as it turns out, will use this 12.4 percent estimate as a baseline by which future payments and losses will be judged. This decision is good in the sense that it has prompted the administration to intensify its crackdown on health care fraud and abuse—a key aspect of health care reform. On the other hand, the 12.4 percent baseline is also a possible political ploy: by overestimating the magnitude of fraud and abuse, the Obama administration has a better opportunity to play the role of hero by reducing the fraud rate to a targeted 8 percent by 2012.[1]

But complex issues have complex causes. We have seen the variety and in-genuity of schemes to abuse and defraud the health care system. Rooting out all of these schemes and preventing perpetrators from inventing new ones is a mission impossible. Nonetheless, measures can be taken to control and reduce health care fraud and abuse. A successful attack on health care fraud and abuse will have to come through the proverbial "death by a thousand cuts." That is, no single measure is going to decrease this major social problem significantly. The battle will have to involve all segments of the health care system—providers, con-sumers, insurers (or other payers), and federal and state governments. Reducing health care fraud and abuse requires developing, implementing, and coordinat-ing antifraud strategies among all these groups.

Three Approaches to Reducing Criminal and Corrupt Acts

Crime and corruption can be reduced by using three strategies: making it more difficult for the individual perpetrator to commit a criminal or corrupt act, in-creasing the risks associated with the commission of a criminal or corrupt act, and increasing the opportunity costs of a criminal or corrupt act.[2]

The first strategy, making it more difficult to commit a crime or to engage in a corrupt act, forces a perpetrator to work harder at completing the fraud. Crimi-nal acts and acts of corruption require physical and mental effort on the part of the perpetrator. The harder he or she has to work to plan, execute, and avoid detection for a crime, the less attractive the crime becomes. Antitheft technology installed in automobiles does not prevent all car thefts, but it forces professional car thieves to exert more effort and be more cunning; it also encourages amateur car thieves to try their hand at something else.

The same rationale applies to reducing health care fraud and abuse. Recall the order by HHS that required DME providers in Southern California and South Florida to resubmit their Medicare applications. Also, DME suppliers in Califor-nia, Florida, Illinois, Michigan, New York, North Carolina, and Texas are being subjected to a thorough examination of their claims as well as to unannounced inspections of their business premises. In addition, the CMS is expanding its recovery audit contractor program. Recovery audit contractors have been in-structed to focus on companies and individuals whose Medicare billings are higher than those normally submitted by providers and suppliers in their com-munities. The CMS is also targeting Florida home health care agencies caring for patients who are extremely ill. In 2007 a suspiciously high 60 percent of all Miami home health care payments were for sicker-than-average beneficiaries, compared to only 6 percent of total home health care payments nationwide.[3] These edicts are raising the cost of committing DME and home health care fraud—they force dishonest suppliers and agencies to work harder and smarter at avoiding the attention of federal investigators.

The second strategy, increasing the risks associated with a criminal or corrupt act, exposes perpetrators to a greater likelihood of punishment—something strongly encouraged here. Individuals convicted of felonies face prison time, fines, civil judgments, forfeiture of assets, revocation of professional licenses, the loss of important rights as citizens, and ostracism. Upping the punishments and raising the degree of risk for white-collar criminals should reduce the incidence of such crimes. A key to fighting health care fraud and abuse—along with other white-collar crimes—is to place the responsibility for these transgressions on the individual perpetrators, not on their organizations.

The third strategy, taking measures to increase the opportunity costs of health care fraud and abuse, is probably the least effective method. Fraud and abuse have become major social problems precisely because of their huge moneymaking potential. Criminals, according to rational-choice theory, are motivated to maximize the benefits of a crime and minimize its costs. Time spent planning, executing, and covering up illegal endeavors takes time away from legal ones. Unfortunately, few lawful opportunities offer the high financial payoffs of health care fraud and abuse.

The Health Care Provider

Most health care fraud and abuse starts with health care providers. Broadly defined, the term "health care provider" encompasses health care executives, hospital administrators and managers, teaching hospital staff and personnel, physicians, nurses, therapists, and ancillary service providers (laboratories, equipment suppliers, medical-imaging firms, transportation companies, consultants), or any other organization or person who participates—or pretends to participate—in the health care system.

Health care providers can be categorized by the extent of their involvement in fraudulent activities and by the damage they cause. I categorize them as follows: small or unintentional violators, deleterious violators, and flagrant violators.

Small or unintentional violators engage in infrequent and small acts of fraud and abuse. Their transgressions are often the result of slipshod and erroneous billings, inattention to detail, or ignorance of an antifraud law.

Deleterious violators lurk below the surface, but the cumulative damage that they inflict on the health care system and on its consumers can be significant. Some providers may violate the law as an expression of contempt for the bureaucratic nuisances created by the "useless" government red tape imposed on them by what they believe to be misdirected legislators and mindless civil servants who—at least in the providers' minds—know nothing about providing quality health care. In addition, physicians and other providers who falsify or upcode insurance claims are not always acting out of greed; rather, they do not want their services to be undervalued and shortchanged by Medicare, Medicaid, or other insurers.

Some deleterious providers want to go the extra mile to ensure an exceedingly thorough level of care for their patients. They go overboard by ordering too many diagnostic tests, prescription drugs, or medical equipment items. But the lines between fraud and abusive overutilization are often blurred. These seemingly pernicious providers are well intentioned, and they place their patients' needs first. Physicians, for example, are aware of the need to proceed with caution when prescribing pain medications. They want to alleviate their patient's suffering, but they fear legal entanglements if their patients abuse the drug, operate a motor vehicle under its influence, or sell the drug to street traffickers. Although such cases are not commonplace, a pain-management physician who operated a clinic in South Carolina received a thirty-year federal prison sentence for drug trafficking. His actions, however, may have been motivated more by his desire to help his patients than by his desire to profit from the purveyance of illegal drugs.[4] Nevertheless, both the deleterious and the small-time offenders assume—often correctly—that their wrongdoing will go undetected.

Flagrant violators steal—or are prepared to steal—hundreds of millions of dollars from the health care system. These individuals often subject their victims to severe physical and psychological trauma, even death. Executives and medical personnel at Tenet and HCA committed numerous illegal and corrupt acts over the course of two decades. The Houston Hospital District came under fire and was the subject of a CBS News investigative report after it was caught double billing private insurers and Medicare. One of the hospital managers told an employee that this practice was "just the way they did it here."[5]

As we have seen, a small percentage of unscrupulous providers are dedicated strongly to their personal financial gain, often to the detriment of patients, health care insurers, investors, and the public. Fraud and corruption seemed to be ingrained in the cultural fabric of these organizations. Crooked pharmacists who dilute or short prescriptions repeatedly, rent-a-patient organizers who prey on the indigent, and pill-mill scam artists who make fraud their full-time job all fall into this category.

Although these offender categories overlap, they call for different kinds and degrees of punishment. The pattern emerging from the cases discussed here is that the offenders who are most likely to see the inside of a prison cell are the imposters who pose as health care providers as well as real providers who are committing fraud or abuse within their own small—usually solo—business or practice. Also, perpetrators such as the Kansas City pharmacist, whose actions directly and recklessly endangered the lives of patients and other consumers, face prison time. But, as we have seen, fraud artists working in large hospital chains and pharmaceutical firms are rarely incarcerated. Perhaps the availability of top-notch legal counsel or the ability of a perpetrator to hide his or her misdeeds within a large and complex corporate structure makes it exceedingly difficult for a jury to determine guilt "beyond a reasonable doubt."

Flagrant offenders who engage in multimillion dollar frauds or frauds resulting in serious injury or death should face lengthy prison sentences. And deleterious offenders should be subject to strong civil monetary penalties and temporary suspension from Medicare, Medicaid, or other federal programs—but not prison time—for a first offense. Both deleterious and small-time offenders should be required to participate in a government-sponsored antifraud educational program. The costs of participating in the program should be borne by the errant provider with the clear understanding that more severe sanctions will be imposed for subsequent violations.

Internal Corporate Compliance Programs

Corporate compliance programs are implemented voluntarily by providers to detect and deter incidents of health care fraud and abuse. These programs are geared toward ensuring compliance with federal and state health care laws and toward decreasing the likelihood of whistle-blower lawsuits. Corporate compliance programs establish guidelines and assign responsibilities for legal and ethical behavior. These programs also require auditing and monitoring activities for federal compliance and taking remedial action when violations occur.[6]

The Department of Health and Human Services has developed a website containing detailed information on corporate compliance programs for eleven kinds of health care entities: hospitals, clinical laboratories, nursing facilities, pharmaceutical manufacturers, ambulance suppliers, physician practices (both individual and group), Medicare Advantage plans (e.g., HMOs), hospices, DME suppliers, third-party billing companies, and home health agencies. Providers interested in a detailed protocol for preventing health care fraud and abuse should consult the HHS website and study carefully the sections pertaining to their institution. A great deal of supplemental advisory information is also available on this site.[7]

The 2004 amendments to the Federal Sentencing Guidelines stipulate that corporate compliance programs should provide for "the exercise of due diligence to prevent and detect criminal conduct" and "the promotion of an organizational culture that encourages ethical conduct and a commitment to compliance with the law." The guidelines set forth seven requirements for corporate compliance programs, covering areas such as performance standards, the selection and responsibility of high-level personnel, training and communication efforts, performance incentives, and disciplinary and remedial actions.[8]

The major risk associated with a corporate compliance program is the danger of generating more—not less—litigation as problems are discovered and as action is taken against the perpetrators. Even though little empirical or anecdotal evidence exists to support the effectiveness of corporate compliance programs, the federal government continues to believe in their efficacy.

The Deprofessionalization of the Health Care Disciplines

The health care professions have traditionally been held in high regard by the public. Professional groups such as the American Medical Association are supposed to develop high standards that are upheld through education, the powers of certification and regulation, and self-monitoring. In theory, all true professionals are expected to place the legitimate interests of clients or patients above all other interests. But some health care providers are uncertain whether they are a professional service with lofty, noneconomic ideals or a business whose mission is to turn a profit.

Part of the discrepancy between the ideal and the real is clients' inability to measure the quality of the services they receive. As a result, patients and clients must trust the judgment of the professional. Furthermore, the services rendered by professionals—especially those working alone or in solo practices—are subject to few double checks. But when provider and patient interests diverge we have a surefire recipe for fraud and abuse.

Professional discretion and autonomy are attractive aspects of health care careers. As long as this discretion and autonomy are exercised through high standards of performance and ethical behaviors, public goodwill for the profession remains high. As public goodwill is enhanced, however, practitioners whose primarily goal is personal gain—not the welfare of their patients or clients—are attracted to the profession. Over time, more and more of these individuals—known as "rent seekers"—enter a profession and create what is known as a "tragedy of the commons." As the public loses faith in the integrity of a professional group, it begins to impose legislation restricting the profession's right to certification and self-regulation. In short, the profession "deprofessionalizes."[9]

The dangers of deprofessionalization should be of major concern to physicians and other health care professionals. Unfortunately, the deprofessionalization process of U.S. health care providers appears to be well under way as witnessed by the proliferation of increasingly restrictive laws and the burgeoning use of antifraud measures by the government and private insurers. The increased oversight of the health care professions also results in costly overregulation that harms honest professionals. The reversal of this unfortunate process will depend heavily on the extent to which the health care professions and professional groups are willing to police their own.

The Health Care Consumer

Educating health care consumers is a frontline defense against health care scam artists and dishonest providers. This educational effort should include helping consumers understand the various forms of fraud and abuse. One of the easiest ways to educate consumers is by making them aware of the tactics employed by phony Medicare or Medicaid representatives and crooked telemarketers. Shysters claiming to represent the Medicare program often gain the confidence of their elderly victims by offering them "free" housekeeping, tests, vitamin supplements, or other health aids. They then use their Medicare number to submit false claims or to commit medical identity theft.

Educating consumers that Medicare does not make cold calls, does not offer free products, and does not provide housekeeping could significantly reduce the number of health care scams. Furthermore, consumers need to be aware of the plethora of quack health remedies that are available through telemarketers and through the Internet. A good example of an educational effort to protect health care consumers is provided by the U.S. Administration on Aging:

> You should be suspicious if a health care provider tells you that:
> - The test is free; he only needs your Medicare number for his records.
> - Medicare wants you to have the item or service.
> - They know how to get Medicare to pay for it.
> - The more tests they provide the cheaper they are.
> - The equipment or service is free; it won't cost you anything.
>
> Be suspicious of providers that:
> - Routinely waive co-payments without checking on your ability to pay.
> - Advertise 'free' consultations to Medicare beneficiaries.
> - Claim they represent Medicare.
> - Use pressure or scare tactics to sell you high priced medical services or diagnostic tests.
> - Bill Medicare for services you do not recall receiving.
> - Use telemarketing and door-to-door selling as marketing tools.
>
> *Never* give your Medicare/Medicaid or Social Security number over the telephone or to people you don't know.

Never allow anyone to convince you to contact your physician requesting a service you don't need.

Never give your Medicare or Medicaid number to anyone for a free service. They don't need your Medicare or Medicaid number if the service is truly free.

Never accept medical supplies or equipment from a door-do-door salesperson. Neither the Federal Government nor Medicare sell supplies or equipment door-to-door.

Never believe anyone who says they are from Medicare or any Federal agency trying to sell you products or services. Neither the Federal Government nor Medicare endorses the products or services of any individual or company.

Always rely on your personal physician to recommend all medical services and equipment for you.

Keep a record of your health care appointments and services.

Read your Medicare Summary Notice (MSN) carefully. Look for:

- Duplicate payments for the same service.
- Dates of service on the MSN that differs from the dates you actually received the service.
- Items or services you do not recall receiving.
- Billings for medical equipment or services that were not ordered by a physician.

Contact your health care provider, supplemental insurance company and/or carrier if you have questions about services listed on your MSN.[10]

Since 1997 the Administration on Aging has funded Senior Medicare Patrol (SMP) programs. Using trained—and often retired and elderly—volunteers, the SMP educates Medicare and Medicaid beneficiaries, family members, and caregivers about fraudulent, abusive, and wasteful health care practices. The SMP program works primarily through senior centers, but the program also uses a variety of media outlets, outreach campaigns, community events, and partnerships with HHS–OIG, CMS, and the U.S. Department of Justice to educate consumers about health care fraud and abuse. In addition, the SMP program helps consumers file complaints relating to the Medicare and Medicaid programs.[11]

The media also plays an important role in educating health care consumers. NBC produced a two-part series on Medicare fraud, exposing the phony DME distributors and rent-a-patient schemes in the Miami area. CBS produced a segment on Tenet Healthcare Corporation that aired on *60 Minutes*. This segment examined the false diagnoses used to entice otherwise healthy patients into undergoing needless open-heart surgeries at Tenet's hospital in Redding, California.

Popular magazines such as the AARP's *Bulletin* and the *Reader's Digest* frequently publish short articles to alert consumers about the latest health care scams. The Administration on Aging has also produced an educational video to inform Medicare beneficiaries about scam artists who go door-to-door peddling nutritional supplements, supposedly at the behest of the federal government. To receive the free supplements, the beneficiary must provide the solicitor with his or her Medicare number. This video also educates consumers about the 299 Medicare scam (described in chapter 3).

Law firms with a clear financial motive have gotten into the act by placing videos on the Internet to educate consumers about the dangers and atrocities of health care fraud. These firms invite parties who suspect frauds against the federal government to call them for a consultation about filing a False Claims Act whistle-blower suit.

Perhaps the most significant measure for preventing health care fraud and abuse is determining whether a patient actually received the health care service or product itemized on his or her health insurance benefit statement or medical billing. Insurers have employed statistical analyses for identifying unusual claims patterns, but the missing ingredient is matching the information on the claim or billing form with the patient's recollection of the services actually rendered. Barring either an honest error—including a patient's lack of awareness about the services or products received—or a fraud, the two should match. Thus, another component of consumer education is to encourage patients to examine carefully their explanation of benefits (EOB) statements. The EOB statement—also known as an explanation of medical benefits statement—lists the health care services and products provided to the patient along with the amounts covered by the patient's insurance plan. It should provide a key that enables the patient to decode the information on the statement, and it should list items such as diagnoses and treatment dates, itemized charges, the amounts covered by the patient's health insurance, and a running summary of deductibles and copayments made by the patient. Inadequate statements can be difficult to decipher, hiding rather than revealing potential health care fraud and abuse.

But getting consumers to patrol fraud and abuse is difficult. Patients are often overwhelmed by an array of health care professionals, workers, treatments, and medications. Sometimes a patient may be asleep or unconscious while being treated. Furthermore, patients often have incomplete knowledge of the services or products they received, especially when they are heavily medicated or disoriented.

And, as noted, health care pricing is based on a seemingly byzantine system that makes it impossible to know when one has been overcharged. According to a study by the credit-rating agency Equifax, over 90 percent of hospital billings contained errors, and most of these errors were overcharges. In Florida and California, the overcharges averaged more than 20 percent of the billing amounts.[12]

Fathoming a bill—particularly if a person is sick or elderly—almost requires a degree in insurance law with a minor in health care economics. And even such educated individuals may find their bills bafflingly complex and nearly impossible to decipher. To complicate matters, patients may have little incentive to question the veracity of the EOB statements when their health insurance plan pays for all or nearly all of the itemized health care services and products.

In 1975 Congress passed the Magnuson-Moss Consumer Product Warranty Act.[13] The law required that warranties must be written in "simple and readily understood language." The Magnuson-Moss law, although not applicable to insurance policies, started a "plain language" movement that was soon adopted by the U.S. insurance industry. That is why you can now understand most of the wording in your life, homeowner, and automobile insurance policies. It does not seem to be much of a stretch—or an unreasonable expectation—for Congress to pass a law that requires plain-language EOB statements. I suggest that these statements include an explanation of each procedure provided to the patient along with the amount charged. In addition, the statement should include information on the average charges for that procedure, drug, or medical supply within the geographical area where it was provided. If I have an appendectomy, for example, it would be helpful for me to know whether I was charged more, less, or about the same as what other providers charge in my locale. A data bank of average regional charges could be established and maintained by a neutral party such as the CMS. Furthermore, the EOB statement should provide a running summary of the patient's deductibles, copayments, and percentage of lifetime benefits used.

Health care consumers must be protected from medical identity theft—a problem that may be easier to address than other kinds of fraud. Patients and their families should be educated regarding the risks of medical identity theft along with the importance of protecting their personal documents and presenting proper identification prior to treatment. In addition, patients lacking photo identification should be willing to be photographed as part of the admissions process. The patient's family should also be asked to verify identifying information, especially if the patient is unable to respond to the queries of admissions personnel.[14]

The Fair Credit Reporting Act directs the Federal Trade Commission and the bank regulatory agencies to issue regulations protecting consumers from identity theft. According to the FTC's Red Flag and Address Discrepancy Rules, financial institutions and other organizations serving as creditors are required to develop identity theft prevention programs.[15] If a hospital, clinic, or other provider allows a patient to make installment payments on an account, then they are regarded by the FTC as a creditor. These regulations have been a source of contention, especially by physicians and attorneys, who do not want to be regarded as creditors—an issue that has led to repeated delays in the effective date of the regulations. Several FTC "red flags" pertain specifically to health care institutions, including:

1. The patient receives bills designated for another individual, bills for products or services not received, or bills from an unknown provider.
2. The patient discovers inconsistencies between his diagnoses or treatments and the information on his medical records.
3. The patient receives unexpected collection agency notices for health care services or products.
4. The patient is denied health insurance coverage because her benefit limits have been exceeded.
5. The patient discovers erroneous credit report information from his health care provider.
6. The patient provides an insurance number (e.g., Medicare number), but never shows an insurance card.[16]

According to the World Privacy Forum, most medical identity theft is the work of insiders such as clerks, nurses, or records personnel who either steal or fail to protect sensitive information. An employee of a South Florida clinic and her cousin were convicted of conspiracy, fraud, and HIPAA violations for stealing patients' names, dates of birth, Social Security numbers, Medicare numbers, and addresses, and then using this information to make more than $2.5 million in fraudulent Medicare claims involving more than 1,100 victims. When the employee exceeded her authorized access limits to the clinic's computer system, the conspiracy began to unravel and an investigation by the FBI ensued.[17]

Checking patient identifications helps to stop fraud by outsiders, but it will not deter insiders who are stealing patient Social Security, insurance, or bank account numbers. Well-intentioned health care providers bent on preventing medical identity theft may be attracted to new technology such as biometrics and digital scans. But collecting and storing more medical information on health care consumers may actually increase the risk of security breaches.[18] According to a European information technology consultant:

> Unfortunately, once a biometric is stored in digital form on a computer, any security offered by the biometric identification is at risk, because it can easily be copied from one computer to another. If an individual's biometric information is compromised or stolen, that individual could no longer use those biometrics to prove his or her identity. Therefore, unless stringent security measures are put in place, the digital storage of biometric data could present a real security risk for facilitating identity theft.[19]

Furthermore, otherwise honest employees may allow unsecured information on laptop computers, flash drives, or other portable data devices to fall into the wrong hands.[20] Computers have been reported stolen from Johns Hopkins University, the regional offices of HCA, and the Allina Hospitals and Clinics (Minnesota). The data breach of celebrity medical records mentioned in chapter 3 initially involved a handful of staff members who had gained illegal access to the medical records of celebrity patients. During 2008 the scandal widened to include some 939 patients and as many as 165 medical center workers.[21]

The HHS has issued new rules required by the Health Information Technology for Economic Clinical Health (HITECH) Act that requires providers to notify individuals if their health information is breached.[22] Under the HITECH Act, the maximum penalty for serious violators has been increased to $1.5 million. Some states have also taken action to safeguard patient privacy. California, for example, has fortified its data breach rules to further protect health care consumers.[23] The California bill provides tougher penalties for patient-privacy breaches and serious medical errors, and it creates an Office of Health Information Integrity with the authority to assess fines of up to $250,000 against hospitals failing to protect confidential patient information.[24] U.S. Congressman Pete Stark (D-Calif.) proposed the Health-e Information Technology Act to enable the federal government to create clear standards for an interoperable health information technology system. The law is designed to improve patient privacy, establish rules for the use of personal medical information, safeguard the security of this information, and hold health care providers responsible for security breaches.[25]

HIPAA, the federal law that is supposed to safeguard the privacy of a patient's medical information, may actually be a hindrance to victims of medical identity theft. According to the *Los Angeles Times*:

> A big reason most people never find out about erroneous records is the Health Insurance Portability and Accountability Act of 1996. The law can make it difficult for patients to see their own medical records, since the penalties for improper disclosure prompt some hospitals to set up roadblocks including demands for multiple forms of identification. The bitter twist on medical identity theft is that once a person tells a keeper of records that someone else's data might be intermingled [with their own], the file becomes even harder to obtain. Why? Because it includes another person's medical history, which many hospitals argue can't be turned over without consent.[26]

Private Health Insurers

The insurance industry is not well regarded by the public. In fact, the National Insurance Fraud Forum believes insurance fraud is precipitated, at least in part, by the public's negative attitude toward the industry.[27] Otherwise honest consumers often condone "soft" frauds—cheating the property insurance company by claiming that hail destroyed an old and crumbling roof—knowing that their dishonesty will go unchallenged or unnoticed. Policyholders may regard insurance premiums as exorbitant, or they may believe insurers will make every effort either to deny their claim or to "slow walk" it as a way of delaying the payment. These elements mark insurance companies as "deserving victims" of fraud.

Antifraud measures taken by insurers have three effects. First, they cost money. Second, they slow claims processing. Third, they do, in fact, detect and reduce fraud. Some private health insurers ignore or deny the severity of health care fraud. When I queried a sales manager of a major private insurer about health insurance fraud, he seemed unsure of its magnitude but did not believe it was a serious threat to his industry. Others are aware of the problem and have put antifraud measures in place, although such measures may be inadequate. Thus, private insurers find themselves in a juggling act of reducing fraud, controlling costs, expediting claims—and making a profit.

As insurance companies try to detect and prevent fraud, fraud perpetrators try to make their claims appear as normal—and as legitimate—as possible. And fraudsters learn from their mistakes; if a claim is rejected, they carefully note the explanations on the claims and then use what they have learned to avoid making the same mistake in the future.[28]

Insurance company special investigation units (SIUs) are supposed to prevent and detect fraud. But SIUs have no standardized methods for assessing the effectiveness of their work. Without baseline data—or at least without an idea of the extent of the problem—health insurers cannot be certain whether their antifraud programs are giving them a good return on their investment. According to a survey by the Coalition Against Insurance Fraud, SIUs focus their efforts primarily on automobile insurance fraud with health insurance fraud having the lowest priority. About the only other clear finding from the survey was that SIUs devote a considerable amount of time to training internal departments about fraud.[29] Thus, fraud prevention—not detection—appears to have the highest priority with SIU managers.

Some insurance companies may be content to take the approach of "anything we do is bound to be an improvement." Other insurers may pay meticulous attention to measuring the effectiveness of their antifraud programs only to be frustrated by a lack of industry standards for judging whether their programs are good, average, or poor. Rather than worrying about the best way to measure the magnitude and scope of health care fraud, insurers may implement antifraud measures, expose enough cases to keep fraud investigators busy, and pass the remaining costs of fraud to consumers in the form of higher premiums. This suboptimal strategy is probably the norm.[30]

Malcolm Sparrow in his classic book *License to Steal* cited an example of this problem. An insurer with an annual claims volume of approximately $2 billion and an estimated $200 million in fraud losses (the 10% fraud estimate described earlier) had an SIU with an $800,000 annual budget. The SIU recovered $2.5 million in fraudulent claims, a wonderful threefold return on its investment. But, as Sparrow pointed out, the effectiveness of the SIU is dismal once one compares its performance against the insurer's $200 million estimate of fraud activity. The company discovered that when the SIU personnel had some spare time, they could do a perfunctory "beating of the bushes" and uncover more than enough fraud activity to stay busy. As Sparrow noted, "The annual budget for their fraud unit ($800,000) represented 0.04 percent of their claims volume. They spend at the 0.04 level to deal with a problem they think might be costing them 10 percent."[31]

By the beginning of the twenty-first century, the vast majority of health care billings were processed either in part or in total by electronic means. In some cases, the billing information is scanned electronically from paper forms. In other cases, the information is processed entirely by computer. So how does the shift from paper to electronic claims processing affect the fight against health care fraud? At first glance, the electronic billing for health care services and products appeared to be a step forward because it eliminated cumbersome paperwork and it expedited the payment of claims. Insofar as fighting health care fraud is concerned, however, electronic billing may have been a step backward.

Electronic billings for health care products and services may be outsourced to physician-management services or to billing agencies. The Internet is full of websites and advertisements by companies offering these services. One billing agency site touting its services compares the supposedly higher expenses of in-house billings—employee training, system- and billing- software updates, billing supplies, postage and claims submissions costs, and office space to name a few—with the supposedly lower expenses of subcontracting the task to an outside firm. But questions about billings become more difficult to resolve as the gap widens between those who provide health care and those who bill for that care. In addition, electronic billing has made the claims and the reimbursement processes vulnerable to computer programming bugs, increasing the chances of both erroneous payments and fraud.

By using processing software, a claim may be received, processed, and paid without any human intervention or oversight.[32] Some claims may be either rejected or checked further only if the software detects an irregularity. Irregularities may include an incorrect data entry, an unauthorized provider or beneficiary, an erroneous diagnostic code or a possible code manipulation, a pricing error, a claim for an uncovered procedure, or evidence of a duplicate claim. If the software program detects no deficiencies, then the claim will be paid, even if it is otherwise bizarre or preposterous.

Furthermore, the codified knowledge of a claims-processing software program is not a good substitute for the intimate knowledge of an experienced human claims processor. Computer software only obeys the commands of the software designer. It is not capable of having "an uneasy feeling" about a claim. Alterations on the claims form, misspelled words, similarities between the handwriting of the patient and the provider, photocopied documents (rather than the original document), a request that the reimbursement check be sent to a post office box rather than to a street address, claims made consistently in whole dollar amounts (no cents), claims made for a large number of prescriptions with no corresponding claims for diagnoses or treatments, and rubber-stamped physician signatures represent danger signals to an experienced health-claims processor.[33]

Finally, electronic billing systems enable perpetrators to file hundreds or even thousands of bogus claims. In the copy-and-paste world of personal computers, fraud perpetrators can submit claims and receive reimbursement checks quickly.

The National Health Care Anti-Fraud Association (NHCAA), a private-public partnership of more than one hundred private insurers and the governmental agencies, investigates health care fraud and abuse cases. The NHCAA Institute for Health Care Fraud Prevention, founded in 2000, is an incorporated, tax-exempt educational foundation that provides training to public- and private-sector antifraud personnel. Its educational activities include the professional development of accredited health care antifraud specialists. The NHCAA is also involved in information sharing with the media and government. In 2008 the NHCAA joined with the Coalition Against Insurance Fraud and the National Insurance Crime Bureau to pool their resources for detecting and preventing health care fraud. This arrangement became known as the Consortium to Combat Medical Fraud. The two associations developed a strategy for sharing information and cross-matching claims and data to uncover fraud schemes.[34] The consortium also includes joint educational and research programs to help health insurers and property casualty insurers better understand each other's fraud detection trends and techniques.

According to Dennis Jay, the consortium's executive director, "Criminals are smart. They leverage cutting-edge technology to probe for the soft under-belly of the health care system. As a result, we need to modernize our approach to combating them." Gary Healy, director of operations for the Mid-Atlantic, National Insurance Crime Bureau, added, "By unleashing this group's collective resources against both organized crime as well as individual perpetrators, the Consortium will intensify the battle against fraud in our insurance system."[35]

The Biggest Players of All: Federal and State Governments

Federal and state governments enact and enforce laws and educate consumers and providers about health care fraud and abuse. With the assistance of state governments, the federal government administers the huge public health insurance programs. Acting in concert, federal and state governments are the major players in fighting health care fraud.

No New Legislation, Just Fewer Big-Dollar Settlements and More Prison Time

Politicians and government officials are already convinced of the seriousness of health care fraud and abuse, and they have responded by enacting the legislation described in chapters 1 and 2. Each state also has laws for fighting health care fraud and abuse. Taken together, this patchwork quilt of legislation has generated an abundant crop of cases for prosecutors. Although the existing federal and state legislation may require periodic adjusting and tweaking, passing additional antifraud laws will complicate and, perhaps, hinder enforcement efforts to fight health care fraud and abuse.

Plato's *Republic* dealt with the overarching question: What is justice? Although Plato obviously did not address health care fraud, the *Republic* did describe the dangers of too much legislation:

> It isn't appropriate to dictate to men who are fine and good. They'll easily find out for themselves whatever needs to be legislated about such things.…If not, they'll spend their lives enacting a lot of other laws and then amending them, believing that in this way they'll attain the best…for such people are surely the most amusing of all. They pass laws on the subjects we've just been enumerating and then amend them, and they always think that they'll find a way to put a stop to cheating on contracts and the other things I mentioned, not realizing that they're really just cutting off a Hydra's head.[36]

The Hydra was a mythical monster—when one head was severed, two or more grew in its place. This metaphor also points to the dangers of imposing another layer of regulation on the health care industry. As law school professor Arti K. Rai has noted: "Because fraud prosecution is a very blunt—and even destructive—tool for addressing cost and quality concerns, prosecutions should probably be limited to intentional deceitful behavior (for example, situations in which institutions bill for services that were never provided)."[37]

The Sarbanes-Oxley Act has made it more difficult for top executives to sidestep responsibility for corporate accounting and financial fraud by requiring the CEO and CFO to attest to the truthfulness and accuracy of corporate financial statements. Perhaps it is time to demand the same degree of accountability from executives whose companies are engaged in widespread health care fraud and abuse. Although corrupt health care providers and others cheating the system dislike paying large civil monetary penalties or having their reputations scarred, they will probably dislike serving time in prison even more. Executive-level health care professionals and prominent physicians should be on notice that they are not immune from lengthy prison sentences if they commit multimillion dollar frauds—or any fraud that endangers patients' lives.

At this writing, a bipartisan bill known as the Medicare Fraud Enforcement and Prevention Act has been introduced by Capitol Hill lawmakers, led by Representative Ron Klein (D-Florida). The Act would double prison sentences and fines for Medicare fraud. It would also create a new offense, and up to three years in prison and fines, for illegally distributing Medicare or Medicaid beneficiary ID or billing privileges. In addition, the proposed act calls for more preventive and oversight measures for Medicare contractors.[38]

The federal government will continue prosecuting the high-profile hospital chains and pharmaceutical firms because these cases offer federal agencies favorable media publicity and huge settlements for government coffers.[39] But federal and state prosecutors should rethink whether the interests of the public are best served by gargantuan settlements and tough corporate integrity agreements. And even when hit with settlements approaching or exceeding $1 billion, the large hospital chains and pharmaceutical companies have not always been deterred from further malfeasance. Tenet, HCA, and Schering-Plough went through periods when the management of these corporations appeared to be incorrigible. Neither huge settlements nor heavy-handed corporate integrity agreements seemed to change their corrupt ways of doing business.

Civil monetary penalties extracted from high-profile cases are like flood waters seeping into the wrong places. If one community builds a flood wall, the water is diverted to an unprotected location. The same analogy may apply to large health care settlements that force consumers to bear the brunt of higher charges for hospitalization, pharmaceuticals, and health care insurance. As prosecuted health care providers quietly raise their prices over a period of several years to offset their settlement losses, providers not prosecuted may seize the opportunity to raise their prices as well. Because of payment limits, Medicare, Medicaid, and TRICARE patients are less apt to suffer from price increases. But at least some of these costs may then be shifted to private-program patients and to their insurers. This dilemma provides yet another example of why big-dollar fraudsters should be put behind bars.

One has to suspect strongly that the huge out-of-court settlements imposed on pharmaceutical companies have contributed to higher drug prices. Pharmaceuticals, especially specialty drugs used to treat conditions such as multiple sclerosis, cancer, and arthritis, often come with over-the-top price tags, forcing many patients to choose between spending their money on drugs or basic necessities. "The largest factor in producing any drug is what the market will bear," says health care analyst Steve Findlay of the Consumers Union. "The industry approach is to price drugs as high as possible and see if the world is willing to go along with that." According to Leonard Saltz, an oncologist at Sloan-Kettering Cancer Center in New York: "Insurance may pay 80 percent of your drug bill, but if a drug costs $10,000 every two weeks, as some cancer drugs do, the patient is left with a huge bill—one that most Americans can't afford."[40]

So here is the critical dilemma: the government's attempt to fight health care fraud and abuse by imposing large civil monetary penalties on violators may be harming the very people it is trying to protect—health care consumers.

And here is the potential solution: rather than imposing huge financial settlements on hospital chains, pharmaceutical manufacturers, and medical equipment firms, prison sentences should be imposed on the people who mastermind the major health care frauds. And the organizations profiting from these crimes should foot the bill for their incarceration.

Prison sentences punish the actual culprits rather than the innocent bystanders—the consumers, insurers, investors, taxpayers, and honest providers. Perhaps prosecutors and judges handling health care fraud and abuse cases should take a cue from the lengthy prison terms meted out to the prominent CEOs and executives at Enron, WorldCom, Adelphia, Tyco, and HealthSouth.

Prison serves several functions. The prospect of a prison sentence serves as a deterrent to crime. Contrary to public perception, even minimum-security federal prisons—the so-called Club Feds—are highly regimented and largely joyless places. Most health care professionals—especially prominent executives, medical school professors, and physicians—covet their financial independence and their status in the community. They are accustomed to the material luxuries of life, to coming and going as they please, and to having others at their beck and call. To trade this existence for one of wearing prison garb, eating bland institutional food, sleeping in an open dormitory, and having their every activity monitored by a federal corrections officer is not a pleasant prospect.

Prison sentences can be viewed as a form of retribution. Health care consumers and the general public may obtain a dark sense of satisfaction from knowing that executives who have bilked the system out of millions of dollars have been locked away, perhaps drawing a brutish street criminal as a cell mate.

Health care executives and providers forced to spend time behind bars have severe restrictions imposed on their freedom. Limitations on visiting privileges, bans on cellular telephones, and prohibitions on Internet usage severely restrict inmate access to the world beyond the prison compound. Incarcerated white-collar criminals may discover that their former business associates want little to do with them—either during the time they are behind bars or after they are released.

Finally, prisons are supposed to rehabilitate inmates, a point of little relevance here since few white-collar criminals recidivate and return to prison. But the prospect of prison time for errant executives and physicians from large firms may put an end to the high-profile cases with megasettlements.[41] Furthermore, a shift from civil to criminal charges will send a stern warning to other scam artists who view the health care system as a lucrative hunting ground.

The Critical Role of the Centers for Medicare and Medicaid Services

As the largest purchaser of health care in the United States, the CMS plays a critical role in reducing fraud and abuse. In 2007 the CMS served over 92 million Medicare, Medicaid, and State Children's Health Insurance Program beneficiaries. The CMS annually oversees the processing of over one billion fee-for-service claims and payments through contracts with private entities.

According to the congressional testimony of the CMS chief financial officer Timothy B. Hill, even small payment errors can have a huge impact on Medicare, Medicaid, and SCHIP expenditures. Between 2000 and 2007, Medicare paid more than $70 million in bogus claims for durable medical equipment based just on the fraudulent use of the personal identification numbers of *deceased* physicians. Despite the large absolute amount of these frauds, the $70 million loss represents only a miniscule fraction of 1 percent of Medicare expenditures during this time frame.[42] Yet, this and other insidious threats can infect the entire Medicare program.

Hill cited the CMS's four-pronged approach to reducing fraud and payment errors: prevention (e.g., educating providers and identifying problems before a claim is paid); early detection (e.g., using data analysis, audits, and postclaims reviews to detect fraud); coordination (e.g., working with contractors, beneficiaries, and state agencies); and enforcement (e.g., coordinating antifraud efforts with the Department of Justice and the HHS–OIG). In line with the second objective, the CMS has initiated Medicare-Medicaid data-matching programs in selected states. Although data mining to detect health care fraud is not a new practice, jointly analyzing Medicare and Medicaid claims has enabled the CMS to discover new patterns of fraud. In line with the third objective, the CMS has established a nationwide network of program-safeguard contractors to perform fraud-detection data analyses, identify vulnerable points in the payment system, investigate fraud cases, and work with federal law enforcement agencies to prosecute those involved in health care fraud and abuse.

The CMS uses both prepayment and postpayment review programs. A May 2008 report, "The Improper Medicare Fee-for-Service Payments Report," indicated that 3.7 percent or $10.2 billion in Medicare reimbursements did not comply with one or more Medicare coverage, coding, billing, or payment rule.[43] The CMS now uses a combination of five payment-review programs. The National

Correct Coding Initiatives (NCCI) Edits and the Medically Unlikely Edits (MUE) are prepayment review programs. The Comprehensive Error Rate Testing (CERT) Program and the expanding Recovery Audit Contractor (RAC) program are post-payment review programs. The Medical Review (MR) program is both a pre- and postpayment review program.

The National Correct Coding Initiative controls improper coding and payment errors and the Medically Unlikely Edits reduces fee-for-service errors for Medicare Part B claims. The purpose of the MUE project is to detect questionable Medicare claims, to stop inappropriate payments, and to improve the accuracy of Medicare payments.

Postpayment reviews use statistical sampling methods to estimate over- and underpayments of Medicare claims. The Comprehensive Error Rate Testing program monitors the accuracy of Medicare fee-for-service payments by using contractors to identify services experiencing high error rates. The Recovery Audit Contractor initiative was used initially in Florida, New York, and California, all high-risk states for Medicare fraud. Because the RACs identified more than $300 million in improper payments, recovering $68.6 million in overpayments from errant providers, the program was expanded to other states. In a related move, the CMS has opened satellite offices in New York City, Los Angeles, and Miami to reinforce fraud-detection efforts in areas where fraud is especially prevalent. In California alone, CMS identified over $2.1 billion in improper payments during 2005 and 2006. The RAC program was scheduled to be up and running in all fifty U.S. states by 2010. Given the massive amounts of fraud described in the opening paragraphs of this chapter, the RAC program—if expanded and funded generously—has the potential to make a major dent in the Medicare fraud problem.

The Medical Review program keeps tabs on providers having a history of billing irregularities. Those submitting erroneous billings may be placed on prepayment review until their billings are deemed once again to be satisfactory by the CMS.[44]

The CMS has emphasized reducing payment-error rates. Specifically, the CMS set an error-rate goal of 7.9 percent in 2005, and the actual rate was 5.2 percent. Similarly, the target rates for 2006 and 2007 were 5.1 percent and 4.3 percent, and the actual rates were 4.4 percent in 2006 and 4.2 percent in 2007.[45] Although decreasing error rates and exceeding performance expectations are laudable, these rates—when compared to those in banks and credit card companies—are still unacceptably high. Furthermore, a reading of the various CMS policies and documents creates the impression that the CMS is going to view incorrect billings as mistakes rather than as forms of fraud.

So what should the CMS do next? As suggested earlier, the CMS should insist on the adoption of a standardized, user-friendly EOM statement for all health care and insurance transactions. And the EOM should list the average cost for a particular treatment in a particular locale so that consumers can benchmark their statement amounts with the amounts charged by other providers. The CMS should also pay close attention to the fraud-detection methods of private financial institutions such as credit card companies. These private firms have a strong incentive to promote fraud detection because fraud diminishes bottom-line profits.

Unfortunately, government agencies do not seem to be as cost conscious as their private counterparts. The sense of urgency behind the government's objective of "staying within budget" is not as compelling as the private sector's objective of "maximizing profits." The CMS has, for example, stepped up its scrutiny of poorly performing nursing homes. But only 136 out of the 16,000 nursing homes throughout the United States have been identified as "special focus facilities." Although the Government Accounting Office recommended that the number of special focused facilities should be subject to more frequent inspections, we hear the usual government agency excuse that "we agree with the idea, but we don't have the resources to accomplish it."

The CMS should also warn providers that detecting fraud and punishing the perpetrators are major priorities, and that no transaction and no provider is immune from scrutiny. But again, the nursing home inspection problem illustrates how government bureaucrats prefer clever analysis and argument over action. In this case, the analyses and arguments center on the "proper methodology" for identifying the worst nursing homes.[46] And, in the meantime, little is done to protect vulnerable nursing home patients.

Additional Statistical Antifraud Measures

Traditionally, antifraud statistical procedures have been retrospective. That is, they have used rules-based data mining to look for potentially fraudulent claims payments—a doctor writes a high volume of prescriptions but has few patient consultations; an ambulance company submits excessive billings for services to clinics that rarely treat seriously ill patients or medical emergencies; or a surgeon in a small Texas town performs an abnormally high number of appendectomies.

Known as the "pay-and-chase" method, the outlier claims discovered retrospectively are sent to an investigative unit where, if errors or frauds are detected, attempts are made to recoup the funds paid. Retrospective methods are effective at detecting known kinds of fraud, but they are ineffective at detecting new and emerging frauds. For example, by analyzing the $2 billion spent by Medicare on 17 million ultrasound services in ambulatory settings during 2007, the OIG discovered a suspicious pattern of activity in twenty U.S. counties. Despite having only 6 percent of the country's Medicare beneficiaries, these twenty counties accounted for 16 percent of all Medicare spending on ultrasound services. The

OIG stopped short of saying that this unusual claims pattern was the result of fraud—it could be that doctors in these locales were practicing a more defensive brand of medicine.[47] But, at least in some cases, analyzing patterns such as these can potentially save millions of dollars in bogus claims.

The prospective approach uses pattern-matching techniques to compare a claim submitted by a provider with claims submitted by the provider's peer group. If fraud is suspected, the claim may be rejected and the payment withheld. As with the retrospective procedures, the prospective procedure depends heavily on the investigator's knowledge of current fraud patterns, and it may not catch fraudulent claims disguised to look like normal claims.

The newest approach, the preventive method, uses statistical techniques to uncover subtle patterns of fraud. This method has been adopted by credit card companies, but it is not yet used extensively in the health care industry.[48] SAS, a vendor of business analytics software and services, has developed a predictive modeling technique to detect emerging fraud schemes and to manage the investigation of these schemes. The company claims the process continually improves the detection of fraud. It cites Highmark, a Blue Cross Blue Shield affiliate in Pennsylvania, as a user of its predictive analytics. Highmark built a model from huge stores of claims, customer data, and provider data. According to SAS, the model "uncovers and prevents costly claims—to the tune of $11.5 million."[49]

It should be remembered that an extremely high percentage of health care transactions and insurance claims are legitimate. A perfect fraud detection system is one that correctly labels legitimate transactions as legitimate and fraudulent transactions as fraudulent. Of course, no system is perfect. One mistake—mislabeling fraudulent transactions as legitimate transactions—may be the result of new frauds that are not yet identifiable by current statistical methods. A second mistake—labeling legitimate transactions as fraudulent—also imposes costs. Accusing an innocent provider or consumer of wrongdoing creates possible litigation costs, loss of customer goodwill, and bad publicity. Finally, systems detecting fraud cases correctly also incur costs as the public or private insurer tries to recoup reimbursements made for false claims, pursues criminal charges against the offender, or absorbs the loss.

Because the health care system generates millions of transactions, the data sets for claims and claim payments are overwhelmingly large. Fraud analysts must integrate and standardize the various data sets and contend with a host of statistical issues, including a large number of irrelevant variables, mixed-variable categories, unbalanced class sizes, and mislabeled classes of variables. Due to the confidentiality of personal health care information, consumer privacy and security must also be monitored. Jing Li and colleagues discuss the importance of meticulous data preprocessing, a stage that can consume approximately 80 percent of the total time for fraud detection. Preprocessing includes determining what kinds of fraud should receive the most attention, "cleaning" the data to ensure consistency and uniformity from one data source to another, and auditing the data to detect nonlinear relationships, clustering patterns, and statistical anomalies.[50]

Once the time-consuming data preprocessing stage has been completed, the selected statistical analysis method is implemented. No "best" statistical method exists for fraud detection. Rather, the effectiveness of each method depends on the data being analyzed and the purpose of the analysis.

A popular statistical application for detecting health care fraud and abuse are neural networks. Neural networks can handle a complex data structure, but the method is plagued by "over-fitting," with error rates increasing as new data are added. Furthermore, neural networks are not well suited to handle a data set skewed heavily by the large number of legitimate health insurance claims.

Another antifraud statistical tool is the decision tree. Decision trees generate rules and enable fraud investigators to focus on claims where fraud is most likely to occur.

Other statistical methods employed to detect health care fraud are the Electronic Fraud Detection system, SmartSifter, and various hybrid methods. The Electronic Fraud Detection system compares the claims of a single health care provider with the claims of the provider's peer group to detect suspicious activity. Similarly, SmartSifter uses continuously revised probability estimates to identify health care providers whose claim submissions are outliers, a possible indication of fraud.[51]

Antifraud techniques must be able to adapt not only to the changing strategies of fraud artists, but also to the changing marketing strategies and clientele of health insurance companies. Furthermore, these measures must detect fraudulent patterns quickly so that losses can be kept to a minimum.[52]

Experienced fraud analysts recognize that some incidents of fraud occur in clusters when perpetrators strike quickly and submit hundreds of phony insurance claims within a few days. Other frauds are either isolated or occur in small, steady amounts over weeks or months. Fraud perpetrators, of course, adapt their strategies based on their knowledge of current fraud-detection systems. Even with the help of sophisticated statistical tools, detecting health care fraud can be a bigger challenge than finding the proverbial needle in a haystack. Haystacks are small in size and do not move. Detecting health care fraud might, instead, be compared to searching for thousands of needles in a fast-flowing river with murky waters.

Investigating and Prosecuting Health Care Fraud and Abuse Cases

Persons accused of health care fraud may become embroiled simultaneously in both criminal and civil cases. A fraud case may involve more than a dozen federal or state statutes, spanning multiple jurisdictions. Prosecutors and defense counsel must be prepared to sort through a confusing mass of evidence, including financial documents, audit reports, statistical analyses, patient records, billings, insurance claims, cancelled reimbursement checks, computers and computer files, and statements from witnesses. Some cases also use evidence such as video surveillance, tape recordings, wiretaps, and even items taken from trash receptacles.

Defendants may not know they are the target of an investigation until they receive either a subpoena from a grand jury or an order from the Inspector General instructing them to hand over documents or other evidence. Once a subpoena is served (or is expected to be served), the defendants must ensure that all documents and other evidence are protected. Persons familiar with the Enron–Arthur Andersen debacle know the dire consequences of destroying documents to hide evidence from prosecutors.

In other cases, the accused parties may not be aware of trouble until law enforcement arrives with a search warrant. Search warrants are based on the "probable cause" that criminal acts have taken place. These warrants, which are issued by a court, specify—often in detail—what investigators are allowed to do when examining and seizing evidence. This strictness can pose a problem in health care cases. Cases of multiple frauds involving potentially dozens of providers and insurers, and possibly thousands of patients, may require the collection of large amounts of evidence that are scattered across a variety of locations—hospitals, clinics, laboratories, and insurance-claims processing centers.[53]

Health care is a document-laden industry, and these documents are often stored electronically. The investigation of white-collar crimes has raised novel legal issues under the Fourth Amendment about the search and seizure of computers and computer files.

> How does the Fourth Amendment apply to the search and seizure of computer data? The Fourth Amendment was created to regulate entering homes and seizing physical evidence, but its prohibition of unreasonable searches and seizures is now being called on to regulate a very different process: retrieval of digital evidence from electronic storage devices. Although obvious analogies exist between searching physical spaces and searching computers, important differences between them will force courts to rethink the key concepts of the Fourth Amendment. What does it mean to "search" computer data? When is computer data "seized"? When is a computer search or seizure "reasonable"?[54]

As is the case with most legal proceedings, defendants in health care fraud cases are protected by attorney-client privilege unless the communications between them will further the commission of a crime (the crime-fraud exception). The statements of witnesses, even when made under oath, can be contradictory, self-serving, and difficult to comprehend. The testimony of whistle-blowers—including those who may not have "clean hands"—is also critical. A whistle-blower who has a tarnished reputation and who stands to receive a substantial reward under the False Claims Act may have little credibility in the eyes of a jury.[55]

Health care fraud investigators must also walk a fine line between obtaining enough evidence to build a case against the defendants in a fraud trial and safeguarding the privacy rights of health care consumers. The seizure of patient medical records and billing documents also imposes an inconvenience on providers who want to continue treating patients during the investigation.

Health care statutes enacted by Congress are written in general language. The regulations associated with these statutes are drafted under the direction of the Secretary of HHS and other agency heads. Medicare manuals, bulletins, fraud alerts, and informal advisory opinions promulgated by federal agencies are supposed to give practical guidance to health care providers and their administrative personnel. Sometimes, however, the volume and detail of these documents can obfuscate rather than clarify. The Medicare 50/50 rule, which regulates the billings for laboratory tests for end-stage renal disease, is a good example of a government policy that is nearly incomprehensible.[56] The interpretation of a regulation may also change over time. A practice such as charging Medicare for certain advertising and marketing costs was deemed acceptable several years ago. Health care providers claiming such costs today, however, may be subject to prosecution for fraud. For these reasons, prosecuting or defending health care fraud and abuse cases requires attorneys with highly specialized knowledge.

Many federal criminal cases never go to trial, ending instead with a guilty plea and plea bargaining. For cases that proceed to trial, the prosecutor tries to develop a theory of the case that is consistent with the evidence. Prosecutors also want to keep the case simple, emphasizing to the jury the big picture of the defendant's fraudulent behavior and not getting bogged down in detailed testimony about intricate medical procedures, complex billing processes, or dense regulatory requirements.

Defense attorneys may employ a dozen or more strategies to convince a jury of their client's innocence or, at least, of their client's minimal culpability. A glaringly obvious defense is to claim that the fraud did not occur. This strategy was used—quite unsuccessfully—by defense attorneys in the trial of former Enron executives Kenneth Lay and Jeffrey Skilling.

If the defense counsel concedes that the fraud did indeed occur, then they may argue that their client was unaware of it. They may, for example, blame the provider's billing service for failing to follow proper procedures. Or they may contend that the billing software contained bugs. Or blame may be placed at the feet of pharmacists, medical laboratories, or other providers. If the defendant claims—or feigns—ignorance of the fraud, prosecutors may attack the defendant for being negligent or for deliberately ignoring the fraudulent practices through "conscious avoidance" or "willful blindness."

A common defense in fraud trials is for the defendant to claim that the applicable federal or state regulations were confusing and ambiguous—"Try as I might, I couldn't understand the intent or meaning of the law." Such a defense might be reasonable in cases involving inadvertent and infrequent billing errors, but it is usually not a tenable defense for the criminal cases that typically find their way into the federal courts. In these cases, the perpetrators are usually guilty of completely ignoring the law. Whether the law was clear or not clear probably made little difference. Only someone who lives in a fantasy world believes that it is okay to submit bills to Medicare for services not provided or to orchestrate a pill-mill scheme or to seek reimbursement for undelivered durable medical equipment.

Similarly, a defendant may argue that his or her interpretation of a federal or state regulation was reasonable, even though it differed significantly from the interpretation of government prosecutors—"I thought I understood the law, but apparently the government disagrees with my view." The defense may call a regulatory expert witness to testify to the ambiguity of the regulation in question. It is then up to the prosecution to demonstrate that the defendant's interpretation of the rules was not reasonable. According to Loucks and Lam, however:

> It is not fair to charge defendants with violating rules that regulators cannot adequately or consistently define. However, it is unjust for a defendant who has identified a billing weakness—sometimes premised on poorly drafted reimbursement rules—and thereafter steals money from a government health care program through deceptive and fraudulent conduct to evade prosecution simply because a governing regulation happens to have ambiguities. Nor is it fair to allow a defendant who has willfully submitted false information to a regulatory agency to gain an economic advantage . . . by using conflicting viewpoints regarding the materiality of information that should be submitted as a tool for evading criminal responsibility.[57]

Defense counsel may contest the testimony of the prosecution's expert witnesses. Expert witnesses are retained because of their specialized knowledge or experience. Under the Federal Rules of Evidence, the judge determines whether an expert is qualified to testify and whether the expert's testimony should be admitted into evidence. Expert witnesses can offer their opinions on matters relevant to the case. These opinions might include the legitimacy of medical treatments, the propriety of billing procedures, or the interpretation of a regulatory matter. Since expert witnesses are paid by the side they are representing, opposing counsel may accuse them of being biased—especially in complex cases where the issues are ambiguous. Although the practice of medicine is viewed as a science, the treatment regimes of patients with nearly identical diagnoses can vary from one provider to another. Not surprisingly, arguments about the propriety and risks of a specific treatment plan may turn into a battle among expert witnesses.

Other (nonexpert) witnesses must confine their testimony to the veracity of relevant facts. Defense attorneys may attack these witnesses because their knowledge of the case facts is inadequate or because their testimony is biased or self-serving. Federal regulators, for example, have a vested interest in promoting the guilt of persons charged with defrauding the government. Similarly, perpetrators involved in plea bargains may fashion their testimony in ways that implicate other defendants and—at the same time—please government prosecutors.

Counsel may argue that the alleged fraudulent act is actually a standard industry practice. This argument is akin to the frequent rationalization of white-collar criminals that "everyone does it." A closer examination of the case facts, however, usually reveals that the fraudulent activities were anything but commonplace.

When statistical evidence is presented by the prosecution, fraud patterns may be discerned by analyzing an entire data set (e.g., all active patient records and billings for the previous three years) or by analyzing random samples of the data. In the latter case, the sample is analyzed and inferences are made about the larger, unanalyzed set of billings. Attacks on the prosecution's statistical evidence may be made on the grounds that the sample size is too small, that the sample does not represent a true cross section of the provider's billings, or that unwarranted inferences were made from the sample data. If prosecutors use summary charts to make it easier for jurors to understand the analyses, the defense counsel may counter by claiming that the charts are too simple and misleading, that they fail to capture the complexity of the data, or that they are based on evidence ruled earlier to be inadmissible.

Defense counsel may accuse the prosecution of making a mountain out of a molehill either by inferring that the defendant engaged in widespread acts of fraud based only on a few isolated incidents or by claiming the government has ignored similar or more serious frauds by other providers. The counsel's objective here is to suggest that prosecutors either "have it out" for the defendant or that they are serving him or her up as a sacrificial lamb. This defense strategy attempts to portray the defendant as a victim rather than a perpetrator.

Defense attorneys may invoke the "happy patient" defense by soliciting testimony from former and current patients who are willing to praise the competent and caring ways of their physician or therapist. A patient may take the witness stand and strongly support her physician even if she suspects that he has committed fraud, especially if the fraud is against a faceless public or private insurer. Another patient, fiercely loyal to his therapist, is not going to provide damning testimony against the very person who has given him such wonderful care over the years.

Finally, counsel may claim the government had approved of the provider's conduct. Rather than denying the charges, a health care provider may contend he or she had no criminal intent because the government expressed or implied that the conduct in question was legal. If a doctor has submitted hundreds of upcoded claims to Medicare over a five-year period, he might argue that the government's payment of these claims was tacit approval that upcoding was an acceptable practice.[58]

These common defenses illustrate two important points. First, health care fraud cases are complex and, second, these cases are often highly contentious. Not only do the defendants want to avoid a large fine or possible incarceration, they also want to protect their personal and professional reputations. If a case goes to trial, it can drag on for weeks or months as potentially thousands of pieces of evidence—computer files, medical records, timelines, video-surveillance tapes, and testimony—are presented and discussed. Both the defendants and their legal counsels are often extremely intelligent. And they will not roll over meekly. Professional persons accused of fraud are far from indigent, and they can employ top-flight counsel at the first sign of trouble—usually well before they are served with a search warrant, summons, or indictment. By settling on the courthouse steps, most defendants avoid prison time even though they—or, more accurately, their corporations—face huge monetary judgments. If a criminal trial ensues, however, the defenses described above will probably be used to the fullest extent. So, the combination of a high-powered legal team and a defendant who can assist ably in his or her defense becomes a formidable opponent for government prosecutors who must demonstrate beyond a reasonable doubt that criminal conduct occurred.

But the skill of government prosecutors must not be underestimated. The government has few financial limits when it comes to prosecuting a major offender—if the government wants to obtain a conviction, it has the financial wherewithal to pull all the stops to nail a major offender. Also, government investigators and prosecutors learn from their successes and failures in health care fraud cases. With experience, they have become more skilled at obtaining, organizing, presenting, or refuting complex evidence, and they have become better able to overcome the tactics of defense counsel.[59]

A Note on the Federal Sentencing Guidelines

A theme of this book is that the federal government should impose criminal sanctions, when possible, on those convicted of flagrant or repeated health care frauds. Persons and organizations convicted of criminal offenses under federal law are subject to the penalties set forth by the Federal Sentencing Guidelines.[60]

The Federal Sentencing Guidelines—with emphasis on the word "guidelines" since judges have flexibility in passing sentence—are an array of sentencing rules with penalties (expressed in months of time served) based on the seriousness of the crime and on the offender's criminal history. The guidelines contain forty-three levels of offenses with overlapping sentence ranges. An increase of six levels roughly doubles the length of a sentence. An act of fraud or deceit is a level 6 offense. Money laundering is a level 8 offense. Antitrust violations are level 12 offenses, whereas obstruction of justice is a level 14 offense. White-collar crimes, including health care fraud, usually involve multiple offenses—maybe wire fraud, conspiracy, lying to investigators, plus, of course, the fraud itself. The sentencing judge adds the offenses, taking into account aggravating and mitigating circumstances, to determine the final sentence level. In extreme cases, the tally may exceed the maximum possible level of forty-three.

Sentencing Individual Defendants

Because the personal and professional stakes for the defendant are high, sentencing hearings in health care fraud cases can be highly argumentative. On receiving a guilty plea by the defendant or on the rendering of a guilty verdict by a jury, the federal court schedules a sentencing hearing, usually two to three months after the completion of the trial. Between the trial and the sentencing, a probation officer conducts a presentence investigation and prepares a presentencing report. Both the prosecutors and the defendant are given the opportunity to provide information for inclusion in the report on matters pertaining to the seriousness of the crime and its impact on the victims.

The genesis of the sentencing guidelines, the Sentencing Reform Act of 1984 (Title II of the Comprehensive Crime Control Act of 1984), called for the development of guidelines to ensure honesty, uniformity, and proportionality in federal criminal sentencing. Honesty refers to the abolition of parole, and it requires an offender sentenced by a federal court to serve his or her full sentence, less approximately 15 percent for good behavior—thus, a person sentenced to 120 months can expect to stay behind bars for at least eight and half years. Uniformity in sentencing refers to reducing disparities among criminal sentences for similar offenses. A person engaging in a $5 million health care scam in Massachusetts should expect to receive a sentence similar to the one received by a person committing a similar $5 million scam in Oregon. Proportionality refers to sentences that reflect the seriousness of the crime. A person who defrauds Medicaid out of $50 million can expect to receive a stiffer sentence than one who defrauds Medicaid out of $5 million, although the sentence of the former offender will not be ten times that of the latter.

Health care fraud is primarily a financial crime. The guidelines contain a table of monetary losses with associated offense levels. A fraud, for example, that results in a $1 million loss results in an increase of sixteen levels, whereas one that causes a $400 million loss (the maximum loss depicted on the table in the guidelines) results in an increase of thirty levels. Two levels are added to the offense if the loss involved 10 to 49 victims, and six levels are added for a loss involving more than 250 victims.

A complicating aspect of health care fraud sentencing is determining the amount of economic damage that can be attributed to a defendant. In general, larger damages or losses lead to longer sentences. The government bears the burden of proving the amount of the loss, although losses need not be determined precisely. Furthermore, the methods for calculating economic losses in fraud cases are not standardized. Government prosecutors favor methods that yield higher loss estimates, whereas defense counsels favor methods that yield lower estimates.

In the most straightforward situation, a defendant who defrauds an insurance company out of $1 million has created a $1 million loss. Most cases, however, are not that simple. The courts have sentenced defendants based on the amounts they have fraudulently billed—the intended loss—and not on the smaller amounts that the defendants actually collected from the victims. Refunds made by the defendant to the victim after the defendant has been charged with a fraud do not reduce the intended loss estimates. But defendants who make refunds before the fraud is detected may be allowed to deduct this amount from the intended losses.

The courts may also reduce intended losses by the value of the defendant's legitimate services to the victim. Victims who obtained health care services from an unlicensed provider posing as a licensed professional, however, are usually viewed by the courts as having suffered a total loss even if the services were of some medical value. Similarly, patients who purchased adulterated health care products or products not approved by the FDA usually have their losses measured in terms of the price paid for the products, regardless of whether the products helped them.

In some cases, the losses may be less direct and more difficult to assess. The losses created by illegal kickbacks are often measured by adding the amounts of all kickback payments made. This calculus, however, does not account for indirect losses suffered by patients who might have received inadequate or poor quality care as the result of the kickbacks. Losses from widespread frauds involving hundreds or thousands of patients over a long period of time are also difficult to measure. Suppose a provider has routinely submitted thousands of false Medicare claims but has also provided care of some value to hundreds of patients over the past decade. Determining the exact amount of the losses would entail a tedious and expensive claim-by-claim analysis for each patient—a nearly impossible task. In such a case, estimates of the total losses might be made using statistical methods of inference. But, of course, these methods are subject to challenge by defense counsel at the sentencing hearing.

When determining the sentence to be served, the sentencing guidelines expect judges to consider the defendant's criminal history.

> A defendant with a record of prior criminal behavior is more culpable than a first offender and thus deserving of greater punishment. General deterrence of criminal conduct dictates that a clear message be sent to society that repeated criminal behavior will aggravate the need for punishment with each recurrence. To protect the public from further crimes of the particular defendant, the likelihood of recidivism and future criminal behavior must be considered. Repeated criminal behavior is an indicator of a limited likelihood of successful rehabilitation.[61]

The guidelines contain six levels of criminal history with points assigned for prior offenses. Offenders with no criminal history are assigned to category 1, and offenders with extensive criminal histories are assigned to category 6. For a level 6 offense such as fraud, a habitual criminal would receive a sentence two to three times the length of one received by a first offender. Certain crimes are exempt from the offender point system, but career criminals and criminals participating in a pattern of crime for a livelihood are placed in a higher offender category.

What about aggravating or mitigating circumstances? If the defendant was an organizer or leader of a criminal activity involving five or more participants—an aggravating circumstance—the seriousness of the crime may be increased by four levels. If the defendant was only a minor participant in the crime—a mitigating circumstance—the seriousness of the crime may be decreased by four levels. Furthermore, the guidelines call for a two-level reduction in the sentence if the defendant accepts responsibility for the crime and either provides complete information about the case to prosecutors or enters a guilty plea and saves the government the expense of a trial.

Sentences against individuals in health care fraud cases are also affected by whether the crime involved a "sophisticated means." A sophisticated means might include the use of an intricate money-laundering scheme designed to baffle federal investigators or the use of computer software designed to file thousands of false insurance claims. Defendants who use mass-marketing techniques to reach multiple victims, who employ special skills to commit an act of health care fraud, or who abuse their position of trust and take advantage of vulnerable victims all stand to have their sentence levels increased. This section of the guidelines is especially relevant to health care because physicians and therapists typically may use their professional skills to treat trusting and, often, defenseless patients. A defendant may also have his or her sentence increased for contempt of court, perjury, subornation of perjury, and obstruction of justice. Destroying documents, intimidating witnesses, and making false statements to federal government investigators are violations that add eleven to fourteen levels to a sentence.

In exceptional cases, judges are allowed to impose sentences that are greater than those stipulated by the guidelines. For many health care cases, the aggravating circumstances outweigh the mitigating circumstances. The guidelines permit deviations for heinous crimes resulting in death, bodily injury, or psychological harm. Inflicting great psychological distress on terminally ill patients probably would qualify for a deviation from the guidelines as would harming patients by subjecting them to unnecessary surgery, recklessly filling prescriptions for addictive drugs, or providing patients with unapproved (by the FDA) or dangerous devices. Deviations are also possible for economic losses that exceed the maximum $400 million.

Besides imprisonment, the guidelines provide for other penalties. These penalties include probation, supervised release, restitution, fines and special assessments, forfeiture of assets, payment of prosecution costs, community confinement, home detention, community service, payments to notify victims of the defendant's conviction, and occupational restrictions (e.g., a loss of licensure or prohibition for working in certain health care fields), among others.

Punishing the Organization

The guidelines also impose sanctions on organizations. An organization may be required to remedy harms caused by conduct of its executives and personnel. Such remedies may include restitution to identifiable victims, remedial orders to prevent future harms (e.g., banning marketing efforts promoting the off-label uses of a drug), mandated services to the community if the organization has special skills and competencies for such services (e.g., a hospital or clinic being ordered to provide free immunizations to children in a city school district), and the implementation of compliance and ethics programs.

Fines may be imposed on health care and other businesses that were organized for criminal purposes or that were operated by criminal means. According to the guidelines, the fines should be large enough to divest the organization of all of its net assets. For organizations not having a pervasive criminal purpose, the guidelines provide for base fines. The first step in this process is to assess whether the organization has the ability to pay the fine. After determining the organization's ability to pay its base fine, the guidelines require a measurement of the organization's culpability. Culpability is determined by the size of the organization, the involvement or toleration of an illegal act by executives, the organization's history of criminal or civil adjudication within ten years of the current offense, whether the organization took measures to obstruct justice, and whether the organization had a compliance program or self-reported the violations. The culpability score of the organization is then used to calculate the range of possible fines. Fines may be increased for frauds causing death or bodily injury as well as for frauds involving the participation of corrupt public officials. Fines may be decreased if the organization provides substantial assistance to the authorities during the investigation and prosecution of the case, if the organization is a public entity, or if members or beneficiaries of the organization are also victims of the fraud. Fines may be payable in installments if the organization on which the fines are being levied is not a criminal organization.

Organizations may be placed on probation for between one and five years. Probation enables federal authorities to monitor the payment of fines or the implementation of compliance efforts. Conditions of organizational probation include avoiding any other violations of federal, state, or local laws as well as providing restitution to victims and notifying victims, shareholders, and the public of the offense though a media outlet determined by the court. Organizations may also be required to file periodic financial statements with federal authorities, to develop adequate compliance and ethics programs, and to refrain from operating in designated locations. Violations of probation may result in an extended probationary period, the imposition of more restrictive conditions, or the revocation of the probation and resentencing.

The federal sentencing process was altered by the U.S. Supreme Court's decision, *United States v. Booker*, in 2005.[62] In *Booker*, the Supreme Court held that an enhanced sentence under the guidelines violated the Sixth Amendment if the sentence was based on a judge's determination of fact (other than a prior conviction) when such facts were neither admitted by the defendant nor found by a jury. Thus, the use of the guidelines by judges is no longer mandatory. Judges, however, are still expected to refer to them for guidance. Sentences deemed to be unreasonable by an appellate court, however, are subject to reversal.

In this book I have described a variety of health care fraud and abuse cases along with some strong suggestions for fighting this most pernicious social problem. But this problem is not new. And, paradoxically, health care fraud and abuse is both incipient and insidious. Many high-profile cases have been prosecuted, but they are the tip of the iceberg. Federal and state legislators have responded by passing laws. In turn, agencies have drafted hundreds—make that thousands—of pages of regulations and procedures that are supposed to provide guidance and enforcement. Yet, because of the plethora of out-of-court settlements, we do not have a large body of knowledge—that is, legal precedent—for understanding and controlling health care fraud and abuse. For a legal area that is so complex and so vexing, the courts have offered little wisdom because so few cases have been subject to a full-blown trial.

The Obama administration's health care reform measures have been passed—amid controversy and dissention. But the noble goal of providing greater access to health care for U.S. citizens by making health insurance available to almost everyone—primarily through greater taxes imposed on businesses—is going to breed more, not fewer, frauds.

CONCLUSION

Back to the Beginning

My father's ambulance ride and the fraudulent charges billed for that ride marked the beginning of an ordeal for my family. He spent the last weeks of his life in and out of hospitals and finally in a nursing home. But at ninety-two his deteriorating health had finally caught up with him, and he passed away quietly one early Sunday morning. Losing an elderly parent is traumatic not only because of the personal grief but because of the complications that follow. My father understood the importance of having good insurance coverage. He also kept detailed records, making sure his affairs were in order so that we could settle matters quickly and get on with our lives.

Trouble began in the weeks following my father's death. My mother received over $150,000 in medical bills for my father's care during his final days. The bills seemed to come from every direction, and they were submitted by a variety of providers, most of whom my mother did not recognize. Were the charges for these services legitimate? My mother had no idea what treatments and drugs my father may have received. They were often given to him when she was not present at the hospital or nursing home. Furthermore, some of the explanations on the EOB statements were so complicated that they were nearly impossible to decipher. How were the amounts listed on the bills calculated? When we contemplate buying a new car, for example, we search the Internet to determine the manufacturer's suggested retail price, and then we get firm quotes from several dealers before deciding on which car to purchase. But in health care, we accept—often blindly—the charges presented to us. The traditional economic forces of supply and demand seem to have little relevance to doctor's bills and hospital charges, and shopping for the best deal and haggling over price are unheard of in health care.

She had to deal with insurance coverage. How much of my father's medical expenses were covered by insurance? Which insurance plan—Medicare or Blue Cross Blue Shield—had primary responsibility for paying the charges? How did the deductibles and copayments apply? Listening to the recorded telephone instructions and getting the runaround from Social Security and health insurers is part and parcel of trying to settle the affairs of someone who has recently died. Should my mother pay the bills she received or wait for the insurers to pay? Could she expect my father's insurers to identify fraudulent charges? If the insurers dragged their feet or refused to pay some of the charges, then what recourse would she have in trying to settle my father's affairs? Once you are faced with the dilemma of losing a loved one and are forced to work "down in the trenches," health care issues and the prospect of fraud take on a new meaning. These issues also bring a deeper meaning to our earlier discussion of the complex—and seemingly criminogenic—U.S. health care system, with its vast flows of money and its many points of accessibility for fraud perpetrators (Fig. 1).

Back to the Basic Questions

At the outset, I delineated several broad questions that are integral to health care fraud and abuse. Now that we have explored the salient issues, I would like to return to these questions.

Are the current definitions of "fraud" and "abuse" too broad? How does one reconcile the dilemma between a physician's zealous advocacy for her patients and her ordering tests and treatments that might be regarded as excessive or unnecessary? Are legal counsel, government officials, prosecutors, judges, and juries with little or no formal training in the health disciplines able to distinguish between quality health care and abusive overutilization?

The definitions of fraud and abuse have broadened over time, and neither these definitions nor the laws designed to stop health care fraud and abuse should be expanded further. But we need to be more persistent and aggressive in using the existing definitions and laws to curtail this major social problem. Federal and state authorities should probably spend their investigative and prosecutorial dollars on the mainstream frauds and avoid venturing into questions of overutilization. The latter should be addressed by the AMA or other professional associations and only when a doctor or other provider clearly places his financial needs above the legitimate needs of his patient or client. Of the cases discussed in this book, almost all involve flagrant violations of the law—usually to the extreme detriment of patient care. Since the vast majority of these cases fall well outside the gray areas, I believe that those working in the criminal justice system should be able to make intelligent evaluations and decisions about health care fraud and abuse. Of course, allowing those without health care education and training to make these decisions hastens the deprofessionalization of the health care professions.

How effective are the current laws and regulations for fighting health care fraud? Do these laws micromanage and hinder the efficient delivery of health care, or do they ignore certain types of health care fraud and abuse? Are more antifraud laws necessary or should greater emphasis be placed on enforcing existing laws? How much money is needed to ensure an optimal level of support for fighting health care fraud and abuse? And how will regulators know when enforcement measures have reached an optimal level?

The current laws, as written, should provide effective measures for dealing with major and repeated violations of fraud and abuse. These laws and their accompanying, regulations, administrative manuals, and advisory opinions, however, go too far in trying—and I emphasize the word "trying"—to cover every conceivable aspect and scenario of health care fraud. Unfortunately, this regulatory quagmire not only leads to micromanaging by government officials, it also imposes severe burdens on the vast number of honest health care providers. Time and money spent on regulatory activities is time and money taken from patient care.

Economic theory posits that we should continue with an endeavor until its marginal costs exceed its marginal benefits. So, following economic theory, the government should continue prosecuting cases until the costs incurred—such as the investigation, court, and imprisonment costs—exceed the benefits derived from these cases. Benefits include settlement payments, the forfeiture and sale of property acquired through criminal means, better patient care, and less fraud in the future. As noted earlier, the government has obtained substantial yields for every dollar spent on prosecuting a high-profile health care fraud and abuse case. Of course, the government has gone after the low-hanging fruit with the deepest pockets—namely, the pharmaceutical firms, the hospital chains, and the large medical supply companies. The government is also just adding up the costs of arresting, investigating, trying, and incarcerating violators and comparing these costs with the settlement amounts they extract—usually on the courthouse steps. They have no way of precisely measuring the economic, psychological, and social toll of health care fraud on its victims.

Even though the economic theory suggests that the government should continue to prosecute fraud and abuse cases until marginal costs equal marginal benefits, such an analysis creates two problems. First, government prosecutors have cases outside the health care arena that are vying for their attention. Prosecutors, whether they admit it or not, are susceptible to public pressure—especially the pressure to give priority to the prosecution of violent crimes (e.g., murders, terrorist activities, and violence induced by drug trafficking). This pressure, in part, explains why nonviolent crimes such as health care fraud often end up in civil courts. Not surprisingly, prosecutors may take action only on those cases where the marginal benefits vastly exceed the marginal costs. Second, no comprehensive, nationwide database exists for tracking health care fraud and abuse. The FBI, however, does have a comprehensive database for violent crimes and property crimes. If we cannot measure the magnitude or the damage caused by a social problem such as health care fraud and abuse, then we cannot know how many resources—in this case, how many hundreds of billions of dollars—should be allocated to fighting it. So, without a solid database on which to build good decisions, and with only the roughest notion as to how to measure the psychological and social impact of health care crimes, we are hard put to know when we have met the cost-benefit threshold.

Are certain institutional arrangements such as fee-for-service or capitation plans more conducive to fraud and abuse? What is the role of for-profit health care in reducing this major problem? What health care arrangements, financial incentives, and technologies can be used to curb fraud and abuse?

In this book I have provided an abundance of examples of health care fraud and abuse in almost every major institutional setting. Logically, fee-for-service arrangements and for-profit institutions should be plagued by frauds on the revenue side of the income statement, whereas capitation plans and not-for-profit institutions should be plagued by frauds on the expense side of the income statement. In reality, this distinction does not hold true. Both the revenue and expense sides of the income statement are highly susceptible to fraud. Although for-profit hospitals and clinics seem to have a stronger incentive to cheat than their not-for-profit counterparts, both segments of the health care system—in the United States and elsewhere—have staggering amounts of fraud and abuse. And, of course, fraud and abuse among for-profit pharmaceutical companies, labs, and equipment manufacturers is especially pernicious.

A major theme of this book is that the individual perpetrators—not the particular characteristics of a health care system—are at the root of fraud and abuse. More aggressive prosecution along with harsher penalties for crooked providers, expanding consumer education, better information technology, improved statistical fraud detection devices, and a greater sense of urgency among health insurers to combat fraud all offer the potential for effectively attacking this major social problem.

To what extent do health care providers, patients, shareholders in private hospitals, fraud-control experts, health insurers, fiscal intermediaries, and government officials share a common ground insofar as reducing health care fraud is concerned? If the interests of these diverse groups are not in sync, what measures can be taken to align them?

The common ground for these diverse groups is twofold: first, reducing health care costs and, second, spending time and money on improving the health of the population rather than on detecting and fighting fraud and abuse. As has been illustrated amply throughout this book, the cost of health care fraud is borne ultimately by the consumer in the form of higher hospital and doctor bills, more expensive pharmaceuticals and other health care products, and escalating health insurance premiums. As long as the health care buck—in the form of higher and higher costs—is passed to the consumer, we will see little headway in reducing health care fraud and abuse. A two-pronged approach will be necessary to reduce the problem.

First, we must recognize that fraud and abuse start with health care providers. So, the message must be sent that harsh penalties—incarceration, fines, and forfeiture of assets—will be imposed on individuals who commit major or repeated violations. Providers must also comprehend, perhaps through their professional associations or industry training programs, how fraud and abuse is leading to their deprofessionalization.

Second, we must understand that the health care consumer is the first line of defense against fraud and abuse. A major mode of attack is to cast a wide educational net—using television and newspaper advertisements, magazine articles, private organizations such as AARP, community volunteer groups, and flyers mailed to Medicare and Medicaid recipients—to inform health care consumers about how fraud and abuse can affect their lives and how they can take an active role in reporting and stopping it.

This two-pronged strategy for reducing health care fraud and abuse is in sync with the interests of public and private insurers and government enforcers. Reducing fraud and abuse should drastically reduce health care costs. But litigation and incarceration costs may rise, at least in the short run, as errant health care providers are prosecuted.

What demographic changes will affect the future of the health care system, and will these changes exacerbate or diminish health care fraud and abuse? Most books about a major social problem end on an optimistic note by suggesting ways to eliminate whatever problem the book was addressing, and I have tried to do the same by suggesting a number of measures that may alleviate the problem. Unfortunately, health care fraud and abuse are not going to disappear—far from it.

Unless preventive efforts are increased substantially, demographic and economic trends suggest that the problem may become even worse. The aging post– World War II baby boomers will be consuming more health care services and products and, within a few years, they will become heavily dependent on the

Medicare program. At this writing, the U.S. economy has plummeted to levels that are unprecedented since the Great Depression. Harsh economic times will place a greater burden on the Medicaid program as unemployment levels rise and as more individuals become eligible for public assistance. Since both the Medicare and the Medicaid programs are major targets for health care fraud, the prospects of reducing the problem appear bleak.

The *World Health Report 2000,* published by the World Health Organization and mentioned briefly in the introductory chapter of this book, proposed three goals for a health care system. The first WHO objective, ensuring the good health of the population across the entire range of ages, is affected by health care fraud and abuse because of its disproportionate impact on low-income and the elderly people. The second WHO objective, health care providers who respond to people's expectations and treat them with respect and dignity, is affected less by fraud and abuse, although one could argue that fraud and abuse are clearly affronts to human dignity. The third WHO objective, developing a system of health care financing that is fair and that is based on a person's ability to pay, is directly affected because fraud and abuse increase all health care—and health care insurance—costs.

Cause for optimism still exists, however. The U.S. health care system and similar systems in other developed countries are amazingly resilient. With size and complexity comes the ability to absorb and jettison problems that, at least in theory, should be catastrophic. But we should not hope that our system of health care will just roll with the punches and absorb the blows of health care fraud and abuse. Fighting back is a far better solution.

APPENDIX: A NOTE ON THE MAJOR U.S. PUBLIC INSURANCE PROGRAMS

The public insurance programs Medicare and Medicaid (including the State Children's Health Insurance Program, SCHIP) are primary targets for criminals committing health care fraud. Public programs have claims budgets amounting to hundreds of billions of dollars. The proposed HHS budget for 2010 was $879 billion, most of which will be consumed by the Medicare and Medicaid programs.[1]

Medicare

Medicare (Title XVIII of the Social Security Act) was enacted primarily for people age sixty—five and older.[2] Medicare Part A, known as hospital insurance or HI, covers inpatient hospital care, including critical—access hospitals and skilled—nursing facilities (but not custodial or long-term care), hospice care, and some home health care. Medicare Part B, supplementary medical insurance or SMI, covers physicians' services and outpatient care. It also pays for physical and occupational therapy, supplies, some home health care, and other services. Part C of Medicare is known as Medicare Advantage (formerly the Medicare+Choice program). The Balanced Budget Act of 1997 gave Medicare recipients under Part C the option of receiving care through private health insurers as long as the insurers provided benefits that were comparable to those offered under the original Medicare plan. In 2007 over forty—four million people were enrolled in one or both of Parts A and B of the Medicare program, and an additional eight million people participated in the Medicare Advantage plan.[3]

The most revolutionary change in Medicare since its inception in 1965 was the enactment of the Medicare Prescription Drug, Improvement, and Modernization Act of 2003 (MMA). This act created Part D of Medicare, and it allows beneficiaries to select from among a number of prescription drug programs and premium options. The program was designed to control prescription drug costs, but it has also become a significant source of fraud.[4]

Medicare is funded primarily through Social Security payroll taxes at the rate of 2.9 percent on all earned income.[5] In addition, recipients also pay certain premiums and deductibles. By 2008, the Medicare program trust fund expenditures were approximately $230 billion. After 2009, the Medicare program trust funds will face a growing deficit. By 2017, Medicare is projected to have $348 billion flowing into the program and $415 billion flowing out.[6] Much of this cash drain could be eliminated if Medicare fraud was curtailed. "We estimate that for every $1 we spend to stop fraud in the system, we save $1.55," said HHS Secretary Kathleen Sebelius. "The president's budget lays out funding for anti-fraud efforts over five years that we estimate could save $2.7 billion."[7]

The program is administered by the Centers for Medicare and Medicaid Services, an entity within the U.S. Department of Health and Human Services. The Social Security Administration maintains and checks Medicare beneficiary records. State agencies—usually state health departments working with CMS— certify and oversee the health care providers, institutions, and suppliers participating in the Medicare program.

Part A, Medicare payments for inpatient hospital services, are made under a reimbursement mechanism called a "prospective payment system." To help contain the rapid increase in health care costs, Medicare PPS reimbursements were converted to a system of "diagnostic-related groups" in 1983. A hospital stay, for example, is categorized in a DRG having a predetermined payment amount. Adjustments are applied to each DRG, including those for excessive labor or other extraordinary costs, to determine the specific amount reimbursed to the hospital. Different DRGs are applied to skilled-nursing care, home health care, inpatient-rehabilitation hospital care, long-term care hospitals, and hospices.

Part B Medicare payments for physicians are defined as the lowest of the physician's submitted charges or, more commonly, the amount determined by a fee based on a relative value scale. Payments for durable medical equipment and clinical laboratory services are also determined by a fee schedule.

"Participating physicians" are those who agree at the beginning of the year to accept assignment for all Medicare services furnished for that year. Once a physician accepts the Medicare-approved rate—known as "taking assignment"— additional payments cannot be requested from Medicare, the patient, or the patient's private insurer. If a physician does not take assignment, then either the patient or the private insurer (or both) are responsible for excess charges, subject to program limits. Medicare Advantage plans under Medicare Part C are paid on a regional capitation basis rather than on the number of services rendered to each patient.

Medicare claims are processed by private organizations or agencies (known as intermediaries) working under contract with the federal government. They process claims, make payments to providers, maintain records, establish controls, monitor costs and reimbursements, conduct audits, and serve as a defense against fraud and abuse. Medical "carriers" handle claims by physicians and suppliers. Carriers are typically Blue Shield and other private commercial insurance carriers. They determine allowable charges, assist and make payments to physicians and suppliers, and perform auditing and fraud-control functions. Of course, the more actors involved in the claim-payment process, the greater the likelihood of fraud and abuse.

Quality-improvement organizations (formerly called peer-review organizations) are groups of practicing health care professionals under contract with the federal government. They supervise the quality of care provided to Medicare beneficiaries, and they educate health care providers in their respective states about Medicare issues. In theory, education and supervision should reduce health care fraud and abuse. Whether quality-improvement organizations actually achieve this objective is open to debate.

Medicaid

Medicaid (Title XIX of the Social Security program) furnishes health care to needy recipients that meet certain age, income, and other eligibility requirements. The program is funded jointly by the federal and state governments with the federal government establishing broad guidelines for state Medicaid programs. Each state then establishes its own eligibility standards, services, reimbursements, and administrative structure within the federal guidelines.

The federal government requires Medicaid coverage for individuals who receive federal assistance, and it provides matching funds to states for other "categorically needy" groups. Examples of such groups include limited-income families with children, pregnant women whose family income is below 133 percent of the federal poverty level, Supplemental Security Income (SSI) recipients, and certain Medicare beneficiaries. The individual states have the option of providing Medicaid coverage to broader, "categorically related" groups (similar to the federally mandated recipients) as well as to "medically needy" persons whose income and resources otherwise make them ineligible for Medicaid. Qualifying for Medicaid also depends on a recipient's status under other federal laws. Not all low—income—or even destitute—individuals are entitled to Medicaid benefits.

Nondisabled adults without dependent children, for example, are not able to obtain Medicaid coverage in most states because they fail to fit into any of the eligibility categories.[8]

Medicaid provides funding for a wide range of health care services, including inpatient and outpatient hospital services, physician services, nurse-midwife services, prenatal and postpartum care, vaccines for children, family planning services, home health care and skilled—nursing services, pediatric and family nurse-practitioner services, among others. States also receive matching federal funds for services such as intermediate care facilities for the mentally disabled, prescription drugs, prosthetic devices, optometrist services, transportation, and hospice care. The receipt of matching funds can lead to accusations of fraud.[9]

Medicaid health care providers are paid either on a fee-for-service basis or through a prepayment plan. The latter is common to managed-care arrangements. Payments to health care providers are tied to rates customarily paid in their respective locales. Hospitals admitting and treating a disproportionate number of Medicaid patients are eligible to receive additional payments. In some states, Medicaid recipients are required to pay a deductible or copayment for certain services. By the end of the first decade of the twenty-first century, more than sixty million persons were receiving annual health care through the Medicaid program.[10]

Medicaid spending is expected to increase at a rate that will significantly outpace U.S. economic growth. A report released by the Centers for Medicare and Medicaid in October 2008 projected the economy will grow at an annual rate of 4.8 percent, whereas Medicaid spending will grow at an annual rate of 7.9 percent (or from $339 billion in 2008 to $674 billion in 2017). Speaking at a 2008 meeting of the National State Budget Officers, then HHS Secretary Mike Leavitt said this rate of growth was "unsustainable" by the federal and state governments and that "the nation's most vulnerable citizens could be threatened."[11] Because of the deteriorating economic conditions during 2008 and beyond, it is likely that the number of citizens needing Medicaid will grow.

State Children's Health Insurance Program (SCHIP)

The State Children's Health Insurance Program (SCHIP) is part of the Social Security program (Title XXI). It was enacted in conjunction with the Balanced Budget Act in 1997.[12] The objective of SCHIP is to provide health insurance coverage to children whose families might not otherwise qualify for Medicaid benefits. Children in families whose income was less than twice the federal poverty level are usually eligible for SCHIP benefits.[13] Like Medicaid, SCHIP is regulated broadly at the federal level and is funded jointly by the federal and state governments. Each state determines it eligibility standards, benefits, and administrative procedures. Approximately $8.7 billion was spent on SCHIP in FY 2007 to cover some 4 million children.[14] Many children who qualify for the program, however, remain uncovered, possibly because of a lack of parental awareness of the program. Days after taking office, President Obama extended SCHIP funding for four years.

TRICARE

The TRICARE program (formerly CHAMPUS) provides medical care for active duty and retired military personnel (including National Guard and Reserve members) and their dependents (including dependents of deceased military personnel). Health care is provided through almost nine hundred military health care facilities worldwide as well as through a network of civilian health care professionals, institutions, pharmacies, and suppliers.

TRICARE is managed by the U.S. Department of Defense, TRICARE Management Activity. It covers approximately 9.2 million eligible beneficiaries and offers them a variety of options. For example, TRICARE for Life is designed for Medicare-eligible beneficiaries, and TRICARE Prime is a managed—care plan. Other TRICARE options are available for military personnel in overseas and remote locations. Private health care providers typically handle billings and claims directly with TRICARE.[15] The U.S. Department of Defense's Criminal Investigative Services is the major investigative agency for TRICARE frauds.

Notes

INTRODUCTION

1. President Bush's 2008 budget provided $1.2 billion in mandatory funding and $183 million from a discretionary cap adjustment for the Health Care Fraud and Abuse Control Program for Medicare integrity activities. In 2008 the HHS Inspector General's Office collected $2.35 billion directly and $1.33 billion indirectly, and the OIG pursued about 2,100 cases stemming from 4,800 health care fraud and abuse complaints. During the same time frame, the Department of Justice recovered $1.12 billion from perpetrators of health care fraud, down from $1.53 billion the previous year.

For FY 2009, the OIG reported that 2,556 individuals and entities were excluded from federal health care programs and 671 criminal actions and 394 civil actions were taken. President Obama's proposed budget added $125 million in discretionary spending to the $1.5 billion that already funded the Health Care Fraud and Abuse Control Program. Total discretionary spending for the program in FY 2010 was projected to be $311 million. See Baumann 2007, 4; U.S. Department of Health and Human Services and U.S. Department of Justice 2007, 1; National Health Care Anti-Fraud Association, n.d.; Fierce Healthcare, Daily News for Health Care Executives 2009e; Fierce Healthcare, Daily News for Health Care Executives, 2008c; U.S. Department of Health and Human Services, Office of the Inspector General 2009; Kaisernetwork 2008a.

2. The degree of cooperation between federal and private agencies is extensive. According to the FBI's *Financial Crimes Report to the Public, Fiscal Year 2006:* "The FBI leverages its resources in both the private and public arenas through investigative partnerships with agencies such as the U.S. Department of Health and Human Services–Office of Inspector General (HHS–OIG), the Food and Drug Administration (FDA), Drug Enforcement Agency (DEA), Defense Criminal Investigative Service, Office of Personnel Management, Internal Revenue Service (IRS), and various state and local agencies. On the private side, the FBI is actively involved with national groups, such as the National Health Care Anti-Fraud Association (NHCAA), the National Insurance Crime Bureau (NICB), the Blue Cross and Blue Shield Association (BCBSA), the American Association of Retired Persons, and the Coalition Against Insurance Fraud, as well as many other professional and grass-roots efforts to expose and investigate fraud within the system."

3. U.S. Department of Health and Human Services 2009c.

4. Kennedy 2009a.

5. Heath 2010.

6. Fierce Healthcare, Daily News for Healthcare Executives 2010.

7. Price Waterhouse Coopers 2009, 9. Also see Fierce Healthcare, Daily News for Healthcare Executives 2008e.

8. Because of the attention given to health care financing arrangements, the broader term "health care fraud" will be used in this book instead of the term "medical care fraud." These terms, however, are often used interchangeably.

9. U.S. Department of Justice, Federal Bureau of Investigation 2006.

10. Ibid.

11. U.S. Department of the Treasury, Internal Revenue Service 2006.

12. Fierce Healthcare, Daily News for Healthcare Executives 2009g; Rockoff and Kendall 2009; Winslow 2009.

13. National Health Care Anti-Fraud Association n.d.

14. European Healthcare Fraud and Corruption Network 2004.

15. European Healthcare Fraud and Corruption Network 2007, 2.

16. Savedoff and Hussmann 2005, 4.

17. BrainyQuote n.d.

18. U.S. Department of Labor, Bureau of Labor Statistics 2007.

19. See National Coalition on Health Care 2009; OECD Health Data 2006; and Seelye 2010.

20. Freking 2008a.

21. Carpenter and Sanders 2007, 115.

22. Defining the boundaries of the health care system can be a problem. Hospitals, physicians, and diagnostic laboratories are always regarded as part of any health care industry. Other health-promoting activities such as health foods, spas, gyms, and exercise equipment are usually excluded from an analysis of health care. This book focuses on the nine segments delineated by the Bureau of Labor Statistics, as well as both private and public sources of health care financing.

23. U.S. Department of Labor, Bureau of Labor Statistics 2007, 3–4.

24. U.S. Department of Labor, Bureau of Labor Statistics 2007, 1.

25. Chua 2006, 1.

26. Freking 2008a.

27. Woolhandler and Himmelstein 1991; Woolhandler, Campbell, and Himmelstein, 2003.

28. Woolhandler and Himmelstein 2007.

29. National Coalition on Health Care 2009.

30. Freking 2008a.

31. United Health Foundation 2008, 1.

32. Kaiser Family Foundation 2007; University of Maine, Bureau of Labor Education 2001, 1–8. It is also noteworthy that health care expenditures are not distributed uniformly. Eighty percent of U.S. health care expenditures are made by 20% of the population, primarily those suffering three serious chronic conditions simultaneously as well as by very ill persons who are in the last six months of their lives. See Bradley 2007, 135.

33. Bonifield 2010.

34. DeNavas-Walt, Proctor, and Smith 2007.

35. Holahan and Cook 2008; Robert Wood Johnson Foundation 2008.

36. Joshi 2008. Citing a survey conducted by the foundation, the *Washington Post* reported: "More than two in five adults in the 19-to-64 age group reported problems paying medical bills or had accumulated medical debt in 2007, up from one in three in 2005. Their difficulties included not being able to afford medical attention when needed, running up medical debts, dealing with collection agencies about unpaid bills, or having to change their lifestyle to repay medical debts." The *Post* described how people had exhausted their savings, incurred large amounts of credit card debt, and were unable to pay for basic necessities such as food, heat, or rent. Limited access to health care is especially devastating for infants and children, and a lack of insurance often forces adults to postpone seeking help until their medical conditions have become serious or even life threatening.

37. Kaiser Health News 2009a.

38. Families USA 2009.

39. Arora et al. 2009, 199–201.

40. World Health Organization 2000, 23–40.

41. Brown 2008, 325–27. Brown defines the U.S. health care "industry" as having three sectors: the well-known private and public sectors and the little known safety-net

sector: "The safety-net sector encompasses public and voluntary hospitals, community health centers, public health clinics, free clinics, and services donated by private physicians." Brown goes on to say that these institutions often live on the financial edge and stay afloat with eleventh-hour infusions of money. But safety-net venues serve as a first line of defense for those without health insurance: "This fact is of paramount importance, for these providers also extend a safety net for the political legitimacy of the health care system as a whole."

42. Chua 2006, 3.

43. The term "criminal" is used to describe anyone who commits a crime by violating a criminal statute or common law doctrine, regardless of whether their actions are detected or prosecuted. "Corruption" refers to an act in which a person uses his or her position of authority to commit a criminal or unethical act.

44. Beam and Warner 2009, 12.

45. Weisburd, Waring, and Chayet 2001, 51–90. These three authors coined the white-collar criminal terms "crisis responder," "opportunity taker," and "opportunity seeker." The fourth category, "inadvertent offender," is my categorization.

46. In some cases, a so-called crisis responder has committed other crimes that have gone either undetected or unreported.

47. 42 U.S.C., sec. 1395.

48. Some physicians may have become scapegoats in the prosecution of health care fraud and drug abuse cases. See Libby 2008.

49. Samenow 2004, 12.

50. Kaiser Health News 2009b.

51. Davis 2003.

52. Tenet Shareholder Committee, LLC 2008.

53. Slater 2008.

54. ITIM International n.d.

55. Felson 2002, 100–101.

56. Nunnally 2006.

57. Barrish 2010.

58. Wilemon 2010.

59. Bradley 2007, 146.

60. U.S. Department of Justice, Federal Bureau of Investigation 2006, 9.

61. The term "non–self-revealing" has been used to describe health care fraud in Sparrow 1996, 20.

CHAPTER 1

1. U.S. Attorney's Office, Northern District of Texas 2009.

2. This chapter provides an overview of the major laws and issues associated with health care fraud. Amendments to federal and state statutes, new court rulings, and changes in regulations and advisory opinions alter the interpretation of health care laws. The expertise and depth of knowledge required to prosecute or defend claims of health care fraud go well beyond the scope of this chapter. Litigants are directed to the Bureau of National Affair's treatises on health care fraud: Baumann 2007 (as well as the 2009 Cumulative Supplement); Loucks and Lam, 2001 and 2007. And they are encouraged to retain the services of an attorney who specializes in the complex area of health care fraud.

3. The terms "fraud" and "abuse" are often used interchangeably. Abuse, however, may occur in the absence of fraudulent intent. The Medicaid Program defines abuse as "provider practices that are inconsistent with sound fiscal, business, or medical practices, and result in an unnecessary cost to the Medicaid program, or in reimbursement for services that are not medically necessary or that fail to meet professionally recognized

standards for health care. It also includes recipient practices that result in unnecessary cost to the Medicaid program" (42 C.F.R., sec. 455.2, "Definitions").

4. Garner 2000, 484.

5. HealthGrades, Inc. 2006, 3. Minnesota, according to the survey, was the safest state, whereas New Jersey was the most dangerous state for medical errors and deaths.

6. Moore, Lesser, and Smith 2009.

7. Even in trials with a morass of evidence and conflicting testimony, proving intent to defraud often hinges on a simple, offhand statement by the perpetrator or an obscure document or e-mail message.

8. National Health Care Anti-Fraud Association 2007.

9. Garner 2000, 530.

10. U.S. Department of Health and Human Services and U.S. Department of Justice 2006.

11. Little 2010.

12. Zwillich 2005.

13. This case received nationwide attention and was later used as the basis for a television movie, *The Babymaker: The Dr. Cecil Jacobson Story.*

14. U.S. Department of the Treasury, Internal Revenue Service 2008a; United States Attorney, Northern District of Ohio 2005; *Fraud Digest* 2005.

15. Wang 2009 and Chicago Tribune 2010.

16. Loucks and Lam 2007, 464 and 506.

17. Rowland 2005.

18. U.S. Department of the Treasury, Internal Revenue Service 2008a.

19. 18 U.S.C. sec. 371. "If two or more persons conspire either to commit any offense against the United States, or to defraud the United States, or any agency thereof in any manner or for any purpose, and one or more of such persons do any act to effect the object of the conspiracy, each shall be fined under this title or imprisoned not more than five years, or both.

If, however, the offense, the commission of which is the object of the conspiracy, is a misdemeanor only, the punishment for such conspiracy shall not exceed the maximum punishment provided for such misdemeanor."

20. Garner 2000, 248.

21. Knaupp 2007.

22. Garner 2000, 249.

23. Associated Press 1987.

24. "Conspiracy—Procedural Rules" n.d.

25. 18 U.S.C. sec. 1961–1968.

26. *Sedima v. Inrex,* 105 Sup. Ct. 3275 (1985). Also see Canade 1985, 1086–1102.

27. *FindLaw for the Public* 2008.

28. Section 1962(a) "makes it unlawful for a person to use an enterprise to launder money generated by a pattern of racketeering activity"; section 1962(b) "makes it unlawful for a person to acquire or maintain an interest in an enterprise through a pattern of racketeering activity"; and section 1962(c) "prohibits any defendant person from operating or managing an enterprise through a pattern of racketeering activity." Grell n.d.

29. Sugerman-Broznan and Woolman 2009.

30. Connecticut Attorney General's Office 2008.

31. *New England Carpenters Health Benefits Fund v. First DataBank, Inc.* 2008. WL 723774 (D.Mass).

32. *New England Carpenters Health Benefits Fund et al. v. First DataBank, Inc. and McKesson Corp.,* Attachment B n.d.

33. Martinez 2006.

34. Tibken 2008; Fierce Healthcare, Daily News for Healthcare Executives 2008f.

35. O'Reilly and Milford 2008.

36. Grell n.d.; Canade 1985.

37. See *McGee v. State Farm Mutual Automobile Insurance Co. et al.*, 1:2008cv00392 (January 30, 2008) and *McGee v. Allstate Insurance Company et al.*, 1:2008cv00842 (February 28, 2008).

38. Turkewitz 2008a and 2008b.

39. U.S. Postal Inspection Service n.d.

40. U.S. Code, Title 18, part 1, chap. 63, sec. 1347, Health Care Fraud: "Whoever knowingly and willfully executes, or attempts to execute, a scheme or artifice—

(1) to defraud any health care benefit program; or

(2) to obtain, by means of false or fraudulent pretenses, representations, or promises, any of the money or property owned by, or under the custody or control of, any health care benefit program, in connection with the delivery of or payment for health care benefits, items, or services, shall be fined under this title or imprisoned not more than 10 years, or both. If the violation results in serious bodily injury (as defined in section 1365 of this title), such person shall be fined under this title or imprisoned not more than 20 years, or both; and if the violation results in death, such person shall be fined under this title, or imprisoned for any term of years or for life, or both." With respect to wire fraud, section 1343 states: "Whoever, having devised or intending to devise any scheme or artifice to defraud, or for obtaining money or property by means of false or fraudulent pretenses, representations, or promises, transmits or causes to be transmitted by means of wire, radio, or television communication in interstate or foreign commerce, any writings, signs, signals, pictures, or sounds for the purpose of executing such scheme or artifice, shall be fined under this title or imprisoned not more than 20 years, or both. If the violation affects a financial institution, such person shall be fined not more than $1,000,000 or imprisoned not more than 30 years, or both."

41. Strader 2002, 59–60.

42. Grell n.d.

43. Ibid.

44. *U.S. v. Jain*, 93 F.3d 436 (8th Cir. 1996).

45. Abrams and Beale 2000, 385–97.

46. Leap 2007, 58–59.

47. U.S. Attorney's Office, Southern District of Florida 2007.

48. Many individuals and organizations withdraw or deposit large amounts of cash in the course of routine, legal business activities. Large withdrawals and deposits are not illegal, and the filing of a currency transaction report does not indicate criminal activity. The Tax Reform Act of 1986 requires organizations to file a report with the IRS when customers make cash purchases over $10,000. Criminals, for example, often pay cash for expensive items such as automobiles.

49. U.S. Department of the Treasury, Internal Revenue Service 2008b.

50. Strader 2002, 219.

51. Tax evasion differs from tax avoidance. Tax evasion involves hiding income, claiming unauthorized exemptions, or taking illegal deductions. Tax avoidance involves taking full advantage of available deductions and exemptions and paying no more tax than necessary while complying fully with tax laws.

52. U.S. Department of the Treasury, Internal Revenue Service 2008c.

53. Manning 2000, 69–92.

54. 18 U.S.C., sec. 1001. False statements include: "(1) falsifying or concealing a material fact by trick, scheme, or device; (2) making a false, fictitious, or fraudulent representation; and (3) making or using a false document or writing."

55. 18 U.S.C., sec. 1621.

56. Garner 2000, 1233. The term "two-witness rule" is a misnomer because it is not necessary for two live witnesses to testify. Rather, one live witness plus corroborative evidence (the second "witness") may be sufficient.

57. Strader 2002, 194–98.

58. Garner 2000, 882.

59. 18 U.S.C., secs. 1503 and 1505.

60. U.S. Department of Health and Human Services and U.S. Department of Justice 2007, 17.

61. O'Connor 2006; *U.S. v. Mikos* 539 F.3d 706 (7th Cir. 2008).

62. U.S. Department of Justice, Federal Bureau of Prisons, Inmate Locator, May 9, 2010.

CHAPTER 2

1. U.S. Department of Health and Human Services and U.S. Department of Justice 2008, 16.

2. U.S. Department of Health and Human Services and U.S. Department of Justice 2008, 17.

3. U.S. Department of Justice 2009.

4. 42 U.S.C. sec. 1320a–7b.

5. 42 U.S.C. sec. 1320a–7b(b)(1),(2). The 1972 statute made an illegal kickback a misdemeanor. In 1977 the antikickback statute made the offense a felony.

6. Baumann 2007, 28; Pub. L. No. 105–93; and 111 Stat. 251 (1997).

7. Burton and Armstrong 2009.

8. *U.S. v. Hancock,* 604 F.2d 999 (7th Cir. 1979).

9. 42 U.S.C. sec. 1320a–7b.

10. Bressert 2006; Mather 2005.

11. Grande et al. 2009.

12. Weintraub 2010.

13. Testerman 2001.

14. Testerman 2002.

15. *U.S. v. Greber,* 760 F.2d 68 (3rd Cir. Pa. 1985).

16. *U.S. v. McClatchey,* 217 F.3d 823 (10th Cir.), cert. denied, 531 U.S. 1015 (2000).

17. Baumann 2007, 30.

18. See "Medicare Fraud and Abuse Physician Self-Referral Prohibition ('Stark Law') and Anti-Kickback Law" n.d., 5–6.

19. Walsh 2009.

20. In *U.S. v. Medica-Rents Co.* 285 F. Supp. 2d 742, 770–71 (N.D. Tex. 2003) the court noted: "Medicare regulations are among the most completely impenetrable texts within human experience." Cited in Baumann 2007, 236.

21. Comment by Salcido 2007 in Baumann 2007, 254.

22. Cashill 2000.

23. 42 C.F.R., sec. 1001.952(v). In theory, safe harbors protect business practices when commercially reasonable items or services are exchanged at a fair market price. The obvious and safe choice is to comply fully with the detailed safe harbor rules. But partial compliance with a safe harbor rule does not necessarily violate the antikickback statute. Arrangements not adhering completely to safe harbor rules must be analyzed on a case-by-case basis. When parties are uncertain whether their arrangements qualify for safe harbor protection, they may request an advisory opinion from the U.S. Department of Health and Human Services, Office of Inspector General.

To help honest providers distinguish between what is and is not legal, the OIG periodically releases special fraud alerts and advisory bulletins pertaining to the antikickback statute. For example, a fraud alert on telemarketing activities by durable equipment manufacturers was released in March 2003. In case you ever wondered why wheelchair and scooter providers are so fond of advertising on television, it is because this OIG alert restricts unsolicited telephone calls by equipment companies to Medicare recipients. Special fraud alerts and advisories do not carry the force of law, but they provide insight into the concerns and views of the OIG. Baumann 2007, 32.

24. 42 U.S.C.S. sec. 1395nn.

25. Kusserow 1989.

26. Amednews.com. 2009b.

27. OANDP.com, O & P Edge n.d.

28. ApatheticVoter.com n.d.

29. 18 U.S.C. sec. 287.

30. Loucks and Lam 2007, 477–81.

31. 18 U.S.C. sec. 286; Loucks and Lam 2007, 480–81.

32. 31 U.S.C. sec. 3729–33.

33. One critical aspect of FCA whistle-blower actions is whether the relator had information already known by the government. Such cases involve the whistle-blower public disclosure jurisdictional bar prohibiting lawsuits in cases where the relator was not the original source of information surrounding the false claim. If the information was already in the public domain, a whistle-blower suit is barred because, at that juncture, citizens expect the government to intervene. The whistle-blower public disclosure jurisdictional bar raises a number of issues, including the meaning of "public disclosure" and the point where relevant information becomes public.

34. Ekstrand 2006; U.S. Government Accountability Office 2005. In the summer of 2008, the U.S. Department of Justice faced a backlog of more than five hundred health care whistle-blower cases (out of a total of nine hundred backlogged cases). Since 2001 whistle-blowers have filed between three and four hundred cases a year, but the staff of seventy—five attorneys assigned to these cases can handle only one hundred or so cases annually. FierceHealthcare, Daily News for Health Care Executives 2008a.

35. Sorrel 2009.

36. Salcido 2007, 228–38.

37. The courts have also construed literal falsities under the FCA in conjunction with violations of the antikickback and Stark laws.

38. McCabe 2007.

39. *United States ex rel. Cox v. Iowa Health Systems,* 29 F. Supp. 2d. 1022 (S.D. Iowa 1998). The nautical mile to statute mile conversion is 1 to 1.15.

40. *Visiting Nurses Ass'n. of Brooklyn v. Thompson,* 378 F. Supp. 2d 75 (E.D.N.Y. 2004).

41. See Park and Pawlitz 2008, 47–61.

42. Landsberg and Keville 2001.

43. Medicare Act, sec. 1320c–5(a) "(2) will be of quality which meets professionally recognized standards of health care…" There may be a great deal of difference, however, between procedures that are perfect versus those that are minimally compliant.

44. *Covington v. Sisters of the Third Order of St. Dominic at Hanford,* 61 F.3d 909 (9th Cir. July 13, 1995).

45. *U.S. v. Krizek,* 859 F. Supp. 5 (D.D.C. 1994).

46. Rosenzweig and England 2003.

47. *Allison Engine Company v. United States,* U.S. Sup. Ct. No. 07–214 (June 9, 2008).

48. Estrada 2008, 5–10. In *Graham County Soil and Water Conservation District et al. v. U.S. ex rel. Wilson,* U.S. Sup. Ct. No. 08–304 (March 30, 2010), the U.S. Supreme Court held that whistle-blowers are barred from filing FCA lawsuits based on information obtained through federal, state, or local reports. An FCA amendment that is part of the Obama health care package, however, will permit such suits as long as the information was not obtained by the whistle-blower from a federal source.

49. 18 U.S.C. sec. 1320a–7b. The HHS Office of Civil Rights enforces the privacy standards, and the Centers for Medicare and Medicaid Services enforces both the transaction and code set standards and the security standards.

50. *U.S. v. Lucien et al.,* 347 F.3d 45 (2nd Cir.), 2003.

51. 42 U.S.C. sec., 1320a–7b.

52. U.S Food and Drug Administration 1981.

53. History of the FDA n.d.

54. 21 U.S.C. 301 et seq.

55. Wax 1995.

56. According to 15 U.S. Code, sec. 55, "Additional Definitions": "The term 'drug' means (A) articles recognized in the official United States Pharmacopoeia, official Homoeopathic Pharmacopoeia of the United States, or official National Formulary, or any supplement to any of them; and (B) articles intended for use in the diagnosis, cure, mitigation, treatment, or prevention of disease in man or other animals; and (C) articles (other than food) intended to affect the structure or any function of the body of man or other animals; and (D) articles intended for use as a component of any article specified in clause (A), (B), or (C). The term "device" (except when used in paragraph (n) of this section and in sections 301(i), 403(f), 502(c), and 602(c)) means an instrument, apparatus, implement, machine, contrivance, implant, in vitro reagent, or other similar or related article, including any component, part, or accessory, which is—(1) recognized in the official National Formulary, or the United States Pharmacopeia, or any supplement to them, (2) intended for use in the diagnosis of disease or other conditions, or in the cure, mitigation, treatment, or prevention of disease, in man or other animals, or (3) intended to affect the structure or any function of the body of man or other animals, and which does not achieve its primary intended purposes through chemical action within or on the body of man or other animals and which is not dependent upon being metabolized for the achievement of its primary intended purposes."

57. See U.S. Food and Drug Administration n.d.b. for a summary of the FDA approval process.

58. U.S. Food and Drug Administration n.d.b.

59. The discussion of the FDCA is based in part on Loucks and Lam 2001, 95–182.

CHAPTER 3

1. U.S. Department of Health and Human Services and U.S. Department of Justice 2008, 18.

2. U.S. Department of Health and Human Services 2009a.

3. U.S. Department of Health and Human Services 2009d.

4. U.S. Department of Health and Human Services 2008b; U.S. Department of Health and Human Services, Centers for Medicare and Medicaid Services 2008g.

5. U.S. Congressional Budget Office 2010, 54–55.

6. U.S. Department of Health and Human Services and U.S. Department of Justice 2007, 9.

7. U.S. Department of Health and Human Services and U.S. Department of Justice 2003.

8. Dutton n.d.

9. U.S. Department of Health and Human Services and U.S. Department of Justice 2004.

10. U.S. Department of Health and Human Services and U.S. Department of Justice 2004.

11. U.S. Department of Health and Human Services and U.S. Department of Justice 2007, 17 and 18.

12. Appleby 2008b.

13. *Los Angeles Times* 2009.

14. Fierce Healthcare: Daily News for Healthcare Executives 2009d.

15. Menn 2006, A1.

16. Dixon 2006, 28.

17. Andrews 2008.

18. U.S. Department of Labor, Office of Employment Disability Policy 2008. If the medical identity-theft victim has a record of a physical or mental impairment, protection against discrimination may be available under the Americans with Disabilities Act. Of course, forcing a victim of identity theft to endure unnecessary litigation is expensive, unfair, and discouraging.

19. Some imposters engage in "looping," a practice in which the health insurance benefits for a family is exhausted one member at a time. Gellman and Dixon 2008, 11.

20. Merisalo 2008.

21. Merisalo 2008, 8.

22. See http://www.medicalaw.net/july_15,_2006_legal.htm and MedLaw.com 2006.

23. Slade 2000.

24. U.S. Attorney's Office, Southern District New York 2006.

25. Tennessee Board of Medical Examiners 2004.

26. Mangano 1997.

27. U.S. Department of Health and Human Services, Office of Inspector General 2003b. Also see, U.S. Department of Health and Human Services, Centers for Medicare and Medicaid Services 2006.

28. Fierce Healthcare, Daily News for Healthcare Executives 2009f.

29. U.S. General Accounting Office 1998.

30. U.S. Department of Health and Human Services and U.S. Department of Justice 2007, 17.

31. Mangano 1997.

32. U.S. Department of Health and Human Services and U.S. Department of Justice 2007, 9.

33. U.S. Department of Health and Human Services and U.S. Department of Justice 2006, 11.

34. *Business First of Buffalo* 2008.

35. Holmes 2008.

36. Associated Press 2008.

37. FierceHealthcare, Daily News for Healthcare Executives 2007b.

38. Fierce Healthcare, Daily News for Healthcare Executives 2005.

39. Prism Innovations, Inc., Caregiver Education Series, N.d.

40. Fraud Guides n.d.

41. U.S. Department of Health and Human Services, Centers for Medicare and Medicaid Services 2008e, 2.

42. U.S. Department of Health and Human Services, Centers for Medicare and Medicaid Services. n.d.a; U.S. Department of Health and Human Services, Office of Inspector General 1998.

43. For a description of a DRG coding-process software used at the Louis A. Weiss Memorial Hospital, a teaching hospital affiliated with the University of Chicago Hospitals, see Kerwin 1995. According to medical economist J. D. Kleinke, "Indeed, the practices of upcoding, and optimizing [revenues] in particular, are so commonplace that they have spawned a cottage industry of software vendors and consulting firms that specialize in them." Kleinke 1998, 21.

44. Phillips and Cohen, LLP n.d.

45. Fierce Healthcare, Daily News for Healthcare Professionals 2009f.

46. Silverman and Skinner 2001.

47. Silverman and Skinner 2004.

48. Morris 2000.

49. U.S. Department of Health and Human Services and U.S. Department of Justice 2001.

50. *U.S. ex. rel. Semtner v. Emergency Physicians Billing Services et al.* (WD OK No. 94–617–C).

51. U.S. Department of Justice n.d.

52. Phillips and Cohen, LLP n.d.

53. U.S. Department of Justice 1997.

54. U.S. Department of Justice n.d.

55. Mangano 1997.

56. Ibid.

57. U.S. Department of Defense, Office of Inspector General n.d.

58. Kelly 2007.

59. U.S. Department of Health and Human Services, Centers for Medicare and Medicaid Services n.d.a., 1.

60. U.S. Department of Justice n.d.

61. U.S. Department of Health and Human Services and U.S. Department of Justice 2001.

62. U.S. Department of Health and Human Services, Centers for Medicare and Medicaid Services n.d.b. From 2000 to 2007, Medicare paid between $60 and $92 million for hundreds of thousands of durable medical equipment claims containing identification numbers of an estimated 16,500 to 18,200 deceased physicians. U.S. Senate 2008; Medical News Today 2008.

63. U.S. Department of Health and Human Services and U.S. Department of Justice 2001.

64. U.S. Department of Health and Human Services, Centers for Medicare and Medicaid Services n.d.a., 9–10.

65. U.S. Department of Health and Human Services and U.S. Department of Justice 2006.

66. Morris 2008, 7.

67. HealthDay: News for Healthier Living 2009.

68. Themedica 2009.

69. Shishkin 2008.

70. Abel 2009.

71. U.S. Department of Treasury, Internal Revenue Service 2009.

72. U.S. Department of Health and Human Services, Centers for Medicare and Medicaid Services 2007, 3.

73. A complicating issue with respect to hospice patients is the uncertain course of their illness. Patients diagnosed with terminal illnesses, contrary to the standard textbook prognosis, sometimes survive indefinitely. This fortunate turn of events creates the impression the provider engaged in Medicare fraud.

74. Halper 2009.

75. Rubin 2003.

76. U.S. Department of Justice n.d.

77. U.S. Department of Health and Human Services and U.S. Department of Justice 2006, 12.

78. U.S. Department of Justice, Federal Bureau of Investigation 2007a.

79. Fierce Healthcare, Daily News for Healthcare Executives 2009a and 2009b.

80. U.S. Department of Justice 2010.

81. Hallam 2005.

82. Zwillich 2005.

83. Office of the New York State Attorney General 2000.

84. Freeman 2008.

85. CBS News 2007; Associated Press 2007, 10.

86. Office of Applied Studies, Substance Abuse and Mental Health Services Administration 2010, 1.

87. Clevenger 2009.

88. Interagency Working Group on Synthetic Drugs 2005, 9–13.

89. U.S. Department of Health and Human Services and U.S. Department of Justice 2007, 20.

90. Freeman 2008.

91. U.S. Drug Enforcement Administration, Last Act Partnership, and the University of Wisconsin, Pain and Policy Studies Group 2004.

92. Kaufman 2004.

93. U.S. Department of Health and Human Services 2007a.

94. U.S. Department of Health and Human Services, Office of Inspector General 2007, 19–26.

95. Clarkson n.d.

96. Cross and Bennett Attorneys 2007.

97. Fierce Healthcare, Daily News for Healthcare Executives 2007a.

98. U.S. Department of Health and Human Services 2007b.

99. Leavitt 2007.

100. Mathias 2004.

101. Russell 2004.

102. U.S Department of Health and Human Services, Centers for Medicare and Medicaid Services n.d.a., 4.

103. Arkansas Division of Aging and Adult Services n.d., 1.

104. U.S. Department of Justice 2007b.

105. These cases were obtained from U.S. Department of Health and Human Services and Department of Justice 2007, 14–15.

106. Jecker and Braddock 2008.

107. Peeno 1996.

108. Serbaroli 1999–2000.

109. Francis 2008, B1 and B2.

110. U.S. Department of Health and Human Services, Centers for Medicare and Medicaid Services n.d.a., 8.

111. Freking 2008b.

112. Ibid.

113. Girion 2006, C2.

114. Girion 2007.

115. Girion 2008.

116. Ibid.

117. Appleby 2008a.

118. Jay 2010.

119. Morris 2007.

120. U.S. Department of Health and Human Services and U.S. Department of Justice 2007, 17.

121. Belluck 2001; de Vries 2002.

122. Draper 2003.

123. Gillam n.d.

124. Draper 2003.

125. Zycher 2007; de Vries 2002.

CHAPTER 4

1. The physician revealed neither the patient's identity nor the name of the hospital where the treatment took place.

2. Fierce Healthcare, Daily News for Healthcare Executives 2009i.

3. *Doulgeris v. U.S.* No. 8:08-cv-00282 (August 3, 2009).

4. Fierce Healthcare, Daily News for Healthcare Executives 2009c.

5. Mamula 2008.

6. Tenet Shareholder Committee, LLC 2005, 2.

7. See "Tenet Healthcare Corporation" n.d.; Goff 2007.

8. Grassley 2003.

9. Gray and Hebert 2007, 283–98.

10. Associated Press 2006.

11. U.S. Department of Justice 2006b.

12. Metropolitan News-Enterprise 2006.

13. Business Services Industry 2004.

14. Goff 2007.

15. Reuters 2009.

16. Tenet Shareholder Committee, LLC 2005, 4.

17. Kleinke 1998, 7.

18. The historical sketch of HCA was based on their website at http://hcahealth care.com/CustomPage.asp?guidCustomContentID=9612D4C4–07A9–4CD6-B271–87D3BF3225F0.

19. Funding Universe n.d.

20. Public Broadcasting System 1997.

21. Eichenwald 1998.

22. U.S. Department of Justice 2000.

23. U.S. Department of Justice 2003b.

24. Johnson 2007, A13.

25. See *New York Times* 2010.

26. Sorkin 2006; Duncan 2007.

27. Hoovers n.d.

28. Farrell 2006, 135.

29. Information obtained from the U.S. Department of Justice, Bureau of Prisons, Inmate Locator website, http://www.bop.gov/iloc2/LocateInmate.jsp.

30. U.S. Department of Justice 2004b.

31. U.S. Department of Justice 2007a.

32. But the $2.88 billion judgment against Scrushy will be paid directly to HealthSouth, and the shareholders will get approximately 40% of the settlement after legal and other expenses.

33. Beam and Warner 2009, 112–14.

34. Esterl and Bauerlein 2009.

35. Bauerlein and Esterl 2009.

36. HealthSouth 2009.

37. HealthSouth 2010.

38. U.S. Federal Trade Commission n.d.

39. Pear 2009.

40. U.S. Federal Trade Commission 2009, 113.

41. U.S. Federal Trade Commission 2009, 113–15.

42. Allen and Farragher 2009.

43. Allen and Bombardieri 2008a.

44. Ibid.

45. Allen and Bombardieri 2008b; Farragher and Kowalczyk 2008.

46. Allen and Bombardieri 2008b.

47. Ibid.

48. Weisman and Kowalczyk 2010.

49. U.S. Federal Trade Commission 2005, 244–77.

50. American Medical Association 2004.

51. Jordan 2009.

52. Kennedy 2009b; Chernoff and Steffen 2009.

CHAPTER 5

1. Ruiz 2009.

2. Market Research.com 2009.

3. Rockoff and Kendall 2009; Winslow 2009; Pfizer n.d.; and O'Reilly 2009b. Note that doctors can prescribe drugs for off-label use, but drug manufacturers are forbidden from engaging in such promotions.

4. Attkisson 2009; National Association of Medicaid Fraud Control Units 2009.

5. Morris 2007.

6. U.S. Department of Health and Human Services, Centers for Medicare and Medicaid Services 2008a.

7. National Health Policy Forum 2009, 1–3.

8. Morris 2007.

9. U.S. Department of Health and Human Services and U.S. Department of Justice 2007, 12.

10. Boyd and Associates and Berg and Androphy 2005.

11. U.S. Department of Health and Human Services and U.S. Department of Justice 2007, 20.

12. U.S. Department of Health and Human Services 2007a, 7–8.

13. FierceHealthcare, Daily News for Health Care Executives 2008h.

14. A Schedule I drug has a high potential for abuse, and it has no safe or accepted medical use in the United States. A Schedule II drug also has a high potential for abuse and it may lead to serious physical or psychological dependence by the user, but it does have a legitimate medical use (possibly with severe restrictions) in the United States. Schedules III, IV, and V all have acceptable medical uses with lower potential for abuse (with Schedule V being the least addictive). See Title 21 "Food and Drugs," chap. 13 "Drug Abuse Prevention and Control," subchap. I, "Control and Enforcement," part B "Authority to Control"; Standards and Schedules, 21 U.S.C. Sec. 812 January 22, 2002, http://www.usdoj.gov/dea/pubs/csa/812.htm.

15. U.S. Department of Health and Human Services and U.S. Department of Justice 2007, 22.

16. U.S. Department of Health and Human Services and U.S. Department of Justice 2004.

17. U.S. Drug Enforcement Administration 2005.

18. U.S. Department of Health and Human Services and U.S. Department of Justice 2007, 21

19. Interagency Working Group on Synthetic Drugs 2005, 12.

20. Yahoo Finance 2008.

21. U.S. Congressional Budget Office 2006.

22. See U.S. Food and Drug Administration n.d.a.

23. False Claims Act Legal Center n.d.

24. "Takeda Pharmaceuticals and TAP Pharmaceutical Products, Inc. Merge" 2008. Reference in this press release is made to TAP, the company's name during the federal investigation and settlement, not to its current name of Takeda.

25. Public Law 100–293 (1987) and Public Law 102–353 (1992).

26. Phillips and Cohen, LLP 2001.

27. Morris 2007, 3.

28. Quitamhelp.com n.d.

29. Business Wire 2001.

30. The quotes by McCallum, Sullivan, Thompson, and Bradley are from U.S. Department of Justice 2001.

31. Petersen 2001.

32. Dembner 2004.

33. Murphy and Dembner 2004.

34. U.S. Department of Justice 2005.

35. See, for example, Value Based Management.net n.d.

36. Both Serostim and the protease inhibitor drugs were introduced to the market in 1996.

37. Spivack 2008.

38. Washingtonpost.com and Associated Press 2005, A12.

39. Lichtblau 2005.

40. McGrath 2005, 14–16.

41. Thompson www.thompson.com 2005, 15.

42. U.S. Department of Justice 2005.

43. Ibid.

44. Kerber 2007.

45. Purdue n.d.

46. Chasen 2007.

47. Online Lawyer Source n.d. For an in-depth discussion of OxyContin, see Jayawant and Balkrishnan 2005, 77–82, and U.S. General Accounting Office 2003.

48. Roth et al. 2000, 853–60.

49. Ibid, 859 (last full sentence of the text).

50. Roth et al. 2000. This quotation can be found in the Comment section of the article, 4th paragraph at the 4th and 5th sentences.

51. U.S. Attorney's Office, Western District of Virginia 2007.

52. Ibid.

53. All quotes are from U.S. Attorney's Office, Western District of Virginia 2007.

54. Schering-Plough home page 2008.

55. Petersen 2002.

56. U.S. Food and Drug Administration 2002.

57. U.S. Department of Justice 2004c.

58. Abelson 2004.

59. U.S. Department of Justice 2006a.

60. Harris 2004.

61. Ibid.

62. Campbell et al. 2007.

63. Rust and Fauber 2009; Wilson 2009.

64. Armstrong and Winstein 2009.

65. Fierce Healthcare, Daily News for Healthcare Executive 2009j.

66. Gellene and Maugh 2008.

67. Carey and Harris 2008.

68. Periodic Table 2009.

69. Shelton 2008.

70. Gardner 2009.

71. Harris 2009.

72. Harris 2008.

73. Wilson 2009.

74. Saul 2008.

75. Tabarrok 2000, 41–47.

76. Kaisernetwork.org 2008b and Tesoriero 2008, B1. The Vioxx case remains in litigation. For the latest developments on the Vioxx settlements, see PointofLaw.com 2010.

77. Fierce Healthcare, Daily News for Healthcare Executives 2009k.

78. O'Reilly 2009a.

79. FierceHealthcare, Daily News for Healthcare Executives 2008b.

80. Association of American Medical Colleges 2010.

81. Harvard Medical School 2010 and Singer and Wilson 2010.

82. Government of the District of Columbia, Office of the Inspector General 2003.

83. U.S. Department of Health and Human Services and U.S. Department of Justice 2005; U.S. Department of Justice 2003a.

84. Hood 2009, 52.

85. Moore 2008.

86. Burns 2008. Information on Zimmer Holdings, list of consultants, deferred prosecution agreement, and compliance hotline can be found at zimmer.com.

87. U.S. Department of Health and Human Services, Office of Inspector General 2003a.

88. Pringle 2006.

89. U.S. Department of Justice 2004a.

90. Pringle 2006.

91. "National News Briefs: Faulty Tubing Is Blamed for Four Dialysis Deaths" 1998.

92. U.S. Food and Drug Administration 2006.

93. U.S. Securities and Exchange Commission 2000.

94. Business Wire 2000.

95. U.S. Federal Trade Commission 2009, 8–9.

96. U.S. Federal Trade Commission 2009, 10–11.

97. This information was derived from tables in Loucks and Lam 2007, appendix A: "Health Care Fraud Settlements of at Least $1 Million (1990–2007)," 519–640.

98. Settlement amounts for the eight-year period were taken from Loucks and Lam 2007, 513; the national health care expenditures were taken from U.S. Department of Health and Human Services, Centers for Medicare and Medicaid Services n.d.b.

99. For a thorough discussion of the dynamics of prosecuting and defending health care fraud and abuse cases, see Loucks and Lam 2007, and Hooper and Abbott 2007 in Baumann 2007, 321–408.

CHAPTER 6

1. Yen 2009; Duhigg 2008.

2. Leap 2007, 161–63.

3. Kaisernetwork.org 2008a.

4. Rosenberg 2007.

5. Attkisson 2008.

6. For a discussion of preventive methods, see Barber 2006 and the U.S. Securities Exchange Commission.

7. U.S. Department of Health and Human Services, Office of Inspector General n.d.

8. U.S. Sentencing Guidelines 2007, chap. 8, part B, and U.S. Sentencing Commission 2004.

9. Nanda 2006.

10. U.S. Administration on Aging 2008. Also see U.S. Department of Health and Human Services, Centers for Medicare and Medicaid Services 2009.

11. U.S. Administration on Aging 2008; U.S. Administration on Aging n.d.

12. Barber and the U.S. Securities Exchange Commission 2006.

13. P.L. 93–637; 15 U.S.C. ch. 50, sec. 2301 et seq.

14. See Gellman and Dixon 2008.

15. Gellman and Dixon 2008, 6–7.

16. U.S. Federal Trade Commission 2007

17. U.S. Department of Justice, Federal Bureau of Investigation 2007b.

18. Best 2006.

19. Bentham 2007.

20. Schultz 2007; Fierce Healthcare, Daily News for Healthcare Executives 2006b; Fierce Healthcare, Daily News for Healthcare Executives 2006a.

21. Fierce Healthcare, Daily News for Healthcare Executives 2008g.

22. U.S. Department of Health and Human Services 2009b.

23. Arkansas Department of Health and Humans Services, Division of Aging and Human Services 2007; Modern Healthcare.com 2008.

24. Modern Healthcare.com 2008.

25. The proposed bill may be viewed at http://thomas.loc.gov/cgi-bin/bdquery/z?d 110:HR06898:@@@L&summ2=m&.

26. Menn 2006.

27. National Insurance Crime Bureau 2000, 14.

28. Sparrow 2000, 39–40.

29. Coalition Against Insurance Fraud 2003.

30. See Hyman 2001 for a discussion of the professional, social, and economic complications surrounding the control of health care fraud.

31. Sparrow 2000, 159–61.

32. For an excellent analysis of the weakness of health insurance claims processing and fraud, see Sparrow 2000.

33. Sparrow 2000, 163–64; Sparrow 1996, 126–27.

34. Gusman 2008.

35. Consortium to Combat Medical Fraud 2008.

36. Grube and Reeve 1992, 101 and 102.

37. Rai 2001.

38. Govtrack.us: A Civic Project to Track Congress 2010.

39. It appears that government prosecutors—from a cost-benefit standpoint—want to pursue potentially high-dollar settlements. In other instances the existence of whistle-blowers dictates which cases are prosecuted.

40. Basler 2008.

41. See Bosworth 2002, Luongo 2004, and Novak 2006 for insights into the routines of inmates in the federal prison system.

42. Hill 2007. Note the discussion in this chapter about the Inspector General's investigation of the veracity of some fraud rates reported by CMS.

43. U.S. Department of Health and Human Services, Centers for Medicare and Medicaid Services 2008b.

44. The description of the CMS pre- and postpayment claim-review programs are from U.S. Department of Health and Human Services, Centers for Medicare and Medicaid Services. 2008d.

45. Hill 2007.

46. Freking 2009.

47. Clark 2009.

48. Galimi 2006.

49. Webwire 2008.

50. Li et al. 2008, 281–85.

51. Li et al. 2008, 285.

52. Li et al. 2008.

53. Obtaining documents or computer files may require a search warrant, but evidence pertaining to billings and reimbursements from Medicare, Medicaid, or other federal programs may be subject to seizure without a warrant.

54. Kerr 2005, 532. Also see Britz 2009, 233–63, and U.S. Department of Justice 2002.

55. Loucks and Lam 2007, 392.

56. To illustrate the confusing language of some Medicare regulations, see U.S. Department of Health and Human Services, Centers for Medicare and Medicaid Services 2004.

57. Loucks and Lam 2007, 648.

58. The discussion of the strategies used by prosecutors and defense counsel is based, in part, on Baumann 2007, 321–408, and Loucks and Lam 2007, 641–90.

59. For an insider's view of how federal prosecutors work, see Kroger 2008.

60. 18 U.S.C. sec. 3553(a). The Federal Sentencing Guidelines and Manual are available at: http://www.ussc.gov/2008guid/TABCON08.htm.

61. U.S. Sentencing Commission 2008, chap. 4, part A, "Criminal History."

62. 543 U.S. 220. 125 S. Ct. 738 (2005).

APPENDIX: A

1 Amednews.com 2009a. For 2009 budget information, see U.S. Department of Health and Human Services 2008a; Kaiser Family Foundation 2007.

2. Persons under the age of sixty-five who receive Social Security disability payments as well as dialysis patients, among others, may also be eligible for Medicare benefits.

3. Hoffman, Klees, and Curtis 2007, 6.

4. For an in-depth discussion of the Medicare program and an explanation of benefits and options, see U.S Department of Health and Human Services, Centers for Medicare and Medicaid Services 2008f, *Medicare and You 2008*. The document is available on the Social Security Administration website (www.ssa.gov) or at: http://www.medicare. gov/Library/PDFNavigation/PDFInterim.asp?Language=English&Type=Pub&PubID=1 0050.

5. Of this, 1.45% is contributed by the employee and 1.45% is contributed by the employer; those who are self—employed pay the entire 2.9%.

6. U.S. Social Security Administration 2008.

7. Amednews.com 2009a.

8. KaiserEDU.org, n.d.

9. Confessore 2009.

10. U.S. Social Security Administration 2008; Center for Health Care Strategies, Inc. 2010.

11. U.S. Department of Health and Human Services, Centers for Medicare and Medicaid Services 2008c.

12. SCHIP had an initial ten-year authorization period.

13. Families USA 2008.

14. Kaiser Family statehealthfacts.org 2007.

15. http://www.tricare.mil/mybenefit/index.jsp.

References

Abel, David. 2009. "Costs, Concerns Rise on Home Health Care." *Boston Globe,* March 28, http://www.boston.com/news/local/massachusetts/articles/2009/03/28/costs_concerns_rise_on_home_healthcare/.

Abelson, Reed. 2004. "Schering Case Demonstrates Manipulation of Drug Prices." *New York Times,* July 31, http://query.nytimes.com/gst/fullpage.html?res=9900E1D91E3DF932A05754C0A9629C8B63.

Abrams, Norman, and Sara Sun Beale. 2000. *Federal Criminal Law and Its Enforcement,* 3rd ed. St. Paul: West.

Allen, Scott, and Thomas Farragher. 2009. "Partners, Insurer Under Scrutiny." *Boston Globe,* January 23, http://www.boston.com/news/local/massachusetts/articles/2009/01/23/partners_insurer_under_scrutiny/.

Allen, Scott, and Marcella Bombardieri. 2008a. "A Handshake That Made Healthcare History." *Boston Globe,* December 28, http://www.boston.com/news/health/articles/2008/12/28/a_handshake_that_made_healthcare_history/.

——. 2008b. "A Healthcare System Badly Out of Balance." *Boston Globe,* November 16, http://www.boston.com/news/local/articles/2008/11/16/a_healthcare_system_badly_out_of_balance/.

Amednews.com. 2009a. "2010 HHS Budget Looks to Use Medicare Savings for Reform." May 18, http://www.ama-assn.org/amednews/2009/05/18/gvsb0518.htm.

——. 2009b. "Stricter Self-Referrals Rules May End Some Physician Contracts with Hospitals." September 28, http://www.ama-assn.org/amednews/2009/09/28/gvl10928.htm.

American Medical Association. 2004. "What Is the Messenger Model?" January, http://www.cms.org/OfficeStaff/HCFD/AntiTrust/WhatIsaMessengerMode.pdf.

Andrews, Michelle. 2008. "Medical Identity Theft Turns Patients into Victims." *U.S. News & World Report,* February 29, http://www.usnews.com/health/family-health/articles/2008/02/29/medical-identity-theft-turns-patients-into-victims.html.

ApatheticVoter.com. n.d. "Defense Contracting Rip-Off." http://www.apatheticvoter.com/DefenseContractingRip-Off.htm.

Appleby, Julie. 2008a. "Regulators Tell HealthMarkets to Improve Practices." *USA Today,* January 7, http://www.usatoday.com/money/companies/regulation/2008-01-07-megalife-healthmarkets_N.htm.

——. 2008b. "Identity Thieves Prey on Patients' Medical Records." *USA Today,* May 7, http://www.usatoday.com/news/health/2008-05-06-privacy_N.htm.

Arkansas Department of Health and Human Services, Division of Aging and Human Services. 2007. "National Program Aimed at Reducing Health Care Fraud Takes on a New Identity." http://www.Healthyarkansas.com/news/pr_01-10-2007.html.

——. n.d. "Durable Medical Equipment (DME) Fraud and Abuse." http://www.arkansas.gov/dhs/aging/6-DurableMedicalEquipmentFraudAndAbuse.pdf.

Armstrong, David, and Keith Winstein. 2009. "Hospital Gets Subpoena Tied to Doctor's Studies." *Wall Street Journal,* April 7, http://online.wsj.com/article/SB123905950162494901.html.

Arora, Vineet, Sandeep Gangireddy, Amit Mehorptra, Ranjan Ginde, Megan Tormey, and David Meltzer. 2009. "Ability of Hospitalized Patients to Identify Their In-Hospital Physicians." *Archives of Internal Medicine* 169(2): 199–201.

Associated Press. 1987. "Podiatrist Is Indicted in Medicaid Fraud Case." *New York Times,* November 13, http://query.nytimes.com/gst/fullpage.html?res=9B0DE0D91138F930A25752C1A961948260.

——. 2006. "Tenet in $900 Million Settlement." June 30, http://www.nytimes.com/2006/06/30/business/30tenet.html.

——. 2007. "'Pill Mill' Caused at Least 4 Deaths, Prosecutors Say." December 20, http://www.msnbc.msn.com/id/22346625/.

——. 2008. "Merck Settlement One of the Largest Ever in Health Fraud." March 7, http://www.denverpost.com/healthcare/ci_8201950.

Association of American Medical Colleges. 2010. "In the Interest of Patients: Recommendations for Physician Financial Relationships and Clinical Decision Making." June, https://services.aamc.org/publications/showfile.cfm?file=version163.pdf&prd_id=303&prv_id=375&pdf_id=163.

Attkisson, Sharyl. 2008. "Meet Medicare Fraud's Whistleblower." CBS News, February 8, http://www.cbsnews.com/stories/2008/02/08/eveningnews/main3811185.shtml.

——. 2009. "Eli Lilly Owes $1.4 B over 'Off Label' Use." CBS News, January 15, http://www.cbsnews.com/stories/2009/01/15/cbsnews_investigates/main4725873.shtml.

Barber, Jeff and Securities and Exchange Commission. 2006. Letter from Accu-Rate Telecom, Inc. to SEC Assistant Secretary Jill M. Peterson. July 19, http://www.sec.gov/comments/s7-11-06/s71106-5.pdf.

Barrish, Cris. 2010. "Delaware Crime: Dr. Earl Bradley Sex Case Ignites Outrage." *News Journal,* February 24, http://www.delawareonline.com/article/20100224/NEWS01/2240356/Delaware-crime-Dr.-Earl-Bradley-sex-case-ignites-outrage.

Basler, Barbara. 2008. "Million-Dollar Medicines." *AARP Bulletin,* October: 12–15.

Bauerlein, Valerie, and Mike Esterl. 2009. "Judge Orders Scrushy to Pay $2.88 Billion in Civil Suit." *Wall Street Journal,* June 19, http://online.wsj.com/article/SB124533875598827811.html.

Baumann, Linda A., ed. 2007. *Health Care Fraud and Abuse: Practical Perspectives.* Arlington, Va.: BNA Books, Bureau of National Affairs.

Baumann, Linda A., ed. 2009. *Health Care Fraud and Abuse: Practical Perspectives: 2009 Supplement.* Arlington, Va.: BNA Books, Bureau of National Affairs.

Beam, Richard, and Chris Warner. 2009. *HealthSouth: The Wagon to Disaster.* Fairhope, Ala.: Wagon Publishing.

Belluck, Pam. 2001. "Prosecutors Say Greed Drove Pharmacist to Dilute Drugs." *New York Times,* August 18, http://query.nytimes.com/gst/fullpage.html?res=990CE6DC103EF93BA2575BC0A9679C.

Bentham, Paul. 2007. "Can Biometrics Secure the Public's Data?" Silicon.com, November 23, http://www.silicon.com/publicsector/0,3800010403,39169254,00.htm.

Best, Jo. 2006. "Biometrics Unreliable, Says EU Privacy Head." CNet News.com, March 15, http://news.cnet.com/Biometrics-unreliable,-says-EU-privacy-head/2100–1029_3–6050024.html.

Bonifield, John. 2010. "Health Care Industry Sick with Medical Waste." CNN Health, March 3, http://www.cnn.com/2010/HEALTH/03/03/prescription.for.waste/index.html.

Bosworth, Mary. 2002. *The U.S. Federal Prison System.* Thousand Oaks, Calif.: Sage.

Boyd and Associates and Berg and Androphy. 2005. "King Pharmaceuticals Pays $124 Million to Settle Medicaid Fraud Charges Involving Pharmacy Benefit Managers." November 1, http://www.taf.org/BogartKingRelease.pdf.

Bradley, Bill. 2007. *The New American Story.* New York: Random House.

BrainyQuote, n.d. http://www.brainyquote.com/quotes/quotes/w/waltercron169605.html.

Bressert, Steve. 2006. "Persuasion and How to Influence Others." American School of Professional Psychology, April 4, http://psychcentral.com/lib/2006/persuasion-and-how-to-influence-others/.

Britz, Marjie T. 2009. *Computer Forensics and Cyber Crime: An Introduction,* 2nd ed. Upper Saddle River, N.J.: Pearson Prentice Hall, 233–63.

Brown, Lawrence D. 2008. "The Amazing Non-Collapsing U.S. Health Care System—Is Reform Finally at Hand?" *New England Journal of Medicine* 358(4): 325–27.

Burns, Greg. 2008. "Hip Deals Put Money in Pocket: Partnerships between Surgeons, Implantmakers Raise Ethical Concerns." Chicagotribune.com, October 26, http://www.chicagotribune.com/business/chi-sun-hip-replacement-zimmer-oct26,0,6406833.story?page=1.

Burton, Thomas M., and David Armstrong. 2009. "Medical-Device Suits Allege Kickbacks." *Wall Street Journal,* July 16, http://online.wsj.com/article/SB124769623201347809.html.

Business First of Buffalo. 2008. "Minn. Co. Pays $75M to Settle Gov't Charges." May 22, http://buffalo.bizjournals.com/buffalo/stories/2008/05/19/daily51.html.

Business Services Industry. 2004. "Tenet Announces Agreement to Sell St. Charles General Hospital to Preferred Continuum Care." December 10, http://findarticles.com/p/articles/mi_m0EIN/is_2004_Dec_10/ai_n8586999.

Business Wire. 2000. "Fresenius Medical Care Fact Sheet." January 19, http://findarticles.com/p/articles/mi_m0EIN/is_2000_Jan_19/ai_58664477.

——. 2001. "Tufts Health Plan Congratulates U.S. Attorney on Settlement with TAP Pharmaceuticals, Inc." October 3, http://findarticles.com/p/articles/mi_m0EIN/is_2001_Oct_3/ai_78864983.

Campbell, Eric G., Russell L. Gruen, James Mountford, Lawrence G. Miller, Paul D. Cleary, and David Blumenthal. 2007. "A National Survey of Physician-Industry Relationships." *New England Journal of Medicine* 356 (April 26): 1742–50.

Canade, Terrence P. 1985. "Civil RICO-Incentive to Litigate: The Court's Rejection of Standing Requirements." *Journal of Criminal Law and Criminology* 76: 1086.

Carey, Benedict, and Gardiner Harris. 2008. "Psychiatric Group Faces Scrutiny over Drug Industry Ties." *New York Times,* July 12, http://www.nytimes.com/2008/07/12/washington/12psych.html.

Carpenter, Mason A., and William Gerard Sanders. 2007. *Strategic Management,* 2nd ed. Upper Saddle River, N.J.: Pearson Prentice Hall.

Cashill, Jack. 2000. "Intolerable Abuse: The Unlikely Persecution of Dennis McClatchey." September, http://www.cashill.com/natl_general/intolerable_abuse.htm.

CBS News. 2007. "Kansas 'Pill Mill' linked to 4 Deaths." December 20, http://www.cbsnews.com/stories/2007/12/20/national/main3636538.shtml?source=related_story.

Center for Health Care Strategies, Inc. 2010. "Medicaid by the Numbers: Opportunities to Improve Quality and Control Costs." May, http://www.chcs.org/usr_doc/Medicaid_Facts.pdf.

Chasen, Emily. 2007. Purdue Frederick Pleads Guilty in OxyContin Case." Thomson Reuters, May 10, http://www.reuters.com/article/healthNews/idUSWBT00695020070510.

Chernoff, Allan, and Sheila Steffen. 2009. "Organized Crime's New Target: Medicare." CNN.com, October 24, http://www.cnn.com/2009/CRIME/10/22/medicare.organized.crime/?iref=polticker.

Chicago Tribune. 2010. "Burr Ridge Doctor Gets 5 Years for Insurance Fraud." August 11, http://articles.chicagotribune.com/2010-08-11/news/ct-met-physician-sentenced-0812-20100811_1_insurance-fraud-health-care-insurance-providers.

Chua, Kao-Ping. 2006. "Overview of the U.S. Health Care System." February 10, http://www.amsa.org/uhc/HealthCareSystemOverview.pdf.

Clark, Cheryl. 2009. "Feds Find Many Docs Are Using Ultrasounds Too Often, Possibly Fraudulently." *Health Leaders Media,* July 24, http://www.healthleadersmedia.com/content/236431/page/2/topic/WS_HLM2_PHY/Feds-Find-Many-Docs-Are-Using-Ultrasounds-Too-Often-Possibly-Fraudulently.html.

Clarkson, Charles. n.d. "Beneficiaries: Beware of Medicare Part D Scams." SMP of New Jersey, http://www.state.nj.us/health/senior/documents/smparticles_partdscams.pdf.

Clevenger, Andrew. 2009. "Feds Probe Pain-Killing Ring in Southern West Virginia: Charleston Doctor's House Searched." WVGazette.com, April 1, http://wvgazette.com/News/200904014966.

Coalition Against Insurance Fraud. 2003. "Study on SIU Performance Measurement." June, http://www.insurancefraud.org/downloads/siu_study.pdf.

Confessore, Nicolas. 2009. "City and State Agree to Repay U.S. for Improper Medicaid Claims." *New York Times,* July 21, http://www.nytimes.com/2009/07/22/nyregion/22whistle.html.

Connecticut Attorney General's Office. 2008. "Attorney General Sues Pharmaceutical Company for Inflating Drug Prices." Press release, May 29, http://www.ct.gov/ag/cwp/view.asp?Q=416338&.

Consortium to Combat Medical Fraud. 2008. "New Consortium Plans Strategies to Combat Medical Fraud." *Insurance Journal,* June 25, http://www.insurancejournal.com/news/national/2008/06/25/91344.htm.

"Conspiracy—Procedural Rules." n.d. http://law.jrank.org/pages/721/Conspiracy-Procedural-rules.html.

Cross and Bennett Attorneys. 2007. "Medical Equipment Fraud: Almost 1 Billion in Medicare Overpayments for Wheelchairs, Oxygen Supplies, etc." Report, July 3, http://www.crossbennett/CM/Articles/Articles139asp.

Davis, Melissa. 2003. "Untangling Tenet's Ties to Watchdog." TheStreet.com, August 7, http://www.thestreet.com/stocks/melissadavid/10106066.html.

Dembner, Alice. 2004. "TAP Officials on Trial Today in Fraud." *Boston Globe.* April 20, http://www.boston.com/news/nation/articles/2004/04/20/tap_officials_on_trial_today_in_fraud_case/.

DeNavas-Walt, Carmen, Bernadette D. Proctor, and Jessica Smith. 2007. *Income, Poverty, and Health Insurance Coverage in the United States: 2006.* Washington, D.C.: U.S. Census Bureau and U.S. Department of Commerce, Economics and Statistics Administration, Current Population Reports, Consumer Income. Report, August, http://www.census.gov/prod/2007pubs/p60-233.pdf.

de Vries, Lloyd. 2002. "Thousands of Diluted Drug Doses: Pharmacist Pleaded Guilty; Now Says There Were More." CBS News, April 19, http://www.cbsnews.com/stories/2002/04/19/national/main506777.shtml.

Dixon, Pam. 2006. "Medical Identity Theft: The Information Crime That Can Kill You." World Privacy Forum report, May 3, http://www.worldprivacyforum.org/pdf/wpf_medicalidtheft2006.pdf.

Draper, Robert. 2003. "The Toxic Pharmacist." *New York Times Magazine.* June 8, http://query.nytimes.com/gst/fullpage.html?res=9502E2DA1230F93BA35755C0A9659C8B63&sec=&spon=&pagewanted=1.

Duhigg, Charles. 2008. "Medicare Fraud Cutting Disputed." New York Times News Service, August 21, http://www.boston.com/news/health/articles/2008/08/21/medicare_fraud_cutting_disputed.

Duncan, Walker. 2007. "Bovender Tells Story of HCA Buyout." *Nashville Post,* June 27, http://www.nashvillepost.com/news/2007/6/27/bovender_tells_story_of_hca_buyout.

Dutton, Jay M. n.d. "Complications of Nasal and Sinus Surgery." American Rhinologic Society, http://www.american-rhinologic.org/patientinfo.surgerycomplications.phtml.

Eichenwald, Kurt. 1998. "U.S. Suit Charges Fraud by 2 Big Hospital Chains." *New York Times,* October 6, http://query.nytimes.com/gst/fullpage.html?res=9800E0D91F3 8F935A35753C1A96E9582.

Ekstrand, Laurie E. 2006. "Information on False Claims Act Litigation." Letter to the Honorable F. James Sensenbrenner Jr. and the Honorable Chris Cannon. U.S. Government Accountability Office, January 31, http://www.gao.gov/new.items/d06320r.pdf.

Esterl, Mike, and Valerie Bauerlein. 2009. "Big Verdict Sends Lawyers on a Treasure Hunt." *Wall Street Journal,* September 5–6, A1 and A10.

Estrada, Linda A. 2008. "Congress to Consider Dramatic Expansion of False Claims Act." *Journal of Health Care Compliance.* March–April:5–10.

European Healthcare Fraud and Corruption Network. 2004. "Health Care Fraud: A Europe-Wide Issue." European Healthcare Fraud and Corruption Conference, November 6, http://goliath.ecnext.com/coms2/gi_0199–2617460/EHFCC-CONFERENCE-Healthcare-fraud-a.html.

——. 2007. Commission of the European Communities Consultation Regarding Community Action on Health Services. January 31, http://ec.europa.eu/health/ph_overview/co_operation/mobility/docs/health_services_co205.pdf.

False Claims Act Legal Center. n.d. "Top 20 Cases." http://www.taf.org/top20.htm.

Families USA. 2008. "Bush FY 2008 Budget: Analysis of SCHIP and Medicaid Provisions." http://www.familiesusa.org/budget/bush-fy-2008-budget-schip.html.

——. 2009. "'Hidden Health Tax' for Family Health Coverage Climbed to $1,017 in 2008. Press release, May 28, http://www.familiesusa.org/resources/newsroom/press-releases/2009-press-releases/hidden-health-tax-for.html.

Farragher, Thomas, and Liz Kowalczyk. 2008. "Fueled by Profits, A Healthcare Giant Takes Aim at Suburbs." *Boston Globe,* December 21, http://www.boston.com/news/local/massachusetts/articles/2008/12/21/fueled_by_profits_a_health care_giant_takes_aim_at_suburbs/.

Farrell, Greg. 2006. *Corporate Crooks.* Amherst, N.Y: Prometheus Books.

Felson, Marcus. 2002. *Crime and Everyday Life.* Thousand Oaks, Calif.: Sage.

Fierce Healthcare, Daily News for Healthcare Executives. 2005. "Calif. Hospitals Accused of Overbilling Medicare." December 18, http://www.fiercehealthcare.com/story/calif-hospitals-accused-of-overbilling-medicare/2005-12-19.

——. 2006a. "Allina Suffers Patient Data Theft." October 22, http://www.fiercehealthit.com/story/allina-suffers-patient- data-theft/2006–10-23.

——. 2006b. "Massive Data Loss at HCA." August 20, http://www.fiercehealthit.com/story/massive-data-loss-at-hca/2006-08-21.

——. 2007a. "Fraud Riddles FL Medical Device Firms." March 29, http://www.fierce healthcare.com/story/fraud-riddles-fl-medical-device-firms/2007–0330.

——. 2007b. "UConn Health Center Settles Medicare Charges." June 26, http://www.fierce healthcare.com/story/uconn-health-center-settles-medicare-charges/2007-06-27.

——. 2008a. "Department of Justice Faces 500-Case Whistleblower Backlog." July 7, http://www.fiercehealthcare.com/story/department-justice-faces-500-case-healthcare-whistle-blower-backlog/2008–07-02.

——. 2008b. "Doctor Gifts Banned by WI Medical Society." October 20, http://www.fiercehealthcare.com/story/doctor-gifts-banned-wi-medical-society/2008-10-20.

——. 2008c. "Justice Department Recovers $1.12 Billion from Fraud." November 11, http://www.fiercehealthcare.com/story/justice-department-recovers-1–12-billion-fraud/2008–11-11.

——. 2008d. "McKesson Agrees to $350 Million Settlement." November 24, http://www.fiercehealthcare.com/story/mckesson-agrees-350-million-settlement/2008-11-24.

——. 2008e. "PricewaterhouseCoopers Identifies the Top Nine Issues for Health Industries in 2009 Financial Crisis." December 12, http://www.fiercehealthcare.com/press-releases/pricewaterhousecoopers-identifies-top-nine-issues-health-industries-2009-financial-cr.

——. 2008f. "States Aren't Reporting Medicaid Provider Sanctions." August 13, http://www.fiercehealthcare.com/story/states-arent-reporting-medicaid-provider-sanctions/2008-08-13.

——. 2008g. "UCLA Snooping Report Released: More Records Compromised Than Previously Thought." October 30, http://www.fiercehealthcare.com/story/ucla-snooping-report-released-more-records-compromised-previously-thought/2008-10-30.

——. 2008h. "Walgreens Agrees to $35M Drug-Switching Settlement." June 5, http://www.fiercehealthcare.com/story/walgreens-agrees-to-35m-drug-switching-settlement/2008-06-05?utm_medium=nl&utm_source=internal&cmp-id=EMC-NL-FH&dest=FH.

——. 2009a. "Another City of Angels Exec Pleads Guilty to Medical Fraud." March 19, http://www.fiercehealthcare.com/story/another-city-angels-exec-pleads-guilty-medical-fraud/2009–03-19.

——. 2009b. "CA Hospital Chair Pleads Guilty to Paying for Referrals." June 18, http://www.fiercehealthcare.com/story/ca-hospital-chair-pleads-guilty-paying-referrals/2009–06-18.

——. 2009c. "Ex-Cardinal Health Execs Settle with SEC." May 28, http://www.fiercehealthcare.com/story/ex-cardinal-health-execs-settle-sec/2009–05-28.

——. 2009d. "FL Hospital Employee Sells Medical Records to Personal Injury Attorney." July 31, http://www.fiercehealthcare.com/story/fl-hospital-employee-sells-medical-records-personal-injury-atty/2009–07-31.

——. 2009e. "HHS Inspector General Collects $2.35B in 2008." http://www.fiercehealthcare.com/story/hhs-inspector-general-collects-2–35b-2008/2009–01-20?utm_medium=rss&utm_source=rss&cmp-id=OTC-RSS-FH0.

——. 2009f. "Johns Hopkins Facility Settles False Claims Allegations." July 2, http://www.fiercehealthcare.com/story/johns-hopkins-facility-settles-false-claims-allegations/2009-07-02.

——. 2009g. "Lilly to Pay $1.4B to Settle Zyprexa Marketing Charges." January 16, http://www.fiercehealthcare.com/story/lilly-pay-1-4b-settle-zyprexa-marketing-charges/2009-01-16?utm_medium=rss&utm_source=rss&cmp-id=OTC-RSS-FH0.

——. 2009h. "NJ University Pays $2M False Claims Settlement. June 10, http://www.fiercehealthcare.com/story/nj-university-pays-2m-false-claims-settlement/2009–06-10.

——. 2009i. "SEC Charges CA Healthcare Finance Firm with Fraud." July 22, http://www.fiercehealthcare.com/story/sec-charges-ca-healthcare-finance-firm-fraud/2009–07-22.

——. 2009j. "Stryker Faces Two New Investigations." May 13, http://www.fiercehealthcare.com/story/stryker-faces-two-new-investigations/2009–05-13.

——. 2009k. "Wyeth Paid Ghostwriters to Pen Journal Articles on Hormone Replacement Therapy." August 6, http://www.fiercehealthcare.com/story/wyeth-paid-ghostwriters-pen-journal-articles-hormone-replacement-therapy/2009–08-06?utm_medium=rss&utm_source=rss&cmp-id=OTC-RSS-FH0.

——. 2010. "Obama Pledges Crackdown on Healthcare Fraud." March 11, http://www.fiercehealthcare.com/story/president-pledges-crackdown-healthcare-fraud/2010–03-11.

FindLaw for the Public. 2008. http://criminal.findlaw.com/crimes/a-z/racketeering_rico. html.

Finklestein, Katherine Eban. 1998. "The Brighton Beach Swindle." *New York Magazine,* January 26, http://nymag.com/nymetro/news/culture/features/2159/.

Francis, Theo. 2008. "Medicare, Medicaid Managed Care Gets Scrutiny for Fraud." *Wall Street Journal,* March 19, B1–B2.

Fraud Digest. 2005. "Health Care Fraud." September 22, http://www.frauddigest.com/ fraud.php?ident=1464.

Fraud Guides. "Hospital Billing Errors and Fraud." n.d., http://www.fraudguides.com/ medical-hospitalbilling-errors.asp.

Freeman, Liz. 2008. "Federal Jury Finds Naples Doctor Guilty of Illegally Prescribing Meds." *Naples Daily News,* March 21, http://www.naplesnews.com/news/2008/ mar/21/federal-grand-jury-finds-naples-doctor-guilty-ille/.

Freking, Kevin. 2008a. "Health-Care Spending Outpacing Inflation Rate." *Greenville News,* February 26, 1A.

———. 2008b. "Medicare Officials to Review Insurers' Commissions." Associated Press, October 24, http://www.newsvine.com/_news/2008/10/24/2037607-medicare-officials-to-review-insurers-commissions.

———. 2009. "Federal Program Misses Problem Nursing Homes." Associated Press, September 27, http://abcnews.go.com/Politics/wireStory?id=8685083.

Funding Universe. n.d. "HCA—The Healthcare Company." http://www.fundinguniverse. com/company-histories/HCA-The-Healthcare-Company-Company-History. html.

Galimi, Joanne. 2006. "Preventing Healthcare Fraud and Abuse." *Gartner Voice* (Dale Kutnick, host), October 9, http://www.gartner.com/it/products/podcasting/ asset_157499_2575.jsp.

Gardner, Amanda. 2009. "Trial Data on Anti-Seizure Drug Might Have Been Manipulated: Report." *HealthDay: News for Healthier Living.* November 11, http://www. healthday.com/Article.asp?AID=632984.

Garner, Bryan A., ed. 2000. *Black's Law Dictionary,* 7th ed. (abridged). St. Paul: West.

Gellene, Denise, and Thomas H. Maugh II. 2008. "Emory University Psychiatrist Accused of Conflict of Interest." *Los Angeles Times,* October 4, http://www.latimes. com/nes/nationworld/nation/la-sci-doctors4–2008oct04,0,5063741.story.

Gellman, Robert, and Pam Dixon. 2008. "Red Flag and Address Discrepancy Requirements: Suggestions for Health Care Providers." World Privacy Forum report, September 24, http://www.worldprivacyforum.org/pdf/WPF_ RedFlagReport_09242008fs.pdf.

Gillam, Carey. n.d. "Bail Denied to Diluted-Cancer-Drug Suspect." Reuters Health Information, http://www.cancerpage.com/news/article.asp?id=3203.

Girion, Lisa. 2006. "Canceled Policies Prompt Lawsuits." *Los Angeles Times,* April 26, C2, http://articles.latimes.com/2006/apr/28/business/fi-cancel28.

———. 2007. "Blue Shield Sued over Revoked Insurance." *Los Angeles Times,* February 16, C1, http://articles.latimes.com/2007/feb/16/business/fi-revoke16.

———. 2008. "State Fines 2 Health Plans over Canceled Coverage." *Los Angeles Times,* July 18, A1, http://articles.latimes.com/2008/jul/18/business/fi-blue18.

Goff, John. 2007. "Critical Condition, Tenet Healthcare Has Been Laid Low by Scandal, Fraud, and Cash-Draining Litigation: Can New CFO Biggs Help Cure the Ailing Hospital Operator?" *CFO: Magazine for Senior Financial Executives.* September, http://www.cfo.com/article.cfm/9689526/c_9747262?f=magazine_featured.

Government of the District of Columbia, Office of the Inspector General. 2003. "$218,731 to Be Paid by Medical Company for Violating Medicaid Rules." Press release, July 23, http://oig.dc.gov/news/PDF/release/Abbott_Press_Release.pdf.

Govtrack.us. A Civic Project to Track Congress. 2010. H.R. 5044: Medicare Fraud Enforcement and Prevention Act of 2010, http://www.govtrack.us/congress/bill. xpd?bill=h111-5044&tab=summary.

Grande, David, Dominick L. Frosch, Andrew W. Perkins, and Barbara E. Kahn. 2009. "Effect of Exposure to Small Pharmaceutical Promotional Items on Treatment Preferences." *Archives of Internal Medicine* 169(9): 887–93.

Grassley, Chuck. 2003. "Grassley Investigates Tenet Healthcare's Use of Federal Tax Dollars." Press release, September 8, http://www.senate.gov/~grassley/releases/2003/ p03r09-08.htm.

Gray, Bradford H., and Kathy Hebert. 2007. "Hospitals in Hurricane Katrina: Challenges Facing Custodial Institutions in a Disaster." *Journal of Health Care for the Poor and Underserved* 18:283–98.

Grell, Jeffrey Ernest. n.d. *RICO in a Nutshell.* http://www.ricoact.com/ricoact/nutshell.asp#mail.

Grube, G. M. A. (translated by), and C. D. C. Reeve (revised by). 1992. *Plato Republic.* Indianapolis: Hackett.

Gusman, Phil. 2008. "P-C, Health Insurance Fraud Fighters Combining Efforts." June 24, http://www.propertyandcasualtyinsurancenews.com/cms/nupc/Breaking%20 News/2008/06/24-PCHEALTHFRAUD-pg.

Hallam, Kristen. 2005. "Health Insurers Allege 'Rent-A-Patient' Fraud." *Washington Post,* March 12, http://www.washingtonpost.com/wp-dyn/articles/A28484-2005Mar11. html.

Halper, Evan. 2009. "Fraud Infects State In-Home Care Program." *Los Angeles Times,* April 13, http://articles.latimes.com/apr/13/local/me-fraud13.

Harris, Gardiner. 2004. "Medical Marketing—Treatment by Incentive; As Doctor Writes Prescription, Drug Company Writes a Check." *New York Times,* June 27, http:// query.nytimes.com/gst/fullpage.html?res=9A0CE3DD1738F934A15755C0A9629 C8B63.

——. 2008. "Stanford to Limit Drug Maker Financing." *New York Times,* August 26, http://www.nytimes.com/2008/08/26/business/26drug.html.

——. 2009. "Senator Grassley Seeks Financial Details from Medical Groups." *New York Times,* December 7, http://www.nytimes.com/2009/12/07/health/policy/ 07grassley.html.

Harvard Medical School. 2010. "Harvard Medical School Dean Accepts Recommendations for Revising Conflicts of Interest Policy." July 23, http://hms.harvard.edu/ public/coi/newsroom/2010/july_newsrelease.html.

HealthDay: News for Healthier Living. 2009. "Not-for-Profit Nursing Homes Fare Better in Studies." August 5, http://www.healthday.com/Article.asp?AID=629686.

HealthGrades, Inc. 2006. "Third Annual Patient Safety in American Hospitals Study." Report, April, http://www.healthgrades.com/media/DMS/pdf/PatientSafety InAmericanHospitalsStudy2006.pdf.

HealthSouth. 2009. "Investor Relations." n.d., http://investor.healthsouth.com/.

HealthSouth. 2010. "HealthSouth Reports Solid Results for Second Quarter 2010 and Increases 2010 Guidance." August 2, http://investor.healthsouth.com/.

Heath, Brad. 2010. "Little Progress Seen against Health Insurance Fraud." *USA Today,* January 29, http://www.usatoday.com/news/washington/2010-01-28-health-care-insurance-fraud_N.htm.

Hill, Timothy B. 2007. "Statement by Timothy B. Hill, Chief Financial Officer, Centers for Medicare and Medicaid Services on Medicare Health Care Fraud and Abuse Efforts before the Committee on the Budget, U.S. House of Representatives." July 17, http://www.dhhs.gov/asl/testify/2007/07/t2007071b.html.

History of the FDA. n.d. "The 1938 Food, Drug, and Cosmetic Act." http://www.fda.gov/ oc/history/historyoffda/section2.html.

Hoffman, Earl Dirk, Jr., Barbara S. Klees, and Catherine A. Curtis. 2007. *Brief Summaries of Medicare and Medicaid: Title XVIII and Title XIX of the Social Security Act.* Washington, D.C.: U.S. Department of Health and Human Services, Office of the Actuary, Centers for Medicare and Medicaid Services, November 1, http://www.mindfully.org/Health/2005/Medicare-Medicaid-Summaries1nov05.htmS.

Holahan, John, and Allison Cook. 2008. "The Decline in the Uninsured in 2007: Why Did It Happen and Can It Last?" Kaiser Commission, October, http://www.kff.org/uninsured/upload/7826.pdf.

Holmes, Chris. 2008. "State Sues 79 Drug Companies, Claims Fraud, Overcharging in Medicaid Drug Billing." WSFA.com, February 5, http://www.wsfa.com/Global/story.asp?S=7822614.

Hood, Lucy. 2009. "Strong Medicine." *Carolina Alumni Review,* September/October.

Hooper, Patric, and Amanda S. Abbott. 2007. "Practical Considerations for Defending Health Care Fraud and Abuse Cases," in Baumann 2007, 321–408.

Hoovers. n.d. "HCA, Inc." http://www.hoovers.com/company/Hca_Inc/rhtyki-1.html.

Hyman, David A. 2001. "Health Care Fraud and Abuse: Market Change, Social Norms, and the Trust 'Reposed in the Workmen.'" *Journal of Legal Studies* 30 (June): 531–69.

Interagency Working Group on Synthetic Drugs. 2005. *Interim Report from the Interagency Working Group on Synthetic Drugs to the Director of National Drug Control Policy.* Attorney General, Secretary of Health and Human Services, May 23, http://www.whitehousedrugpolicy.gov/publications/pdf/interim_rpt.pdf.

ITIM International. n.d. "Geert Hofstede Cultural Dimensions: United States." http://www.geert-hofstede.com/hofstede_united_states.shtml.

Jay, Dennis. 2010. "Fraud Bureaus Report Sharp Rise in Fake Health Plans." *Insurance Journal, July 7,* http://www.insurancejournal.com/news/national/2010/07/07/111349.htm.

Jayawant, Sujata S., and Rajesh Balkrishnan. 2005. "The Controversy Surrounding OxyContin Abuse: Issues and Solutions." *Therapeutics and Clinical Risk Management* 1 (June), http://www.pubmedcentral.nih.gov/articlerender.fcgi?artid=1661612.

Jecker, Nancy S., and Clarence H. Braddock III. 2008. "Managed Care." Ethics in Medicine, University of Washington School of Medicine, April 11, http://depts.washington.edu/bioethx/topics/manag.html.

Johnson, Carrie. 2007. "Frist Not Charged as Investigators Close Probe of His Hospital Stock Sales." *Washington Post,* April 27, http://www.washingtonpost.com/wp-dyn/content/article/2007/04/26/AR2007042602343.html.

Jordan, Don. 2009. "11 Alleged Mafia Members Indicted on Slew of Federal Charges." *Palm Beach News,* May 21, http://www.palmbeachpost.com/localnews/content/local_news/epaper/2009/05/21/0521ricoindict.html.

Joshi, Sopan. 2008. "Lack of Insurance, High Medical Costs Put More in a Bind." *Washington Post,* August 30, A02, http://www.washingtonpost.com/wp-dyn/content/article/2008/08/19/AR2008081902638.html.

KaiserEDU.org. n.d. "Children's Coverage and SCHIP Reauthorization." http://www.kaiseredu.org/topics_im.asp?id=704&imID=1&parentID=65.

Kaiser Family Foundation. 2007. *Health Care Spending in the United States and OECD Countries.* Report, January, http://www.kff.org/insurance/snapshot/chcm010307oth.cfm.

Kaiser Family statehealthfacts.org. 2007. "Monthly SCHIP Enrollment." June, http://www.statehealthfacts.org/comparemaptable.jsp?ind=236&cat=4.

Kaiser Health News. 2009a. "Study: Medical Bills Underlie 60 Percent of U.S. Bankrupt-cies." June 4, http://www.kaiserhealthnews.org/Daily-Reports/2009/june/04/Medical-Bankruptcies.aspx.

Kaiser Health News 2009b. "White House Reform Chief Was on Boards of Health Companies with Suspect Practices." July 2, http://www.kaiserhealthnews.org/Daily-Reports/2009/July/02/DeParle.aspx.

Kaisernetwork.org. 2008a. "Acting CMS Administrator Weems Announces Efforts to Reduce Medicare Fraud in Seven States." *Kaiser Daily Health Policy Report,* October 7, http://www.kaisernetwork.org/Daily_Reports/rep_index.cfm?DR_ID=54872.

——. 2008b. "Merck Agrees to Pay $58M to Settle Multistate Lawsuit that Claimed Advertisements for Vioxx." *Kaiser Daily Health Policy Report,* May 21, http://www.kaisernetwork.org/DAILY_REPORTS/rep_index.cfm?DR_ID=52276.

——. 2009. "Administration News: President Obama's Budget Request Includes $828B for HHS." May 8, http://www.kaisernetwork.org/Daily_reports/rep_index.cfm?DR_ID=58379.

Kaufman, Marc. 2004. "New DEA Statement Has Pain Doctors More Fearful: Agency Reneges on Guidelines Worked Out for Narcotics." *Washington Post,* November 30, A17.

Kelly, G. Christopher. 2007. "Are You a Fraud?: Avoiding Abuse in Ambulance Billing." EMSResponder.com, January 31, http://www.emsresponder.com/print/Emergency-Medical-Services/Are-You-a-Fraud/1$3229.

Kennedy, Kelli. 2009a. "Dozens Arrested in Medicare Fraud Busts across U.S." Associated Press, July 29, http://www.google.com/hostednews/ap/article/ALeqM5j1-e3AW6RglZGaSK98EdgH97WgKQD99O9QSG4.

——. 2009b. "Mafia, Violent Criminals Turn to Medicare Fraud." Associated Press, October 6, http://www.breitbart.com/article.php?id=D9B5OKO01&show_article=1.

Kerber, Ross. 2007. "Jury Acquits 4 in Serono Kickback." *Boston Globe,* May 4, http://www.boston.com/business/globe/articles/2007/05/04/jury_acquits_4_in_serono_kickback_case/.

Kerr, Orin S. 2005. "Searches and Seizures in a Digital World." *Harvard Law Review* 119:531–85.

Kerwin, JoAnne. 1995. "Hospital Integrates DRG Coding and Optimization with Information System." *IRP: Innovative Resources for Payors,* March 10, http://www.drg.irp.com/articles/jk_hosp.htm.

Kleinke, J. D. 1998. "Deconstructing the Columbia/HCA Investigation." *Health Affairs* 17 (March/April): 7–26, http://content.healthaffairs.org/cgi/reprint/17/2/7.

Knaupp, Casey. 2007. "Medicare Fraud Case Lands Couple in Prison." *Tyler Morning Telegraph,* September 27, http://www.tylerpaper.com/article/20070927/NEWS08/709270301.

Kroger, John. 2008. *Convictions: A Prosecutor's Battles against Mafia Killers, Drug Kingpins, and Enron Thieves.* New York: Farrar, Straus and Giroux.

Kusserow, Richard P. 1989. "Financial Arrangements between Physicians and Health Care Businesses: Perspectives of Health Care Professionals." *Management Report,* May, http://oig.hhs.gov/oei/reports/oai-12-88-01411.pdf.

Landsberg, Barry S., and Terri D. Keville. 2001. "Nursing Homes Face Quality-of-Care Scrutiny under False Claims Act." *Health Care Financial Management,* January, http://findarticles.com/p/articles/mi_m3257/is_1_55/ai_69297986.

Leap, Terry L. 2007. *Dishonest Dollars: The Dynamics of White-Collar Crime.* Ithaca: Cornell University Press.

Leavitt, Michael. 2007. "Remarks as Delivered at the Durable Medical Equipment (DME) Fraud Press Conference." U.S. Department of Health and Human Services, Secretary, May 9, http://www.hhs.gov/news/speech/2007/sp20070509a.html.

Li, Jing, Kuei-Ying Huang, Jionghua Jin, and Jianjun Shi. 2008. "A Survey on Statistical Methods for Health Care Fraud Detection." *Health Care Management Science* 11:275–87.

Libby, Ronald T. 2008. *The Criminalization of Medicine: America's War on Doctors*. Westport, Conn.: Praeger.

Lichtblau, Eric. 2005. "Settlement in Marketing of a Drug for AIDS." *New York Times*, October 18, http://www.nytimes.com/2005/10/18/business/18drug.html?_r=1&oref=slogin.

Little, Robert. 2010. "Patients Learn They Might Have Unneeded Stents." Baltimoresun.com, January 15, http://articles.baltimoresun.com/2010–01-15/health/bal-md.cardiac15jan15_1_stents-heart-patients-cardiac-catheterization.

Los Angeles Times. 2009. "Kaiser Bellflower Is Fined $187,500 for Privacy Breach." July 16, http://latimesblogs.latimes.com/lanow/2009/07/kaiser-fine.html.

Loucks, Michael K., and Carol C. Lam. 2001. *Prosecuting and Defending Health Care Fraud Cases*. Washington, D.C: BNA Books, Bureau of National Affairs.

———. 2007. *Prosecuting and Defending Health Care Fraud Cases, 2007 Cumulative Supplement*. Appendix A: "Health Care Fraud Settlements of at Least $1 Million (1990–2007)." Arlington, Va.: BNA Books, Bureau of National Affairs.

Luongo, Gerald J. 2004. *Surviving Federal Prison Camp: An Informative and Helpful Guide for Prospective Inmates*. Chapel Hill, N.C.: Professional Press.

Mamula, Kris B. 2008. "SEC Probes West Penn Allegheny's $73 Million Revenue Write-Down." *Pittsburgh Business Times*, August 27, http://pittsburgh.bizjournals.com/pittsburgh/stories/2008/08/25/daily18.html.

Mangano, Michael F. 1997. "Testimony on Fraud in Medicare Programs before the Senate Committee on Governmental Affairs, Permanent Subcommittee on Investigations." June 25, http://www.hhs.gov/asl/testify/t970626b.html.

Manning, George A. 2000. *Financial Investigation and Forensic Accounting*. Boca Raton, Fla.: CRC Press.

Market Research.com. 2009. "Special Report: 2009 Chartbook of International Pharmaceutical Prices." June 23, http://www.marketresearch.com/product/display.asp?productid=2303158.

Martinez, Barbara. 2006. "How Quiet Moves by a Publisher Sway Billions in Drug Spending." October 6, http://www.natap.org/2006/newsUpdates/110906_34.htm.

Maruca, William H. 2006. "Fraud Enforcement under Medicare Part D." *Physician's News Digest*, February, http://www.physiciansnews.com/law/206maruca.html.

Mather, Charles. 2005. "The Pipeline and the Porcupine." *Social Science and Medicine* 60(6): 1323–34.

Mathias, Robin. 2004. "7 Charged in Florida DME Fraud." Mathias Consulting, September 5, http://mathiasconsulting.com/cases/2004/FL/DME/7charged.

McCabe, Scott. 2007. "Ambulance Company Faces Medicaid Fraud Trial," Examiner.com National, March 22, http://www.examiner.com/a-632633~Ambulance_company_faces_Medicaid_fraud_trial.html.

McGrath, William A. 2005. "Serono Settlement Should Highlight Need for Compliance, Not Chill Legitimate Off-Label Communication." Thompson www.thompson.com. FDA Advertising and Promotion, Food and Drug Series 13, December, http://www.wileyrein.com/docs/publications/12471.pdf.

Medical News Today. 2008. "CMS Official Kuhn Tells Panel New System Will Prevent Fraudulent Medicare Claims from Using Dead Doctors' Names." July 11, http://www.medicalnewstoday.com/articles/114653.php.

"Medicare Fraud and Abuse Physician Self-Referral Prohibition ('Stark Law') and Anti-Kickback Law." n.d., http://www.gthm.com/index/pdfs/medfraud.pdf:

MedLaw.com. 2006. "Physician Pleads Guilty to Double Billing." June 29, http://www.
medlaw.com/healthlaw/Fraud/5_4/physician-pleads-guilty-t.shtml.

Menn, Joseph. 2006. "ID Theft Infects Medical Records." *Los Angeles Times,* September 25, A1, http://articles.latimes.com/2006/sep/25/business/fi-medid25.

Merisalo, Laura J. 2008. "Medical Identity Theft." *Healthcare Registration* 17 (June), http://www.patientsecure.com/htsys_docs/HCR062008.pdf.

Metropolitan News-Enterprise. 2006. "Tenet Healthcare to Pay Record Whistleblower Settlement." June 30, http://www.metnews.com/articles/2006/tene063006.htm.

Modern Healthcare.com. 2008. "Schwarzenegger Inks Bills Bolstering Patient Privacy." October 1, http://www.modernhealthcare.com/apps/pbcs.dll/artcle?AID=/20081001/REG/310019976&nocache=1.

Moore, Janet. 2008. "Eye on Partnership of Doctors, Heart Research Group." StarTribune.com, September 13, http://www.startribune.com/business/28302424.html.

Moore, Tina, Benjamin Lesser, and Greg B. Smith. 2009. "Daily News Investigates Faked Records and Fatal Blunders at City-Run Hospitals." *New York Daily News,* July 28, http://www.nydailynews.com/ny_local/2009/07/26/2009–07-26_faked_records_and_fatal_blunders_at_cityrun_medical_centers.html.

Morris, Lewis. 2000. "Medicare: Third-Party Billing Companies." U.S. Department of Health and Human Services, Office of Inspector General, Testimony of Lewis Morris, Assistant Inspector for Legal Affairs before the House Committee on Oversight and Investigations, April 6, http://www.oig.hhs.gov/reading/testimony/2000/00406fin.htm.

——. 2007. "Allegations of Waste, Fraud and Abuse in Pharmaceutical Pricing: Financial Impacts on Federal Health Programs and the Federal Taxpayer." U.S. Department of Health and Human Services, Testimony of Lewis Morris, Chief Counsel to the Inspector General before the House Oversight and Government Reform Committee, U.S. House of Representatives, February 9, http://www.oig.hhs.gov/testimony/docs/2007/020907tmy.pdf.

——. 2008. "In the Hands of Strangers: Are Nursing Home Safeguards Working?" U.S Department of Health and Human Services, Office of Inspector General, Testimony of Lewis Morris, Chief Counsel to the Inspector General before the Subcommittee on Oversight and Investigations Committee on Energy and Commerce, U.S. House of Representatives, May 15, http://www.oig.hhs.gov/testimony/docs/2008/testimony051508.pdf.

Murphy, Shelley, and Alice Dembner. 2004. "All Acquitted in Drug Kickbacks Case: Jury Deals a Blow to U.S. Prosecutors." *Boston Globe,* July 15, http://www.boston.com/news/local/articles/2004/07/15/all_acquitted_in_drug_kickbacks_case/.

Nanda, Ashish. 2006. "The Ethics of Professionalism." Harvard Business School lecture video, February 1, http://harvardbusinessonline.hbsp.harvard.edu/b01/en/common/item_detail.jhtml?referral=1145&id=5860C.

National Association of Medical Fraud Control Units. 2009. "Eli Lilly to Pay More Than $1.4 Billion for Off-Label Drug Marketing." http://www.namfcu.net/press/eli-lilly-to-pay-more-than-1–4-billion-for-off-label-drug-marketing.

National Coalition on Health Care. 2009. "Health Insurance Costs." http://www.nchc.org/facts/cost/shtml.

National Health Care Anti-Fraud Association. 2007. "The Problem of Health Care Fraud. Consumer Alert: The Impact of Health Care Fraud on You!" http://www.nhcaa.org/eweb/DynamicPage.aspx?webcode=anti_fraud_resource_centr&wpscode=TheProblemOfHCFraud.

National Health Care Anti-Fraud Association. n.d. *The Problem of Health Care Fraud.* Report, http://www.nhcaa.org/eweb/DynamicPage.aspx?webcode=anti_fraud_resource_centr&wpscode=TheProblemOfHCFraud.

National Health Policy Forum. 2009. "The Basics: The Medicaid Drug Rebate Program." April 13, http://www.nhpf.org/library/the-basics/Basics_Medicaid DrugRebate_04–13-09.pdf.

National Insurance Crime Bureau, International Association of Special Investigation Units, National Insurance Fraud Forum, Coalition Against Insurance Fraud. 2000. October, http://www.insurancefraud.org/downloads/white_paper.pdf.

"National News Briefs: Faulty Tubing Is Blamed for Four Dialysis Deaths." 1998. *New York Times,* June 19, http://query.nytimes.com/gst/fullpage.html?res=9C05E4D71 F3DF93AA25755C0A96E958260.

New England Carpenters Health Benefits Fund et al. v. First DataBank, Inc. and McKesson Corp. n.d. Attachment B to Class Plaintiffs' Amended Memorandum of Law in Support of Joint Motion for Preliminary Approval of Proposed First DataBank Settlement, Certification of Settlement, Class and Approval of Notice Plan. http://www.hagens-berman.com/files/Attachment_B_Class_%20Plaintiffs_Amended_ Memorandum1164664165632.pdf.

New York Times. 2010. "A Historic Moment for Health Care?" August 16, http://room-fordebate.blogs.nytimes.com/2010/03/21/a-historic-moment-for-health-care/.

Novak, David. 2006. *Downtime: A Guide to Federal Incarceration,* 8th ed. Salt Lake City: David Novak Consulting.

Nunnally, Derrick. 2006. "Psychiatrist Charged in Sex Case." *Milwaukee Journal Sentinel,* November 10, http://www.jsonline.com/story/index.aspx?id=529742.

OANDP.com, O & P Edge. n.d. "Lincare Settles with OIG, Pays $10 Million." http://www.oandp.com/edge/issues/articles/NEWS_2006-05-17_02.asp.

O'Connor, Matt. 2006. "Podiatrist Speaks Out at Death Sentencing." *Chicago Tribune,* April 28, http://newsgroups.derkeiler.com/Archive/Alt/alt.true-crime/2006–04/msg05672.html.

OECD Health Data. 2006. "How Does the United States Compare?" Report, http://www.oecd.org/dataoecd/29/52/36960035.pdf.

Office of Applied Studies, Substance Abuse and Mental Health Services Administration. 2010. "The TEDS Report: Substance Abuse Treatment Admissions Involving Abuse of Pain Relievers: 1998 and 2008." July 15, http://oas.samhsa.gov/2k10/230/230PainRelvr2k10.htm.

Office of the New York State Attorney General. 2000. "Brooklyn Pharmacist Gets 1–3 Years in Prison for Selling Drugs to Dealers." Press release, August 16, http://www.oag.state.ny.us/press/2000/aug/aug16b_00.html.

Online Lawyer Source. n.d. "OxyContin." http://www.onlinelawyersource.com/oxycon tin/index.html.

O'Reilly, Cary, and Phil Milford. 2008. "McKesson Will Pay $350 Million to End Pricing Claims (Update 4)." Bloomberg.com, November 21, http://www.bloomberg.com/apps/news?pid=20601103&sid=aaxeMbikKBhA&refer=us.

O'Reilly, Kevin B. 2009a. "Journal Editors Propose Detailed Disclosure Form for Authors." Amednews.com, November 9, http://www.ama-assn.org/amednews/2009/11/09/prsa1109.htm.

——. 2009b. "Pfizer Pays Record $2.3 Billion in Off-Label Drug Marketing Settlement." Amednews.com, September 14, http://www.ama-assn.org/amednews/2009/09/14/prl20914.htm.

Park, S. Sandra, and Katie C. Pawlitz. 2008. "False Claims Act and False Certifications: An Old Dog with a New Trick." *Journal of Health Care Compliance* (May–June): 47–61.

Pear, Robert. 2009. "Antitrust Laws a Hurdle to Health Care Overhaul." *New York Times,* May 26, http://www.nytimes.com/2009/05/27/health/policy/27health.html.

Peeno, Linda. 1996. "Managed Care Ethics: The Close View." Testimony before the U.S. House of Representatives Committee on Commerce, Subcommittee on Health and Environment, May 30, http://www.thenationalcoalition.org/DrPeenotesti mony.html.

Periodic Table. 2009. "Dr. David Polly—On Chuck Grassley's Hit List?" July 28, http://ptable.blogspot.com/2009/07/dr.html.

Petersen, Melody. 2001. "2 Drug Makers to Pay $875 Million to Settle Fraud Case." *New York Times,* October 4, http://query.nytimes.com/gst/fullpage.html?res=9C02EED C1F3DF937A35753C1A9679C8B63.

——. 2002. "Drug Maker to Pay $500 Million Fine for Factory Lapses." *New York Times,* May 18, http://query.nytimes.com/gst/fullpage.html?res=9801E0DF1738F93BA25 756C0A9649C8B63.

Pfizer. n.d. "Pfizer Reports Fourth-Quarter and Full-Year 2008 Results and 2009 Financial Guidelines." http://media.pfizer.com/files/investors/presentations/q4perfor mance_january012609.pdf.

Phillips and Cohen, LLP. 2001. "Settlement of $875 Million Medicare/Medicaid Drug Fraud Yields New Funds for Trust Fund and Could Deter Overcharging." Press release, October 3, http://www.phillipsandcohen.com/CM/NewsSettlements/ TAP_Oct3_2001.asp.

Phillips and Cohen, LLP. n.d. "False Claims Act." http://www.phillipsandcohen.com/CM/ Custom/TOCFalseClaimsAct.asp.

PointofLaw.com. 2010. "Vioxx/Drug Litigation." http://www.pointoflaw.com/vioxx_ drug_litigation/.

Price Waterhouse Coopers. 2009. "Top 10 Health Industry Issues in 2010: Squeezing the Juice out of Healthcare." December, http://www.pwc.com/us/en/healthcare/publi cations/top-ten-health-industry-issues-in-2010.jhtml.

Pringle, Evelyn. 2006. "Gambro Healthcare: Dialysis Fraud Pays Big Bucks." Lawyers AndSettlements.com, March 29, http://www.lawyersandsettlements.com/ articles/00153/gambro.html.

Prism Innovations, Inc., Caregiver Education Series. n.d. Chapter 2, "Medicare Fraud Schemes: Hospitals." http://www.ec-online.net/CGE5/pfs2.htm.

Public Broadcasting System. 1997. "Doctoring the Books." *Online Newshour,* July 31, http://www.pbs.org/newshour/bb/medicare/july-dec97/mdicare_fraud_7-31a. html.

Purdue. n.d. "Who We Are." http://www.pharma.com/html/Who_We_Are/Who_We_ Are.htm.

Quitamhelp.com. n.d. "Qui Tam Stories: TAP Pharmaceuticals, $559 Million, 2001, AstraZeneca $291 Million, 2003." http://www.quitamhelp.com/static/stories/tap. html.

Rai, Arti K. 2001. "Health Care Fraud and Abuse: A Tale of Behavior by Payment Structure." *Journal of Legal Studies* 30 (June): 579–87.

Reuters. 2009. "Hospitals Slash Costs to Offset Falling Admissions." July 28, http://www. reuters.com/article/healthNews/idUSTRE56R6RZ20090728?pageNumber=1&virt ualBrandChannel=0.

Robert Wood Johnson Foundation. 2008. "Cover the Uninsured." Facts and Research, January 5, http://covertheuninsured.org/factsheets/display.php?FactSheetID=101.

Rockoff, Jonathan D., and Brent Kendall. 2009. "Pfizer to Plead Guilty to Improper Marketing." *Wall Street Journal,* September 3, http://online.wsj.com/article/ SB125190160702979723.html.

Rosenberg, Tina. 2007. "When Is a Pain Doctor a Drug Pusher?" *New York Times Magazine,* June 17, http://www.nytimes.com/2007/06/17/magazine/17pain-t. html?pagewanted=1.

Rosenzweig, Paul, and Trent England. 2003. "The Doctor Won't See You Now." Heritage Foundation, October 23, http://www.heritage.org/Press/Commentary/ed102303c.cfm.

Roth, Sanford H., MD; Roy M. Fleischmann, MD; Francis X. Burch, MD; Frederick Dietz, MD; Barry Bockow, MD; Ronald J. Rapoport, MD; Joel Rutstein, MD; and Peter G. Lacouture, PhD. 2000. "Around the Clock, Controlled-Release Oxycodone Therapy for Osteoarthritis-Related Pain: Placebo-Controlled Trial and Long-Term Evaluation." *Archives of Internal Medicine* 160(6): 853–60.

Rowland, Christopher. 2005. "Insurer Accuses Worker of Theft: Blue Cross Alleges Longtime Manager Took $600,000." *Boston Globe,* March 10, http://boston.com/business/articles/2005/03/10/insurer_accuses_worker_of_theft/.

Rubin, Paul. 2003. "Rent a Patient." *Phoenix News Times,* April 24, http://www.phoenixnewtimes.com/2003-04-24/news/rent-a-patient/.

Ruiz, Rebecca. 2009. "America's Most Medicated States." Forbes.com, August 17, http://www.forbes.com/2009/08/17/most-medicated-states-lifestyle-health-prescription-drugs.html.

Russell, Betsy. 2004. "Wheelchair Fraud Trial to Go Ahead." Spokesman Reivew.com, July 6, http://www.healthandwelfare.idaho.gov/_Rainbow/Documents%5Cabout/wheelchair_fraud_trial.pdf.

Rust, Susanne, and John Fauber. 2009. "Drug Firms' Cash Skews Doctor Classes." *Milwaukee, Wisconsin, Journal Sentinel* (JSOnline), November 8, http://www.jsonline.com/news/42064977.html.

Salcido, Robert. 2007. "The False Claims Act in Health Care Prosecutions: Application of the Substantive, *Qui Tam,* and Voluntary Disclosure Provisions," in Baumann 2007, 221–319.

Samenow, Stanton E. 2004. *Inside the Criminal Mind,* rev. and updated ed. New York: Crown.

Saul, Stephanie. 2008. "F.D.A. Plan on Medical Articles Takes More Heat." *New York Times,* April 19, http://www.nytimes.com/2008/04/19/business/19ghost.html?ref=health.

Savedoff, William D., and Karen Hussmann. 2005. *Global Corruption Report 2006. Part One: The Causes of Corruption in the Health Sector; A Focus on Health Care Systems.* "Why Are Health Care Systems Prone to Corruption?" Transparency International, August 11, http://www.transparency.org/publications/gcr/download_gcr/download_gcr_2006.

Schering-Plough home page. 2008. http://www.schering-plough.com/schering_plough/about/about.jsp.

Schultz, Susan. 2007. "Stolen Hospital Computer Returned; Hopkins Hires Investigator to Probe Data Breach." *Baltimore Business Journal,* September 4, http://www.bizjournals.com/baltimore/stories/2007/09/03/daily6.html?b=1188792000^1515454.

Seelye, Katharine Q. 2010. "Health Care's Share of the U.S. Economy Rose at a Record Rate." *New York Times,* February 4, http://prescriptions.blogs.nytimes.com/2010/02/04/us-health-care-spending-rose-at-record-rate-in-2009/.

Serbaroli, Francis J. 1999–2000. "Fraud in Managed Care, Parts I, II, and III." Cadwalader, Wickersham and Taft, LLP, http://library.findlaw.com/1999/Sep/1/127138.html, http://library.findlaw.com/1999/Dec/1/131799.html, and http://library.findlaw.com/2000/Feb/1/127264.html.

Shelton, Stacy. 2008. "Emory Will Punish Psychiatrist Nemeroff." *Atlanta Journal Constitution,* December 23, http://www.ajc.com/metro/content/metro/dekalb/stories/2008/12/23/Emory_punishes_Nemeroff.html.

Shishkin, Philip. 2008. "Cases of Abuse by Home Aides Draw Scrutiny." *Wall Street Journal* (wsj.com), July 15, http://www.charmeckcoa.org/docs/Article07.15.08Abuse. pdf.

Short, Larri A., and Richard S. Liner. 2007. "Controlling Fraud, Waste, and Abuse in the Medicare Part D Program," in Baumann 2007, 860–65.

Silverman, Elaine, and Jonathan S. Skinner. 2001. "Are For-Profit Hospitals Really Different? Medical Upcoding and Market Structure." NBER Working Paper W8133, February, http://ssrn.com/abstract=260546.

——. 2004. "Medicare Upcoding and Hospital Ownership." *Journal of Health Economics* 23:383, http://www.dartmouth.edu/~jskinner/documents/silvermanskinner.pdf.

Singer, Natasha, and Duff Wilson. 2010. "Debate over Industry Role in Educating Doctors." *New York Times,* June 23, http://www.nytimes.com/2010/06/24/ business/24meded.html?_r=1.

Slade, Shelley R. 2000. "False Claims Act and Health Care Fraud." Vogel, Slade, and Goldstein, a Washington, D.C., law firm handling false claims act and antifraud litigation nationwide, December, http://www.false-claims-act-health-care-fraud-whistleblower-attorney.com/articles/false-claims-act-health-care-fraud.php.

Slater, Dan. 2008. "UnitedHealth Settles 'Historical Stock Options Practices' Case for $895 Mil." *Wall Street Journal* law blog, July 2, http://blogs.wsj.com/ law/2008/07/02/unitedhealth-settles-historical-stock-options-practices-case-for-890-mil/.

Sorkin, Andrew Ross. 2006. "HCA Buyout Highlights Era of Going Private." *New York Times,* July 25, http://www.nytimes.com/2006/07/25/business/25buyout. html?_r=1&oref=slogin.

Sorrel, Amy Lynn. 2009. "Health Care Fraud Still Main Focus of False Claims Act." Amednews.com, December 14, http://www.ama-assn.org/amednews/2009/12/14/ gvsb1214.htm.

Sparrow, Malcolm K. 1996. *License to Steal: Why Fraud Plagues America's Health Care System,* updated ed. Boulder, Colo.: Westview.

——. 2000. *License to Steal: How Fraud Bleeds America's Health Care System.* Boulder, Colo.: Westview.

Spivack, Peter S. 2008. "Off-Label Promotion under Scrutiny by DOJ: The Department of Justice Is Aggressively Pursuing Healthcare Fraud Allegations." *Genetic Engineering and Biotechnology News* 28 (June 1), http://www.genengnews.com/ articles/chitem_print.aspx?aid=2487&chid=0.

Strader, J. Kelly. 2002. *Understanding White-Collar Crime.* Newark, N.J.: LexisNexus.

Sugerman-Broznan, Alex, and James Woolman. 2009. "Drug Spending and the Average Wholesale Price: Removing the AWP Albatross from Medicaid's Neck." Bureau of National Affairs, *Health Care Policy Report* 13(36), http://healthcenter.bna.com/ pic2/hc.nsf/id/BNAP-6G8NPZ?OpenDocument.

Tabarrok, Alexander T. 2000. "Assessing the FDA via the Anomaly of Off-Label Drug Prescribing." *Independent Review* 5 (Summer), http://www.independent.org/pdf/ tir/tir_05_1_tabarrok.pdf.

"Takeda Pharmaceuticals and TAP Pharmaceutical Products, Inc. Merge." 2008. Press release, July 1, http://www.tap.com/.

"Tenet Healthcare Corporation." n.d. http://www.fundinguniverse.com/company-histo ries/Tenet-Healthcare-Corporation-Company-History.html.

Tenet Shareholder Committee, LLC. 2005. "Greed, Scandal and Wrongful Deaths at Tenet Healthcare Corp." January 31, http://www.tenetshareholdercommittee.org/ images/Articles/pdf/part_one.pdf.

——. 2008. "Reports and Observations: The Tenet Shareholder Committee Says Goodbye and Good Luck." December 29, http://www.tenetshareholdercommittee.org/.

Tennessee Board of Medical Examiners. 2004. Teleconference, May 21, http://health.
    state.tn.us/Downloads/g5054247.pdf.

Tesoriero, Heather Won. 2008. "Vioxx Rulings Raise Bar for Suits against Drug Firms."
    Wall Street Journal, May 30, B1.

Testerman, Jeff. 2001. "Patient-Broker Gets Prison in Scam." *St. Petersburg Times* (tam-
    pabay.com), April 20, http://www.sptimes.com/News/042001/TampaBay/Patient_
    broker_gets_p.shtml.

———. 2002. "Last of Patient Brokers Gets Two Years." *St. Petersburg Times* (tampabay.
    com), March 29, http://www.sptimes.com/2002/03/29/TampaBay/Last_of_pa
    tient_broke.shtml.

Themedica. 2009. "The U.S. Home Healthcare Industry Overview and Trends." March 23,
    http://www.themedica.com/articles/2009/03/the-us-home-healthcare-industr.html.

Thompson www.thompson.com. 2005. FDA Advertising and Promotion, Food and
    Drug Series.

Tibken, Shara. 2008. "Suit against McKesson Is Dismissed." *Wall Street Journal,*
    August 29, http://online.wsj.com/article/SB121996942015181777.html?mod=2_
    1566_leftbox.

Turkewitz, Eric. 2008a. "Allstate Slammed with RICO Charge over Sham Medical
    Exams." New York Personal Injury blog, March 2, http://www.newyorkpersonalin
    juryattorneyblog.com/2008/03/allstate-slammed-with-rico-charge-over.html.

———. 2008b. "State Farm Hit with Civil RICO Claim over Sham Medical Exams." New
    York Personal Injury blog, February 14, http://www.newyorkpersonalinjuryattor
    neyblog.com/2008/02/state-farm-hit-with-civil-rico-claim.html.

United Health Foundation. 2008. *America's Health Rankings: A Call to Action for Individ-
    uals and Their Communities.* n.d., http://www.americashealthrankings.org/2008/
    index.html.

U.S. Administration on Aging. 2008. "Consumer Protection Tips." Senior Medical Pa-
    trols, September 18, http://www.aoa.gov/smp/consprof/consprof_resources_tips.
    asp.

———. n.d. "AoA Programs, SMP Program (Senior Medicare Patrol)." http://www.aoa.
    gov/prof/aoaprog/SMP/senior_medicare_patrols.aspx.

U.S. Attorney's Office, Northern District of Ohio. 2005. Press release, August 30, http://
    www.usdoj.gov/usao/ohn/news/30 August2005.htm.

U.S. Attorney's Office, Northern District of Texas. 2009. "Two Women Sentenced in
    Health care Case: Defendants Also Ordered to Pay nearly $1 Million in Restitu-
    tion," Press release, May 1, http://dallas.fbi.gov/dojpressrel/pressrel109/d1050109.
    htm.

U.S. Attorney's Office, Southern District of Florida. 2007. "Health Care Fraud Money
    Laundering Found Guilty by Jury All Other Defendants in Large Conspiracy Have
    Plead Guilty." Report, September 26, http://www.justice.gov/tax/usaopress/2007/
    txdv07070926-02.pdf

U.S. Attorney's Office, Southern District of New York. 2006. "Harlem Hospital Agrees to
    Pay $2.3 Million to Settle Charges That It Defrauded Medicare." Report, May 17,
    http://www.justice.gov/usao/nys/pressreleases/May06/harlemhospitalsettlement
    pr%20.pdf.

U.S. Attorney's Office, Western District of Virginia. 2007. "The Purdue Frederick Com-
    pany, Inc. and Top Executives Plead Guilty to Misbranding OxyContin: Will
    Pay Over $600 Million." Press release, May 10, http://www.usdoj.gov/usao/vaw/
    press_releases/purdue_frederick_10may2007.html.

U.S. Congressional Budget Office. 2006. *Research and Development in the Pharmaceutical
    Industry: A CBO Study.* October, http://www.cbo.gov/ftpdocs/76xx/doc7615/
    10–02-DrugR-D.pdf.

——. 2010. "The Budget and Economic Outlook: Fiscal Years 2010 to 2020." January, http://www.cbo.gov/ftpdocs/108xx/doc10871/01–26-Outlook.pdf.

U.S. Department of Defense, Office of Inspector General, Defense Criminal Investigative Service Fraud Alerts. n.d. "Ambulance Fraud: Schemes Including Billing for Services Not Provided, Double Billing, etc." http://www.dodig.osd.mil/inv/dcis/alerts.htm.

U.S. Department of Health and Human Services. 2007a. *FY 2007 Financial Report, Section III, Other Accompanying Information.* http://www.hhs.gov/afr/information/afr-section3.pdf.

——. 2007b. "HHS Fights Durable Medical Equipment Fraud." Press release, July 2, http://www.hhs.gov/news/press/2007pres/07/pr20070702a.html

——. 2008a. "HHS Proposes $737 Billion Budget for Fiscal Year 2009." February 4, http://www.hhs.gov/news/press/2008pres/02/20080204a.html.

——. 2008b. "Statement by Richard S. Foster, FSA, Chief Actuary on 2008 Medicare Annual Report, Financial Portion" before the Committee on Ways and Means, Subcommittee on Health, U.S. House of Representatives." April 1, http://www.hhs.gov/asl/testify/2008/04/t20080401b.html.

——. 2009a. "Eight Miami-Area Residents Charged in $22 Million Medicare Fraud Scheme Involving Home Health Care Agencies." June 26, http://www.hhs.gov/news/press/2009pres/06/20090626a.html.

——. 2009b. "HHS Issues Rule Requiring Individuals be Notified of Breaches of Their Health Information." August 19, http://www.hhs.gov/news/press/2009pres/08/20090819f.html.

——. 2009c. "Medicare Fraud Strike Force Operations Lead to Charges against 53 Doctors, Health Care Executives and Beneficiaries for More Than $50 Million in Alleged False Billing in Detroit." Press release, June 24, http://www.hhs.gov/news/press/2009pres/06/20090624a.html.

——. 2009d. "Miami Physician Sentenced to 97 Months in Prison for Role in $10 Million Medicare Fraud Scheme." June 29, http://www.hhs.gov/news/press/2009pres/06/20090629b.html.

U.S. Department of Health and Human Services, Centers for Medicare and Medicaid Services. 2004. "Emergency Change to Carrier Instructions for End Stage Renal Disease (ESRD) 50/50 Rule Implementation." *MLN Matters,* December 17, http://www.cms.hhs.gov/MLNMattersArticles/downloads/MM3609.pdf.

——. 2006. "CMS Manual System, Pub. 100–04 Medicare Claims, Transmittal 811, Subject: Teaching Physician Services." January 13, http://www.cms.hhs.gov/transmittals/downloads/R811CP.pdf.

——. 2007. "Medicare and Home Health Care." September, http://www.medicare.gov/Publications/Pubs/pdf/10969.pdf.

——. 2008a. "Growth in National Health Expenditures Projected to Remain Steady Through 2017." Press release, February 26, http://www.cms.hhs.gov/apps/media/press/release.asp?Counter=2935.

——. 2008b. "The Improper Medicare Fee-For-Service Payments Report." May, http://www.cms.hhs.gov/apps/er_report/preview_er_report.asp?from=public&which=long&reportID=9.

——. 2008c. "Medicaid Spending Projected to Rise Much Faster Than the Economy." Press release, October 17, http://www.hhs.gov/news/press/2008pres/10/20081017a.html.

——. 2008d. "Medicare Claim Review Programs: MR, MCCI Edits, MUEs, CERT, and RAC." October, http://www.cms.hhs.gov/MLNProducts/downloads/MCRP_Booklet.pdf.

——. 2008e. *The Medicare Recovery Audit Contractor (RAC) Program: An Evaluation of the 3-Year Demonstration.* Report, June, http://www.cms.hhs.gov/RAC/Down loads/RAC_Demonstration_Evaluation_Report.pdf.

——. 2008f. *Medicare and You 2008.* Report, http://www.medicare.gov/Library/PDFNav igation/PDFInterim.asp?Language=English&Type=Pub&PubID=10050.

——. 2008g. "2008 Actuarial Report on the Financial Outlook for Medicaid." October 17, http://www.cms.hhs.gov/ActuarialStudies/downloads/MedicaidReport2008.pdf.

——. 2009. "Protecting Medicare and You from Fraud." May, http://www.medicare.gov/ Publications/Pubs/pdf/10111.pdf.

——. n.d.a. "Current Medicare Fraud Schemes." http://www.trustsolutionsllc.com/Bene/ schemes.pdf.

——. n.d.b. "National Health Expenditure Data." http://www2.cms.gov/NationalHealth ExpendData/.

U.S. Department of Health and Human Services and U.S. Department of Justice. 2001. *Health Care Fraud and Abuse Control Program, Annual Report for FY 2000.* January, http://www.usdoj.gov/dag/pubdoc/hipaa00ar21.htm.

——. 2003. *Health Care Fraud and Abuse Control Program, Annual Report for FY 2002.* September, http://oig.hhs.gov/reading/hcfac/HCFAC%20Annual%20Report%20 FY%202002.htm.

——. 2004. *Health Care Fraud and Abuse Program, Annual Report for FY 2003.* December, http://oig.hhs.gov/reading/hcfac/hcfacreport2003A.htm.

——. 2005. *Health Care Fraud and Abuse Control Program, Annual Report for FY 2004.* September, http://usdoj.gov/dag/pubdoc/hcfacreprot2004.htm.

——. 2006. *Health Care Fraud and Abuse Control Program, Annual Report for FY 2005.* August, http://www.oig.hhs.gov/publications/docs/hcfac/hcfacreport2005.pdf.

——. 2007. *Health Care Fraud and Abuse Control Program, Annual Report for FY 2006.* November, http://www.oig.hhs.gov/publications/docs/hcfac/hcfacreport2006.pdf.

——. 2008. *Health Care Fraud and Abuse Control Program, Annual Report for FY 2007.* November, http://oig.hhs.gov/publications/docs/hcfac/hcfacreport2007.pdf.

U.S. Department of Health and Human Services, Office of Inspector General. 1998. "Using Software to Detect Upcoding of Hospital Bills." August, http://oig.hhs.gov/ oei/reports/oei-01–97-00010.pdf.

——. 2003a. "Home Dialysis Payment Vulnerabilities." May, http://www.oig.hhs.gov/oei/ reports/oei-07-01-00570.pdf.

——. 2003b. "Johns Hopkins University Will Pay $800,000 to Resolve Medicare Fraud Case." Report, February 14, http://oig.hhs.gov/publications/docs/press/2003/ 021403release.pdf.

——. 2003c. "Publication of OIG Special Fraud Alert on Telemarketing by Durable Medical Equipment Suppliers." *Federal Register* 68(42): 10254, http://www.oig. hhs.gov/authorities/docs/03/030403FRSFADMETelemarketing.pdf.

——. 2007. *Fiscal Year 2008 Work Plan.* September, http://www.oig.hhs.gov/publica tions/docs/workplan/2008/Work_Plan_FY_2008.pdf.

——. 2009. "OIG Reports $20.97 Billion in Savings and Recoveries in FY 2009." December 3, http://oig.hhs.gov/publications/docs/press/2009/SemiannualFall2009Press Release.pd.

——. n.d., "Fraud Prevention and Detection, Compliance Guidance," http://www.oig. hhs.gov/fraud/complianceguidance.html#1, and "Corporate Responsibility and Corporate Compliance: A Resource for Health Care Boards of Directors." http:// oig.hhs.gov/fraud/docs/complianceguidance/040203CorpRespRsceGuide.pdf.

U.S. Department of Health and Human Services, Office of Management and the Budget. 2008. *Strengthening Program Integrity in Medicare.* http://www.whitehouse.gov/ omb/budget/fy2008/hhs.html.

U.S. Department of Justice. 1997. "DOJ and HHS Highlight Latest Effort to Fight Fraud by Clinical Laboratories." February 24, http://www.justice.gov/opa/pr/1997/February97/082ag.htm.

——. 2000. "HCA—The Health Care Company and Subsidiaries to Pay $840 Million in Criminal Fines and Civil Damages and Penalties." Press release, December 14, http://www.usdoj.gov/opa/pr/2000/December/696civcrm.htm.

——. 2001. "TAP Pharmaceutical Products, Inc. and Seven Others Charged with Health Care Crimes; Company Agrees to Pay $875 Million to Settle Charges." Press release, October 3, http://www.usdoj.gov/opa/pr/2001/October/513civ.htm.

——. 2002. "Searching and Seizing Computers and Obtaining Electronic Evidence in Criminal Investigations." July, http://www.usdoj.gov/criminal/cybercrime/s&smanual2002.htm.

——. 2003a. "Justice Depart. Civil Fraud Recoveries Total $2.1 Billion for FY 2004; False Claims Act Recoveries Exceed $12 Billion since 1986." Press release, November 10, http://www.usdoj.gov/opa/pr/2003/November/03civ_613.htm.

——. 2003b. "Largest Health Care Fraud Case in U.S. History Settled: HCA Investigation Nets Record Total of $1.7 Billion." Press release, June 26, http://www.usdoj.gov/opa/pr/2003/June/03_civ_386.htm.

——. 2004a. "Gambro Healthcare Agrees to Pay Over $350 Million to Resolve Civil & Criminal Allegations in Medicare Fraud Case." Press release, December 2, http://www.usdoj.gov/opa/pr/2004/December/04_civ_774.htm.

——. 2004b. "HealthSouth to Pay United States $325 Million to Resolve Medicare Fraud Allegations." Press release, December 30, http://www.usdoj.gov/opa/pr/2004/December/04_civ_807.htm.

——. 2004c. "Schering-Plough to Pay $345 Million to Resolve Criminal and Civil Liabilities for Illegal Marketing of Claritin." Press release, July 30, http://www.usdoj.gov/opa/pr/2004/July/04_civ_523.htm.

——. 2005. "Serono to Pay $704 Million for the Illegal Marketing of AIDS Drug." Press release, October 17, http://www.usdoj.gov/opa/pr/2005/October/05_civ_545.html.

——. 2006a. "Schering-Plough to Pay $435 Million for the Improper Marketing of Drugs and Medicaid Fraud." Press release, August 29, http://www.usdoj.gov/usao/ma/Press%20Office%20-%20Press%20Release%20Files/Schering-Plough/press%20release.pdf.

——. 2006b. "Tenet Healthcare to Pay U.S. More Than $900 Million to Resolve False Claims Act Allegations." Press release, June 29, http://www.usdoj.gov/usao/cac/pressroom/pr2006/088.html.

——. 2007a. "HealthSouth and Physicians Pay $14.9 Million to Settle Health Care Fraud Claims." Press release, December 14, http://www.usdoj.gov/opa/pr/2007/December/07_civ_1007.html.

——. 2007b. "Miami Durable Medical Equipment Company Owner Pleads Guilty to $2 Million Medicare Fraud." Press release, July 18, http://www.usdoj.gov/opa/pr/2007/July/07_crm_515.html.

——. 2009. "Texas Hospital Group Pays U.S. 27.5 Million to Settle False Claims Act Allegations." Press release, October 30, http://www.jusstice.gov/opa/pr/2009/October/09-civ-1175.html.

——. 2010. "Former Los Angeles Medical Center Owners Agree to $10 Million Consent Judgment for Medicare and Medi-Cal Fraud Scheme." January 25, http://www.justice.gov/opa/pr/2010/January/10-civ-082.html.

——.U.S. Department of Justice. n.d. *Health Care Fraud Report, Fiscal Year 1998.* http://www.usdoj.gov/dag/pubdoc/health98.htm.

U.S. Department of Justice, Federal Bureau of Investigation. 2006. *Financial Crimes Report to the Public, Fiscal Year 2006.* http://www.fbi.gov/publications/financial/fcs_report2006/financial_crime_2006.htm.

———. 2007a. "Doctor Involved in 'Rent-a-Patient' Scam Sentenced to Nearly Five years in Federal Prison." Report, December 11, http://losangeles.fbi.gov/dojpressrel/pressrel07/la121107usa.htm.

———. 2007b. "Two Defendants Sentenced in Health Care Fraud, HIPAA, and Identity Theft Conspiracy." Press release, May 3, http://miami.fbi.gov/dojpressrel/pressrel07/mm20070503.htm.

U.S. Department of Justice, Federal Bureau of Prisons, Inmate Locator. n.d. http://www.bop.gov/iloc2/LocateInmate.jsp.

U.S. Department of Labor, Bureau of Labor Statistics. 2007. "The 2008–2009 Career Guide to Industries Health Care." Report, December 18, http://www.bls.gov/oco/cg/print/cgs035.htm.

U.S. Department of Labor, Office of Employment Disability Policy. 2008. "Title I of the Americans with Disabilities Act. Significant Court Cases." September 22, http://www.dol.gov/odep/archives/ek99/title1.htm.

U.S. Department of the Treasury, Internal Revenue Service. 2006. *Examples of Health Care Fraud Investigations, FY 2006.* "Miami Doctor Sentenced on False Claims and Tax Evasion Charges." http://www.irs.gov/compliance/enforcement/article/0,id=148267,00.html.

———. 2008a. *Examples of Health Care Fraud Investigations, FY 2008.* "Two Ohio Men Sentenced on Health Care Fraud Conspiracy and Money Laundering Charges" and "Former Blue Cross/Blue Shield Account Manager Sentenced for Health Care Fraud Scheme and Tax Evasion." http://www.irs.gov/compliance/enforcement/article/0,id=174637,00.html.

———. 2008b. "Help Yourself by Filing Past-Due Tax Returns." January, http://www.irs.gov/newsroom/article/0,id=178194,00.html.

———. 2008c. "Suspicious Activity Reports." October 21, http://www.irs.gov/businesses/small/article/0,id=154555,00.html.

———. 2009. "Examples of Healthcare Fraud Investigations 2008." http://www.irs.gov/compliance/enforcement/article/0,id=174637,00.html.

U.S. Drug Enforcement Administration. 2005. "International Internet Drug Ring Shattered." Press release, April 20, http://www.justice.gov/dea/pubs/pressrel/pr042005.html.

U.S. Drug Enforcement Administration, Last Act Partnership, and University of Wisconsin, Pain and Policy Studies Group. 2004. "Prescription for Pain Medications: Frequently Asked Questions and Answers for Health Care Professionals, and Law Enforcement Personnel." August 12, http://headaches.about.com/library/meds/pain_meds_faqs.pdf.

U.S. Federal Trade Commission. 2005. "In the Matter of Partners Health Network, Inc." September, http://www.ftc.gov/os/decisions/docs/Volume140.pdf#page=250.

———. 2007. *Federal Register.* "Identity Theft Red Flags and Address Discrepancies under the Fair and Accurate Credit Transactions Act of 2003; Final Rule." 16 C.F.R. Part 681, November 9, http://www.ftc.gov/os/fedreg/2007/november/071109redflags.pdf.

———. 2009. "Overview of FTC Antitrust Actions in Health Care Services and Products." June.

———. n.d. "In the Matter of Evanston Northwestern Healthcare Corporation and ENH Medical Group, Inc." http://www.ftc.gov/os/adjpro/d9315/index.shtm.

U.S. Food and Drug Administration. 1981. "Taste of Raspberries, Taste of Death: The 1937 Elixir Sulfanilamide Incident." June, http://www.fda.gov/oc/history/elixir.html.

——. 2002. "Schering-Plough Signs Consent Decree with FDA: Agrees to Pay $500 Million." Press release, May 17, http://www.fda.gov/bbs/topics/NEWS/2002/NEW00809.html.

——. 2006. "FDA Updated Public Health Notification: Gambro Prisma Continuous Renal Replacement System." Updated Public Health Notification, February 27, http://www.fda.gov/cdrh/safety/022706-gambro.html.

——. n.d.a. "Device Classes." http://www.fda.gov/CDRH/devadvice/3132.html.

——. n.d.b. "The New Drug Development Process: Steps from Test Tube to New Drug Application Review." http://www.fda.gov/CDER/HANDBOOK/DEVELOP.HTM.

U.S. General Accounting Office. 1998. *Medicare: Concerns with Physicians at Teaching Hospitals (PATH) Audits.* Report to the Chairman, Subcommittee on Health, Committee on Ways and Means, House of Representatives, July, http://www.gao.gov/archive/1998/he98174.pdf.

——. 2003. "Prescription Drugs: OxyContin Abuse and Diversion and Efforts to Address the Problem." Report to Congressional Requesters, December, http://www.gao.gov/new.items/d04110.pdf.

U.S. Government Accountability Office. 2005. "Information on False Claims Act Litigation." Briefing for Congressional Requesters, Report, December 15.

U.S. Postal Inspection Service. n.d. "Fraudulent Health and Medical Products." http://www.usps.com/postalinspectors/fraud/quack.htm.

U.S. Securities and Exchange Commission. 2000. Fresenius Medical Care Holding, Inc. NY, 8-K For 1/8/0, http://www.secinfo.com/dS997.546.htm.

U.S. Senate. 2008. "Medicare Vulnerabilities: Payments for Claims Tied to Deceased Doctors." Permanent Subcommittee on Investigations, Committee on Homeland Security and Governmental Affairs, Hearing, July 9, http://hsgac.senate.gov/public/_files/PSIReport070908.pdf.

U.S. Sentencing Commission. 2004. "Commission Tightens Requirements for Corporate Compliance and Ethics Programs." Press release, May 3, 2004, http://www.USSC.gov/PRESS/rel0504.htm.

——. 2008. "Amendments to the Sentencing Guidelines." November 1, http://www.ussc.gov/2008guid/finalamend08.pdf.

U.S. Sentencing Guidelines. 2007. Chapter 8, Part B: "Remedying Harm from Criminal Conduct; Effective Compliance and Ethics Program." http://www.ussc.gov/2007guid/8b2_1.html.

U.S. Social Security Administration. 2008. "Status of the Social Security and Medicare Programs: A Summary of the 2008 Annual Reports." Social Security Online, http://www.ssa.gov/OACT/TRSUM/trsummary.html.

U.S. Social Security Administration, Office of Retirement and Disability Policy. 2008. *Annual Statistical Supplement, 2008.* http://www.ssa.gov/policy/docs/statcomps/supplement/2008/8e.html#table8.e1.

University of Maine, Bureau of Labor Education. 2001. *The U.S. Health Care System: Best in the World, or Just the Most Expensive?* Report, Summer, http://dll.umaine.edu/ble/U.S.%20HCweb.pdf.

Value Based Management.net. n.d. "Product Life Cycle–Industry Maturity Stages." http://www.valuebasedmanagement.net/methods_product_life_cycle.html.

Walsh, Mary Williams. 2009. "Senators Investigate Hospital Purchasing." *New York Times,* August 13, http://www.nytimes.com/2009/08/14/health/policy/14purchasing.html?pagewanted=1&_r=2&src=twt&twt=nytimespolitics.

Wang, Andrew L. 2009. "Chicago-Area Doctors Charged with Fraud." *Breaking News,* January 30, http://www.chicagobreakingnews.com/2009/01/chicago-area-doctors-charged-with-fraud.html.

Washingtonpost.com and Associated Press. 2005. "Maker of AIDS Drug Fined for Kickbacks." October 18, A12, http://www.washingtonpost.com/wp-dyn/content/article/2005/10/17/AR2005101701870.html?nav=rss_nation.

Wax, Paul M. 1995. "Elixirs, Diluents, and the Passage of the 1938 Federal, Food, Drug, and Cosmetic Act." *Annals of Internal Medicine* 122 (March 15): 456, http://www.annals.org/cgi/content/full/122/6/456.

Webwire. 2008. "SAS' Healthcare Fraud Solution Helps Reduce Healthcare Spending by Millions." November 17, https://www.webwire.com/ViewPressRel.asp?aId=80079.

Weintraub, Arlene. 2010. "New Health Law Will Require Industry to Disclose Payments to Physicians." *Kaiser Health News,* April 26, http://www.kaiserhealthnews.org/Stories/2010/April/26/physician-payment-disclosures.aspx.

Weisburd, David, Elin Waring, and Ellen F. Chayet. 2001. *White-Collar Crime and Criminal Careers.* New York: Cambridge University Press.

Weisman, Robert, and Liz Kowalczyk. 2010. "US Investigates Partners' Contracts: Health Network Examined for Possible Antitrust Violations." Boston.com, April 29, http://www.boston.com/business/healthcare/articles/2010/04/29/justice_department_launches_antitrust_review_of_partners_healthcare/.

Wilemon, Tom. 2010. "Good Deed Punished." *Daily News,* February 10, http://www.memphisdailynews.com/editorial/Article.aspx?id=47751.

Wilson, Duff. 2009. "Steps to Greater Accountability in Medical Education." *New York Times,* October 21, http://www.nytimes.com/2009/10/21/business/21medic.html.

———. 2010. "Using a Pfizer Grant: Courses Aim to Avoid Bias." *New York Times,* January 11, http://www.nytimes.com/2010/01/11/business/11drug.html.

Winslow, Ron. 2009. "Pfizer Sets $2.3 Billion Settlement." *Wall Street Journal,* January 27, http://online.wsj.com/article/SB123301757444517869.html.

Woolhandler, Steffie, Terry Campbell, and David U. Himmelstein. 2003. "Costs of Health Care Administration in the United States and Canada." *New England Journal of Medicine* 349 (August 21), http://content.nejm.org/cgi/content/short/349/8/768.

Woolhandler, Steffie, and David U. Himmelstein. 1991. "The Deteriorating Efficiency of the U.S. Health Care System." *New England Journal of Medicine* 324 (May 2), http://content.nejm.org/cgi/content/abstract/324/18/1253.

———. 2007. "Woolhandler and Himmelstein on Competition and Public Funds: Competition in a Publicly Funded Health Care System." Physicians for a National Health Program, December 1, http://www.pnhp.org/news/2007/november/woolhandler_and_himm.php.

World Health Organization. 2000. *The World Health Report 2000—Health Systems: Improving Performance.* Geneva: WHO. http://www.who.int/whr/2000/en/whr00_en.pdf.

Yahoo Finance. 2008. Yahoo.com, July 23, http://biz.

Yen, Hope. 2009. "Govt: Medicare Paid $47 Billion in Suspect Claims." Associated Press, November 14, http://news.yahoo.com/s/ap/20091114/ap_on_bi_ge/us_medicare_fraud.

Zwillich, Todd. 2005. "FBI Cites Massive Medical Fraud Investigation." March 14, http://www.foxnews.com/story/0,2933,150209,00.html.

Zycher, Benjamin. 2007. "Drug Imports: The Unappreciated Downside." Investors.com, March 7, http://www.investors.com/editorial/editorialcontent.asp?secid=1502&status=article&id=263428863204858.

Legal Cases

Allison EngineCompany v. United States, U.S. Sup. Ct. No. 07–214 (June 9, 2008).

Covington v. Sisters of the Third Order of St. Dominic at Hanford, 61 F.3d 909 (9th Cir. July 13, 1995).

Doulgeris v. U.S. No. 8:08-cv-00282. U.S. District Court Middle District of Florida, Tampa Division. (August 3, 2009).

Graham County Soil and Water Conservation District et al. v. U.S. ex rel. Wilson, U.S. Sup. Ct. No. 08–304 (March 30, 2010).

McGee v. Allstate Insurance Company et al., 1:2008cv00842 (February 28, 2008).

McGee v. State Farm Mutual Automobile Insurance Co. et al., 1:2008cv00392 (January 30, 2008)

New England Carpenters Health Benefits Fund v. First DataBank, Inc. 2008. WL 723774 (D.Mass).

Sedima v. Inrex, 105 Sup. Ct. 3275 (1985).

U.S. v. Booker, No. 04–104 (U.S. Sup. Ct. 2005).

U.S. ex rel. Cox v. Iowa Health Systems, 29 F.Supp. 2d 1022 (S.D. Iowa 1998).

U.S. v. Greber, 760 F.2d 68 (3rd Cir. Pa 1985).

U.S. v. Hancock, 604 F.2d 999 (7th Cir. 1979).

U.S. v. Jain, 93 F.3d 436 (8th Cir. 1996).

U.S. v. Krizek, 859 F.Supp. 5 (D.D.C. 1994).

U.S. v. Lucien et al., 347 F.3d 45 (2nd Cir. 2003).

U.S. v. McClatchey, 217 F.3d 823 (10th Cir.), cert. denied, 531 U.S. 1015.

U.S. v. Medica-Rents Co., 285 F.Supp. 2d 742 (N.D. Tex. 2003)

U.S. v. Mikos, 539 F.3d 706 (7th Cir. 2008).

U.S ex rel. Semtner v. Emergency Physicians Billing Services et al. (WD OK No. 94–617–C).

Visiting Nurses Ass'n. of Brooklyn v. Thompson, 378 F.Supp. 2d 75 (E.D.N.Y. 2004).

Index

AARP, 181; *Bulletin,* 152
Abbot Laboratories, 136–37
Accounting fraud, 98
Acupuncture, 73
Adelphia, 98, 161
Alaska Plumbing and Pipefitting Industry Pension Trust, 16
Alderman, James D., 111
Allegra, 130–31
Allina Hospitals and Clinics, 155
Allison Engine Co. v. U.S., 53–54
Alpharma, 140
Ambulance companies, 1–2, 42, 48, 52, 71, 74
American Cancer Society, 134
American College of Cardiology, 137
American Medical Association, 134, 149, 178
American Psychiatric Association, 134
American Trade Association, 94
Anti-kickback statute, 42–48, 55, 119, 194–95
Anti-trust violations, 17, 109–13, 140
Apotex, 140
Archives of Internal Medicine, 10, 128
Arthur Andersen, 167
Association of American Medical Colleges, 136
AstraZeneca, 121, 122

Bain Capital, 107
Baker, Charles, 112
Balanced Budget Act of 1997, 43, 183
Banbar, 56
Banks, 35
Barbakow, Jeffrey, 100
Baucus, Max, 92
Beam, Aaron, 12
Befaseron, 32
Bextra, 117
Billing errors, 22, 71
Bioengineering, ix
Blue Cross Blue Shield of Illinois, 27
Blue Cross Blue Shield of Massachusetts, 17, 28, 82, 111–12
Blue Cross of California, 53
Boards of directors, inadequate oversight by, 15–16

Bonanno crime family, 114
Boston Globe, 78
Braddock, Clarence H., III, 90
Bristol-Myers Squibb, 140
Bullock, Sandra, 64
Bureau of Prisons, 96
Bush (George W.) Administration, 2–3, 37, 189

Calhoun, A. S., 56
California Department of Managed Care, 93
California Employees' Retirement System, 16
California Office of Health Information Integrity, 155
Campbell, Terry, 8–9
Cardinal Health, 98
Cardiovascular Research Foundation, 137
Carlat, Daniel, 133
CBS, *60 Minutes,* 151
Center for Science in the Public Interest, 136
Centers for Medicare and Medicaid Services (CMS). *See under* U.S. Department of Health and Human Services
Chantix, 133
Chemotherapy, dilution of, 94–96
Cialis, 120
Cigna Healthcare, 130–31
Civil cases, 23, 160–61
Claritin, 130–31
Clayton Act, 110
Cleveland Foundation, 134
Clinton Administration, 2–3
Clooney, George, 65
Collection agencies, 2, 66
Collins, Sara R., 10
Columbia/HCA. *See* Hospital Corporation of America
Commonwealth Fund, 10
Comprehensive Crime Control Act of 1984, 172
Comprehensive Error Rate Testing program, 163
Consortium to Combat Medical Fraud, 158
Conspiracy, 22, 28–30, 40, 42, 58, 75, 78, 105, 192
Consumers Union, 160